REV. JOSHUA THOMAS,

THE PARSON OF THE ISLANDS

THE

PARSON OF THE ISLANDS

A BIOGRAPHY

OF THE

REV. JOSHUA THOMAS

EMBRACING

SKETCHES OF HIS CONTEMPORARIES

AND

REMARKABLE CAMP MEETING SCENES, REVIVAL INCIDENTS, AND REMINISCENCES OF THE INTRODUCTION OF METHODISM ON THE ISLANDS OF THE CHESAPEAKE AND THE COMMUNITIES OF THE DELMARVA PENINSULA

By ADAM WALLACE

OF THE PHILADELPHIA CONFERENCE,

WITH AN INTRODUCTION BY THE REV. JAMES A. MASSEY

MARYLAND
HISTORY PRESS
www.marylandhistorypress.com

MARYLAND
HISTORY PRESS
www.marylandhistorypress.com

Printed in the United States of America

Library of Congress Catalog Card Number: 2001090708

ISBN 0-9703802-2-4

Reprint 2001

TO

THE VENERABLE WIDOW, THE ESTEEMED FAMILY, AND
NUMEROUS FRIENDS

Of the

Rev. JOSHUA THOMAS

And

ALL IN EVERY PLACE, WHO KNEW AND LOVED THIS
SOMEWHAT ECCENTRIC
BUT SINGULARLY EXCELLENT

SERVANT OF GOD,

AND WHO WERE PLEASED AND PROFITED BY
HIS LONG, DEVOTED,
AND SUCCESFUL MINISTRY;

WITH

ALL WHO LOVE OUR LORD JESUS CHRIST, AND ADMIRE
A TYPE OF OLD-FASHIONED METHODISM,
IN ITS SIMPLICITY AND POWER,

THIS VOLUME IS RESPECTFULLY
DEDICATED BY

THE COMPILER

CONTENTS.

CHAPTER IV.

CHAPTER V.

CHAPTER VI.

CHAPTER VII.

CHAPTER XVI.

CHAPTER XVII.

CHAPTER XVIII.

CHAPTER XIX.

10 CONTENTS.

PREFACE.

"MAY God bless and prosper you in this labor of love," writes an intelligent brother minister, on learning that a biography of the Rev. Joshua Thomas was in contemplation.

Another ardent friend wrote, "Go a-head. The work should be accomplished *now*. If longer neglected it may never be done."

Still others,—"Give us a book ; it has been long desired by all who knew the dear old Island Preacher."

"The life of such a man ought not to be confined to his neighborhood, or to his brief sojourn on earth."

"You are now providentially placed on the 'field of his fame," and can glean the rich and abundant materials, in anecdote and incident, that will make a useful volume, and perpetuate the memory of his eventful life, and stirring times."

Thus urged and encouraged, the writer ventured, a few months ago, to take this work in hand ; and, devoting the intervals of leisure allowed on a large and laborious circuit to its arrangement, it has assumed the form in which the reader finds it.

An abler and more practiced pen should have been employed
in this undertaking, but for demands which had to be met in
the active service of the church, and in other departments of
duty.

The apology which may be due, as to why " what was found
worth doing at all is not done better ?" is simply this : the
writer offered his material and services, in vain, to others,
hoping to occupy a subordinate position merely, as co-worker
in its accomplishment ; and not until every request and tender
failed did he assume the responsibilities involved in his own
name.

Appointed to the Princess Anne Circuit in 1860 for the
second time, after the lapse of ten years, he found the vacant
chair and silent grave of his former, greatly beloved, " Father
in Israel," and the hearts of his friends full of cherished
memories of the departed saint.

When formerly on the circuit, it was oftentimes his privilege
and always his delight to visit Bro. Thomas at his Island home,
and listen while he recounted the story of his earlier days, and
told the wonders of redeeming mercy, which had marked his
pathway through a long life. After repeated conversations
with him on the subject of a memoir and history of his times,
he laid his trembling hands on the head of the " young
preacher," and charged him by the love he bore him, *to see
that such a thing was done.*

He had been disappointed greatly, and so had his friends,
that none of the preachers who had talked of, or attempted,
this work, had persevered in its performance.

The Rev. Levin M. Prettyman of the Philadelphia Conference, about twenty years ago, commenced—as the amanuensis

and intimate friend of Bro. Thomas—to prepare an autobiography. This work was continued at such intervals as could be devoted to it, until the manuscript narrative reached the year 1815, where it abruptly terminates, remaining in this unfinished state until both these beloved men had gone " the way of all the earth."

That Mr. Prettyman intended to publish a volume is more than probable. On a fly leaf of his papers there is " a plan to write by," and an outline of topics, or chapters, to guide him in completing his design.

His removal to other scenes of ministerial duty, doubtless, interfered with this purpose, and deferring his work until leisure could be obtained, he fell at his post, a faithful herald of salvation.

Some years since a brother—eminently qualified for the department of literature, such a volume as the present is intended to occupy—Rev. A. Manship, author of " Thirteen years' experience in the Itinerancy"—at the instance of Bro. Thomas' family and numerous friends, was applied to; and, surveying the field, found it " white unto the harvest," but, to their regret, could not devote that time to the preparation of a biography, which the Church required for other and important duties.

In this regret the writer cannot but concur. Brother M., however, with characteristic generosity furnished us the " Prettyman Papers," which had been confided to his care, with every " aid and encouragement" possible, in the prosecution of this task, which, as intimated by another, seems to have devolved, by providential appointment, on the present compiler. This was made apparent to him by a vivid recollection of the obligation imposed by Bro. Thomas himself, the many concurring circumstances thrown around the case, and the hearty "God speed!" he has received, while collecting his material from widely varying sources.

It will not be surmised that Father T. was actuated by a vain ambition, in the desire he felt, and so often expressed, to see a publication of this kind; though he prized the thought—who does not?—that his name should be remembered, and his memory blessed, after he had been "gathered to his fathers."

His true motive was to make memorial of the mercy of his God, and tell to generations following, the mighty works and wonders of his gracious hand.

The following extract from the papers alluded to, and designed for the same purpose as that to which it is devoted here, will reveal his motive:

"The Lord has been so good to me, my family, and friends on these islands, I have had for a long time a great desire to publish an account of the astonishing things he has done for us; that many may be encouraged to seek, and all to praise, him for the great mercy and goodness which we have received.

"It is not to boast, *understand*, of what *I* may have done, but of what my God has done for us, poor ignorant sinners. I give him all the glory and praise for the gracious work he has wrought among us for a great many years past. And as I have now a friend (Bro. Prettyman) to write for me, I will proceed to tell you what a condition we were in before the gospel was preached to us in its convincing energy and saving power; and what a wonderful and happy change it has produced."

It is to be regretted that this " desire of his eyes" was not accomplished before he " fell asleep."

The plan and details of the work were matters of conversation, prior to that last interview, when, receiving his blessing, the writer received also the charge which he has now *affectionately*, if feebly, tried to fulfill.

This duty would have been onerous in the extreme, if not entirely impossible to him, but that " many hands," able, accomplished, and willing, have made comparatively " light work ;" and contributed greatly to whatever value and interest may be found in the following pages.

The sketches of contemporary characters introduced may not be deemed irrelevant to the general design.

Those incorporated with the main narrative were found to be inseparably and worthily associated with the subject, and will revive the memory of names that are still precious throughout the peninsula; connected, as they are, with the rise and rappid progress of Methodism, to that prominence which it has gained in Maryland and Virginia.

In the arrangement of the earlier parts of the work, the Prettyman manuscript has been used entire, and will be found marked all along by a beautiful simplicity and truthfulness in its statement of facts.

The communications of Rev. Brothers Kemp, Dr. Townsend, Brindle, Price, J. Hargis, Nottingham, and others, contribute greatly to the completeness of the book; and, as will be found, to the pleasure and profit of the reader.

The sermon by Rev. Z. Webster, recalled and written at our request, and also the report from memory of the last public discourse delivered by our " Parson," will stand as simple memorials of the man, and may revive useful reflections in the minds of many, who heard with throbbing hearts the lessons of love and meekness from those lips now sealed and silent for ever.

On the question of a *title*, there was, in the mind of the writer, no misgiving. That which has been adopted appeared to be most appropriate and expressive. "THE PARSON OF THE ISLANDS" was the name given to Mr. Thomas by the chief officers of the British army and fleet, when their rendesvous was the Island where he resided, and exercised the simple functions of his office.

He was emphatically the "Parson of the Islands;" extending to all, and over all (in that vicinity), an unwearied watchfulness. Through heat and cold, in storm and sunshine, by day or night, he was prompt to action in every call of duty; performing, as a father and friend, those ministrations of religion that have endeared his name to the hearts of the people. The fastings he endured, the perils he braved, the tears he shed, and the personal sacrifices he made, in attendance wherever sickness or suffering needed sympathy; whenever bereavement and sorrow called for comfort or condolence; in all the varying phases of human ill, there was he, the counselor, pastor, friend of all. He took the little children in his arms, and named them for God and the Church. He joined the hands of united happy hearts, and gave them his blessing. He cheered the dying by his encouraging presence and sublime faith. He stood by their coffins and at their graves to point the living to a home beyond the dark valley. In their disputes and difficulties he was "the son of peace."

Many of the incidents collected and presented here, illustrative of his singularities and strong faith, will, it is probable, tax the credulity of those who have not personally known him. His inward impressions, abrupt movements, dreams, and revelations, may be pronounced "the vagaries of a weak mind," or, "the impulses of fanaticism and folly." To those who were intimately acquainted with the man, the solution is not difficult. "He walked," yea, and *talked*, "with God!" According to his ready, implicit faith, so was it done unto him, or unto those in whose behalf he became oft a pleader at the throne of grace.

The Divine word, to his mind, was an unalterable verity, in all it declared of God, and man, and Christ the Mediator. He believed in the Holy Ghost, and when in perplexity, or indecision, on any matter of duty, invariably asked light from above, and found it "liberally."

"*It comes to me*," was a frequent utterance with him, and that he had access unto the Father, none could doubt, when he spake with "boldness of confidence," the things that were in his heart.

In all reports of what he said or did, after the manuscript from which quotations are made fails, the aim has been to give his language in substance.

However difficult the undertaking to put *such* a man, in a book; this, there is some reason for supposing, has, to a good degree, been done. This, at least, was the primary aim of the writer. His success, others must determine. He congratulates himself, and his readers, that older heads and abler hands have mainly contributed to secure this result.

The "Introduction," by Rev. J. A. Massey, and a descriptive sketch of the Islands, also from his pen, claim special acknowledgment, and will be found both interesting and instructive, not only to the stranger, but to those familiar with the localities and people, to which reference is made.

The engravings, secured at considerable trouble and expense, for this volume, will speak for themselves. It was an oft expressed wish of Father Thomas that the event of his preaching to the British on the eve of their attack on the city of Baltimore should be represented in an engraving. It is here, just as he described the scene, and will make the reader familiar with that notable circumstance.

Many a preacher of the Philadelphia Conference will recognize at a glance the canoe "Methodist," and admit with pleasure the crowding associations therewith connected.

The portrait introduced, is the nearest approach possible to a satisfactory likeness. Memory was our only " original."

Justice to the subject and the compiler, demanded a much longer time in arrangement and completion than could be commanded for the purpose. The "dangers of delay" have prompted a rather premature and hurried publication. For all defects, inaccuracies, and errors of style or fact, he must claim the largest possible forbearance.

Without ambition, except to accomplish good, and with his might, to obey duty's call, he has cheerfully given the toil attendant on the preparation of this book. Among the Island people, at least, what has been done will meet with an appreciative welcome; here, the man they venerated will still preach and point souls to Jesus; and in these pages his friends will see his form, hear his teachings, and become happy, as in the days of other years, in the companionship of "the Parson of the Islands."   ADAM WALLACE.

Princess Anne, Maryland, 1861.

INTRODUCTION,

By The Rev. James A. Massey.

SOME extended biographical notice of that faithful Christian, and useful laborer in the vineyard of the Lord, Rev. Joshua Thomas, ought to have been given long ago. He was very desirous, himself, that "the way which the Lord led him many years in this wilderness" world, should be published in a book. Several of our ministers, at various times, have thought of preparing such a memoir. Many years since, *I* occasionally entertained a thought of engaging in the effort to prepare a work, somewhat similar, in plan and detail, to the present undertaking. If simultaneous leisure could have been possessed by both him and me, when I was situated near him, I might have spent some weeks at his residence, and have accomplished a more minute and thorough biography than can now be furnished as there are no journals, diaries, or other memoranda left by him or his old friends, to aid in this good work. But while he was alive to furnish material, I was not only deterred by his and my own want of leisure, but by a conscious incompetency for the kind of writing that would do justice to such a thrilling subject.

I was glad when Rev. Levin M. Prettyman undertook this work, many years ago. I anticipated such a production from his pen as would meet the requirements of the case, and satisfy the demand of the public. But, after making considerable progress, he never completed his design, and the memoir remained unfinished. What he did write, however, has been placed in the hands of the present biographer, and is, I presume, fully and fairly used in the following pages.

It may be, that my inability, and also that of Bro. P., to accomplish the labor of love that was in our hearts, is all for the best; as Bro. Wallace is better qualified for this service than either of us were. Though not personally conversant with Father Thomas, except for a brief period before his decease, yet Bro. W. retains a sufficiently vivid impression of those traits, which distinguished him, to delineate with accuracy his remarkable character; besides, his present position, and pastoral intercourse with those who knew him best, and loved him most, may enable him, with the descriptive adaptation he possesses, to accomplish the work to which he has addressed himself, with industry and zeal, so as to secure completeness, as far as such a thing can be attained at the present time.

The "*everlasting remembrance,*" in which the "*righteous*" are held, is not dependent on books or biographers. "*Their record is on high.*" Yet, "the memory of the just is blessed" to generations following; and it becomes a grateful, and a useful task, to perpetuate the influence and example of a good life.— such a life as that of Joshua Thomas.

In this form, "being dead," he may yet live, and preach in

his simple way, to thousands who never saw, or knew the man, —and who, by a perusal of these pages, may be induced to " glorify God in him," and " follow him as he followed Christ."

Memorials of his contemporaries, among both ministers and members of the Church, will add greatly to the interest of the volume ; while they will preserve from the oblivion of the past, names that were " as ointment poured forth," and characters that illustrate, in an eminent degree, the power and precious-ness of the gospel to save.

The father of Joshua Thomas, though in humble circum-stances, was a man highly respected in his day, and made an honest living by his industry.   He died while Joshua was quite young, and left his widow and children not entirely destitute. Unfortunately, while Joshua was still a small boy, his mother married a second husband, who turned out to be both indolent and intemperate.   He soon squandered what little property they possessed, and reduced the family to great straits,—and often to extreme suffering, for want of necessary food and com-fortable clothing.   To get along in the difficulties, to which drinking and idleness brought him, this step-father would some-times appropriate what was not his own.   One way of catching drum fish, was to anchor a long cable, by heavy stones at each end, and have a number of hooks attached, with about a fathom of cord to each, and these cords about a fathom apart on the cable.   These hooks were large and strong, and were baited with pieces of crab.   The owner of the cable and lines would make two or three visits to them every day, to take off all the fish that might be hooked.   This wretched man would take his little boys, late at night, and make them row him to some of these drum lines, set by his neighbors, and take off all the fish

that he found on them.   But, although exposed to the corrupt-
ing influence of the example and commands of *such* a stepfather, Joshua retained a tender conscience.   He thoroughly
despised and heartily hated the man's dissipation and dis-
honesty, and resolved that he would pursue a different course.
He desired to serve God, as well as he knew how.   The Pro-
testant Episcopal minister who occasionally visited the Islands,
had no more eager and attentive hearer than young Joshua.
Though he was naturally of a cheerful and lively temperament,
and his company was greatly sought after in the convivial gatherings of his neighbors, he kept up a constant desire and aim
to do right.   He married while young, and succeeded in main-
taining his family comfortably by honest industry.   He was at
this period directed by the minister, during one of his visits to
the Islands, to procure a prayer book and have family worship.
He had the appropriate places pointed out, and promptly engaged in this duty.

He frequently related in after years a circumstance, which
strongly illustrates both his firm resolution to do what he thought
to be his duty, (even though it involved something that was
very unpleasant,) and how extremely poor a reader he was.
One of his neighbors, who was a much better reader than
himself, visited him one evening.   As the usual hour for worship approached, he began to fear that his friend was about to
stay all night.   He dreaded the thought of praying before him.
At length, after waiting until a late hour, he ventured to tell
his visitor that he had established family prayer, and requested
him, as he was the better reader, to take his place in conduct-
ing the service.   His neighbor was very much startled at

this proposal, and insisted that Mr. Thomas should proceed as usual, for he could not think of officiating in his place.

"Well then," said Mr. T., "as you have better *larning* than I, I will place a candle in a chair between us, and you must look over the book, and when I cannot make out the words, you must tell me."

To this proposition the neighbor consented. It was not long before they reached a word which neither of them could decipher. He never afterwards forgot the word : it was "*particular*."

His good minister did not seem to give him any very loud or strong warning against the Methodists, who were making great headway at that time, for he appeared to be open to conviction, when he first was led to attend one of the camp meetings held on the main land in Accomac Co., Va., and began to seek privately the same happy experience which he saw many profess to obtain in public. This blessing he continued to seek, and ere long received.

My acquaintance with him began in August, 1828, at the *first* camp meeting held on Deal's Island. While the tents were being erected on the day on which service was to commence at night, as I sauntered about, a plain, solid built man, with his pants rolled up and his feet bare, came up to the place where several of the ministers who had arrived, were standing or sitting. One of these was Rev. Henry White, then P. E. of the district, who had consented to take charge of the meeting, although it was not a Quarterly Meeting. Brother White introduced the stranger to me, as Brother Joshua Thomas. I had often heard of him, and had formed some opinion of his probable appearance. But I was utterly disappointed in my expectations. I had heard of him so frequently as "Father Thomas, the Tangier Island Preacher," that I anticipated something much more venerable in his looks and bearing. But I had before me only a rough, awkward, stammering Islander. The acquaintance which I formed with him during that meeting, elevated him greatly in my estimation, and endeared him to my heart. I was then in the second year of my Itinerancy, and a few days over twenty years of age. My youth seemed to give this dear man particular interest in me: but my being one of the "*itenery*" preachers was itself a great recommendation to him; for, of the Itinerant ministers and preachers of the Methodist E. Church, he had long been, and continued through life, a devoted friend.

As he attended several camp meetings every year, my acquaintance with him was renewed the following year, which I spent on Salisbury Circuit.

In the year 1830, I was stationed at Asbury Church, West Philadelphia, and was thus cut off from seeing him that year. But in 1831, immediately after my marriage, I was sent to Annamessex Circuit, which, as then constituted, included Deal's Island. Though there was then no church, or regular appointment for preaching on that Island, yet at every appointment at Rock Creek, the nearest church on the main land, I met Bro. Thomas. The appointment was on Tuesdays; and though he was remarkably industrious, he never was too busy to lay aside his fishing, canoe-building, or the cultivation of his corn or "taters," (as he, and the Island people called their noble sweet potatoes,) to attend the week day preaching. We frequently spent some hours together, where I stopped for dinner. The circuit was so large that the week in which we preached at Rock Creek, had an appointment for nearly every day; (there was no spare half day in it, until near its close, and then I would be far off, on another part of the circuit,) so that I did not get to see him at his own house, on little Deal's Island, during my two years on this circuit.

But he usually attended the Quarterly Meetings, as well as the camp meetings of the circuit; and he would time his visits in the "Methodist"—(his big canoe,) to different parts of the circuit, so as to meet me occasionally at several other appointments; and he sometimes visited me at my own house, in Potato Neck—so that the intimacy between us became very considerable, by the expiration of my two years' term.

My colleague and myself visited Smith's Island together each year, about its close. Bro. Thomas took us carefully across the sound, and by his entertaining company, greatly added to the interest and enjoyment of those trips.

During the seven following years, I was on Accomack Circuit, (twice,) and on Cambridge and Salisbury Circuits, and I had more or less intercourse with him if I recollect aright, each of these years.

In 1840, I was made Presiding Elder of Snow Hill District, and met with him every quarter, on his own circuit and occasionally on others, during the three years I remained on the District.

After leaving the District in 1843, I never saw him again, though I occasionally wrote to him, and received messages from him.

Bro. Thomas had a mind of great natural sprightliness and shrewdness. His education was barely sufficient to enable him to read his Bible with satisfaction and profit. In other books he never read much, from lack of time, of books, and of ability to read to advantage. Except in books that were carefully prepared for such as had a very limited vocabulary, he would soon be reading in what, to him, was quite an unknown tongue. But he 'read nature; he studied facts; and was ever learning something from men and things that would help him in his exhortations (as he always called his discourses,) to explain the Bible and Christian experience.

He was remarkable for his prayerfulness, for strong faith, and for sunny cheerfulness. He carried religion into all places and circumstances. He regarded every locality as a suitable place for prayer. In the public office of a Register of Wills, on the road side, in the sedge grass and the silent woods, as well as in the pulpit or altar, the closet or at the fireside of his friends.

But though religion was more or less his theme in all companies and places, yet there was nothing repulsive to the young and cheerful, in his manner of introducing that subject. It was a cheerful, happy thing with him. He always could make his discourses attractive to persons of all ages and characters. He was very loquacious; and might frequently be found, during the intervals of worship, at a camp meeting, surrounded with a small circle, entertaining and instructing them with his sprightly conversation, about religion and the incidents of his own life and experience. I never knew him to take a text when other preachers were present.

At camp meetings, he delighted in the privilege of exhorting, just when he felt like doing so, in the prayer-meetings or at the close of sermons. Whenever he did so, (however able or long the sermon that had preceded)—instead of a retreat from the congregation, when he would arise to exhort, there was sure to be a considerable increase of attentive listeners; and those who were already in the congregation, in considerable numbers, would draw near the stand. This they were induced to do, partly because his voice was not very loud and strong, and partly because they seemed to be attracted towards *him*. His natural facetiousness would frequently produce considerable laughter; but without being in the least disconcerted thereby, he would proceed, until tears would often be as plentiful as preceding smiles and laughter had been.

His own family had great reason to stand in awe of some of his sallies. He felt it his privilege to introduce so much of home matters, of their blunders and faults, (in a way which he thought would do them and others good,) that they might well fear something was coming out, that they would rather he should have kept to himself; but they were so accustomed to it that they did not seem much alarmed by his disclosures, or feel apprehensive beforehand of his personalities.

The late Rev. Henry White once gave him a kind, public reproof, in reference to this matter. He was speaking at a camp meeting on Deal's Island, of prominent, faithful Christian men, in a neighborhood, as being invaluable—" Your old friend, Joshua Thomas," said he, " by his life and labors among you, is of the greatest service to you. I have frequently heard *more divinity in his unpretending exhortations, than in long sermons from able men*—though I do not like the way he has of talking about his family so much in public."

I am writing this introduction without having seen the memoir which it is intended to precede, and can hardly give anecdotes of him—as they readily recur to me—without incurring the risk of saying what the biographer may have inserted, from other sources.

His promptness in doing what good people urged upon him as his duty, is illustrated by some circumstances of his early religious life. He came in contact with some Baptists, who insisted on immersion, in adult years, as the only valid baptism. Reflecting upon what they taught him, when alone in his canoe, with prayer for the Divine blessing, he suddenly plunged into the water, intending it for what he was told was the correct mode of baptism. When he next met with his Baptist friends, he told them that he had been immersed. When asked who had performed the ceremony, he told them that he did it himself. They told him that it must be done by a minister, who had himself been immersed. He then consented to be immersed by a Baptist minister, which at his request was soon done. He was very much distressed however when he found that his Methodist brethren were about to consider this act as a withdrawal from the church of his affections; and though suddenly induced thus to submit to immersion, he soon settled down in the firm persuasion that baptism in infancy and by sprinkling was scriptural.

His second marriage is an illustration of his carrying out the injunction, "In everything by prayer and supplication let your requests be made known to God." While the British were encamped on Tangier Beach, he lost his first wife. She left three small children, one of them an infant at the breast. That there might be no occasion for scandal, he employed two female members of the church to keep his house and attend to his children; but the British officers visited the house so much that these ladies became unwilling to stay there. He put out the babe to a nurse, who in a week or two returned it on his hands. He then began to think that though his wife had been dead only a few weeks he should have to marry again very soon. He prayed the Lord, that if this were best, He would direct his mind to a suitable person for his wife, and a mother to his little children.

A Miss Bradshaw was presented to his mind's eye as the right person. But he replied, "Lord, she is too young." Repeated prayer brought the same answer. Friends began to tell him he would have to contract an early second marriage; and every one of them, without his naming his impressions in answer to prayer, recommended the same person.

He determined to visit the family. When his canoe came in sight of her father's residence, the old people, seeing the approaching sail, tried to ascertain whose canoe it was. The daughter arose, and, on looking, determined in a moment who was coming, and was suddenly impressed that he was coming for a purpose in which she was deeply interested. He was kindly received, and after supper and family worship, the children retired. The old people began to condole with him in his desolate condition, and asked him what he intended to do? He told them that all his friends thought that he would soon have to marry again. In this they coincided, and asked him whom he thought of seeking as his second wife?

He told them of his impressions, in answer to prayer, and of the corroborating advice of his friends. They said their "Lotty" was too young for him, but if she were willing, they would not oppose. When he arose next morning, he saw her engaged in milking a cow. After his secret devotion, he went out of doors to where she stood, straining her milk. He asked

her "if she loved his late wife well enough to undertake to be
a mother to her children." She replied in the affirmative.
"Well then," said he, "old Brother Aydelott will be at his appointment, on Holland's Island, on such a day, (naming a day a
week or so distant,) and I will come and take you up, and get
him to marry us." To this arrangement she gave her consent,
and they were married accordingly. This match contracted
with as little parley or delay as the betrothal of Rebekah by
Abraham's servant, for his young master Isaac, was an eminently happy one. She did him good and not evil all the days
of his life.

One of the most happy exhortations I ever remember to
have heard him deliver, was at a Sabbath morning prayer-
meeting during the progress of a camp at Deal's Island in August, 1838 or '39. There had been a tremendous storm the
previous night, which had blown down some 20 or 30 tents,
and driven ashore about 150 vessels.

Everybody was gloomy and discouraged. Brother Thomas
told the people they ought to be full of gratitude and confidence. "While several large trees had been blown down *near*
the encampment, not a single limb of any size had fallen
within the circle of tents. Though the vessels had been
driven ashore, not a single life had been lost, and only one
vessel had been wrecked outright, and that was an old rotten
craft, which, if it had not been disabled there, might have cost
its owner and crew their lives, for they would have continued
to sail in her until she would have sunk, and they would have
gone to the bottom.

"Besides," said he, "there is no place where these vessels
could have been scattered about in the sound and bay, in pur-

suit of their business, in which some of them, in all probability, would have been lost if they had not been here at the camp meeting during this gale. Instead, then, of giving up holding camp meetings here, we ought to take encouragement, and look for God's blessing upon the closing part of this meeting, and come here every year while we live, to wait upon God with his people."

One part of this address was thrillingly eloquent. He represented himself as looking out at the pines during the storm, "and they bent like bows, but God said unto them, 'Hold on !' and hold on they did, though one of them in the midst of the tents was half cut through, and though outside the ground large trees were blown up by the roots."

This exhortation produced a most astonishing effect. Almost every person cheered up, and the meeting went on very pleasantly to its close.

About 1840, at a camp on Tangier Beach, a missionary service was held. After an appropriate sermon by Rev. C. Karsner, Brother Thomas volunteered to add a few remarks. He told the congregation of a wealthy, corpulent man, whom he once, in vain, solicited to give a dollar at a Missionary meeting. " You had better do so," he told him, "for if you don't you may expect that God will send on you the ' billus !' (the bilious fever;) and the unconscionable doctor will come, and he will charge you five dollars or more. But if you will give a dollar or more to this cause I think God will keep the ' billus' away from you." He could not induce the corpulent gentleman to pay the demanded dollar, but sure enough the " billus" did soon seize upon this penurious sinner, and he drew a most graphic and laughable picture of the manner in which the

" billus," the doctor, and the medicine combined, tortured and pulled down the flesh of the fat man, leaving him, in his appearance, a perfect contrast to his looks in health.

He then drew (in something like the manner of the Psalmist and the Prophet Isaiah), a picture of an Idolater cutting down a tree, carving out an image, painting it, and setting it up to be worshiped. " And then, with the balance of the tree, he makes a fire, cooks a meal, and, before he will eat it, he falls down before the image he had just made and set up, thanks it for his food, and asks it to help him and bless him. " Why," said he, " ignorant as we are, if such an image were set up here for a god, our island boys would stone it, or batter it down with brick bats !" He then went on to insist on their obligation, as having been so favored with gospel light, to send it on to the " heathen" who, " in their blindness bow down to wood and stone."

Many of the happiest illustrations in his discourses were drawn from fishing and sailing in which he had spent most of his life. But, though they were most eminently clear and happy hits, I cannot give any of them so as to afford a proper view of his manner.

He was very fond of carrying the preachers to their Island appointments in his big canoe. And it was usually a treat to be with him. In his cheerful manner he was all the time seeking to gain or give instruction. Finding him so fond of this employment, the societies at Smith's and Holland's Islands, several years after I left the circuit, engaged him to bring the preachers regularly every two weeks during the summer and early autumn. He continued this practice until he became disabled by bodily infirmity. Then one of his sons took his place, and rendered good service, as a careful and competent ferryman.

As long as he lived he evinced a deep interest in the Island people, and claimed an hour or two from the preacher on the occasion of his visits to them that he might inquire about their temporal and spiritual prosperity.

His name is a household word, and his sayings are repeated day after day among them, as the maxims of their business and intercourse. His influence over them was great and for their good, while living; and it is my hope and ardent prayer that "being dead," he may yet speak, with authority and success, in doing good to generations yet unborn, by the publication of the present memoir.

THE PARSON OF THE ISLANDS.

CHAPTER I.

Sketch of the Islands—First discovery—Captain Smith—Settlements formed in Northampton—Accomac and Somerset—Elzey and Revel—Original names—Rev. Mr. Massey's sketch—Hooper's Island—Straits—Light Boat—Holland's, Smith's, and Tangier Islands—Kedge's Straits—Tangier Sound—Oystering—Fishing—Dwellings—Population—Deal's Islands—Spring Island—Watt's and Saxe's Islands—Pocomoke Sound—Somers' Cove.

THE "Islands" which form the scene of our good "Parson's" life and labors, demand some descriptive notice, before entering fully on the narrative, to which the following pages are intended to be devoted.

As early as 1607, Captain Smith, in a history of his first voyage of exploration, in the Chesapeake Bay, recounts having crossed from the new settlement at Jamestown, Va., to the Eastern Shore, and after various adventures, discovered certain "Isles, Rivers, Straits, and places for harbors and habitations," which we have no difficulty in identifying as the present Tangier, Smith's, Holland's, and Deal's (or Devil's) Islands, with the Sounds, Straits, and prominent landmarks, thereunto belonging.

Their modern names do not correspond with the original, but of the localities there can be no doubt from a perusal of the quaint narrative of this expedition.

For half a century after this first intrusion of the white man, both the Islands and adjacent main were left in the comparative solitude in which they were found: early colonization had encountered so many difficulties and reverses.

A few settlers had, after the lapse of years, approached the inviting coast of Northampton and Accomac Counties, Va., and gave such good report of the heritage they had found, that, about the year 1650, the population in those places had become sufficiently numerous to admit of emigration farther up the course of this noble Bay; and we find by reference to the early histories of Maryland, settlements were made in what shortly after was called Somerset County. Two adventurers named Elzey and Revel led the van, and were speedily followed by a considerable number of settlers. Somerset County was formed in 1666; and included many of the Islands to which allusion will be made. For two hundred years, therefore, this part of the State has had a settled society, inheriting from their ancestors, who, by reference to the original names, were all English, a quiet, thrifty, and enterprising character.

The first dwellers on the Islands, were principally families from the settlements in Somerset, and the Virginia main, bearing similar names, and keeping up their affinity and intercourse by the common interests that bound them together. Of these names, the more prominent about the period of the American Revolution were Thomas, Tyler, Evans, Crockett, and Parks, whose descendants remain, and are the most numerous at the present day.

Within the memory of many now living, the population of these Islands has largely increased, not only in numbers, but in enterprise, wealth, and intelligence. For a description of the characteristics of the inhabitants, and their modes of gaining "a comfortable livelihood," in the isolated situation which they occupy, we are indebted to a careful paper prepared and furnished by Rev. J. A. Massey, who has for many years been intimate with the places and people he describes. He writes:

"The south eastern part of the Chesapeake Bay is called Tangier Sound. This beautiful sheet of water is about forty miles in length, from north to south, by about five to ten miles in width, from east to west. It abounds with fish and fowl, and is separated from the main bay by numerous small islands. The most northern of these is called Hooper's Island, in Dorchester County, Maryland. This is a long, narrow strip of land, occupied by a hardy and active population. Hooper's Straits, to the south of this Island, separates it from a small group called Holland's Islands, as fertile and pleasantly situated as any in the Chesapeake Bay. The arable land is not very considerable, hence the population is not large. They have a small Methodist Church, where meetings are regularly kept up, and a good society is maintained.

"Hooper's Straits are a great thoroughfare for vessels bound up the Bay, from the Nanticoke, Wicomico, Manokin, Annamessex, and Pocomoke Rivers, and the various creeks along the Eastern Shore, emptying into the Tangier and Pocomoke Sounds. The channel of these Straits is narrow and crooked; and, to aid in their safe navigation, a Light Boat, having an excellent lantern at the top of its masts, is moored on the point of one of its bars.

South of Holland's Islands, and separated therefrom by Kedge's Straits, lie Smith's Islands. This group is densely populated, notwithstanding the great area of marsh land which it includes. In these Straits a desperate engagement took place in the days of the Revolutionary struggle, which ended disastrously to the Americans.

There is a light-house on Fogg's Point, commanding Kedge's Straits; and centrally situated, there is a neat Methodist Episcopal Church, at which there is an average membership of about one hundred. Richard Evans, (long known as King Richard,) and his brother Solomon, were the leading men in this society for a great many years. Both are now gathered home. A broad expanse of shallow water, about five to ten miles wide, separates Smith's Islands from the group called Tangier, in Accomac Co., Va. I do not know whether this group gave name to the Sound, or the Sound to it. This was the early residence of Joshua Thomas, and the scene of his first public labors, as an Exhorter and Local Preacher. Here was the site of many large, popular, and gloriously successful camp meetings. It is also famous as the place where Cockburn's forces were encamped, during his predatory warfare on the villages near the Chesapeake. On the spot where the camp meetings were formerly held, the Chesapeake House, for the accommodation of persons seeking health and pleasure, in the heat of summer, from pure air, and salt water bathing, has recently been erected, by one of our brethren. This house is well conducted on temperance principles. It contains twenty commodious chambers for boarders, besides full accommodations for the family; and, as the bathing place is very fine and safe, it furnishes first rate inducements to moral and religious people, to choose it as a summer retreat.

The inhabitants of Smith's and Tangier Islands may almost be called an amphibious race; for nearly all the men and boys spend fully half their time (if not *in* yet) *on* the water. Canoes, skilfully hollowed out of pine logs, and constructed with due regard to the purposes intended, are very numerous. They are rigged with two masts, with sails attached, which can be easily taken down or put up, and can outsail every vessel on these waters, that is not propelled by steam. When there is not sufficient wind for them to sail, the islanders are very dexterous in managing them with paddles.

As a large part of these islands consists of marsh, there is not sufficient arable land to sustain the population. Almost every family has, therefore, a small schooner, of the class familiarly known as "Pungy," which is made the most fruitful means of its support. Much of the time the male part of the population, with their schooners and canoes, are employed in catching and conveying to market the excellent oysters that abound in the Sound and Bay. These were formerly almost all (except those consumed by the islanders themselves) conveyed to the Baltimore market; but of late years, numerous Philadelphia, New York, and New England vessels come to this part of the Chesapeake for oysters; and the Island craft, released from the business of transportation, do a very remunerative trade in "dredging."

This is a mode of catching oysters in deep water, by means of large iron bags, formed of a kind of chain work, with a firm open mouth, the bottom part of which is a kind of rake. One of these dredges is slung to each side of the vessel engaged in this work, so as to drag on the bottom, as she glides under easy sail to and fro, across the surface of the "oyster rocks," or immense beds, which lie beyond the reach of the rake or "tongs." As the dredges fill, they are successively raised and emptied on deck, to be "culled," and stowed away for delivery on board the northern schooners, that are lying at anchor, ready to receive them.

The other and former mode of catching oysters, is with tongs, which are formed of two iron rakes, united to long wooden handles, which move on a pivot like pincers or scissors, and open or shut by the movement of the hands. They are frequently so large that they will take up at one time, about a peck of unculled oysters. In this business more than half the year is spent by these islanders. Even a part of the hot weather of summer, when the oysters are not so good or wholesome, and when it is unlawful for them to be taken to the cities, the Island schooners are employed in taking oysters from their natural beds, where frequently they lie too thickly to thrive, and in "planting them out," in new situations, more favorable for their growth. These new beds are staked out and claimed as the property of those who planted them. In a few months the oysters may be raised again, (for their improvement under such circumstances is very rapid,) and sold to the northern vessels or conveyed to the cities.

When watermelons are in season, the island vessels are employed in carrying them to Baltimore and elsewhere, and across the Chesapeake. They grow abundantly in Annamessex, Virginia, and on the islands, and are profitable to those who cultivate them.

But the oyster business is their main dependence. It has been conjectured that the supply, in the Chesapeake waters, must soon fail, in view of the immense quantities taken up annually, and the increasing facilities with which they are obtained. But they have held out for scores of years; and there seems very little probability that this providential product for these interesting islanders, will be cut off for many generations, if ever.

The islanders are all expert fishermen, and manage to catch a good supply, of numerous delicious kinds of the finny tribes, as they come and go, in their waters. The principal mode is with hooks attached to long hand lines, so that when a very large and strong fish takes hold, they can let a considerable length of line run off, and allow the fish to weary itself, before they attempt to pull it into the canoe.

Sometimes as the fishing season advances, the vessels make trips to the best fishing grounds of the bay, and catch large quantities of fish; these they salt away in barrels for their own use and for sale.

In these various ways the hardy islanders generally make a good livelihood, and not a few of them amass considerable property. They are much attached to their island homes, and by relationship, are closely allied to each other. As the children grow up and marry, a part of the paternal acres is set off for the new family,— another little dwelling is erected, and soon adorned with its surroundings of shrubbery, garden, potato patch, and lot of Indian corn. By degrees each island is thus assuming the appearance of a scattered village. On Tangier Islands, there is hardly a point from which some twenty or more dwellings may not be seen, each freshly painted white, with fancy colors to set off the contrast.

In the youth of Brother Thomas, when he resided here, dwelling houses were comparatively few and far between, and much inferior, as to style and comfort to the present class of residences.

Deal's (or as they were formerly called Devil's) Islands, are two in number, and are situated to the N. E. of Tangier, near the main, and not between the Sound and the Bay. Though the name by which they are now known is a contraction of "Devil's;" yet the orthography for thirty years has been quite well settled in "Deal's." Rev. D. Dailey while P. E. of the District, used to insist on spelling the name in this way, lest there should seem to be a recognition of Satan's having some right to, or property in them.

The larger one, (on which there is a good sized Methodist Church, and where camp meetings have been held most of the years since 1828,) is about three miles in length, by one in width. It is a very productive soil, suitable for almost any species of grain, fruit, or vegetables. An immense quantity of sweet potatoes is raised there, as also a large yield of corn, and some excellent wheat.

But the population, (numbering nearly one thousand,) like that on the smaller islands, has to depend more on the water than on the land for support.

This larger island is separated from the main land by a narrow strait, formerly crossed by a ferry—now by a substantial bridge. The little Deal's Island, where Brother Thomas spent many of the last years of his life, is separated from the larger, by a similar strait or " thoroughfare." This island contains about twenty acres of arable land, besides a large body of marsh. It was purchased a number of years ago by Mr. Thomas, and his brother-in-law, Aaron Bradshaw, and was divided between them; each erecting a dwelling on his part of the island. Subsequently, Mr. T. let his son Seymour have a part of his end of the island, and ever since, there have been three residences on it. Their occupants at the present time are Mrs. Thomas, widow of Rev. Joshua Thomas, Wm. Seymour, his son, and Solomon Evans.

There are several other islands near those that have been described above, that may be worthy of notice. The principal of these are Spring Island, a beautiful spot near Holland's, and for many years the residence of Bro. T. Parks; and Great, and Little Watts' Islands, midway between Tangier and the Accomac shore. On Little Watts' Island, there is a beautiful Light House, and a neat residence for its keeper. It has no other dwelling on it. Great Watts' Island has three families.

These islands separate between the Tangier and the Pocomoke Sound. This latter sound runs from east to west, from the mouth of Pocomoke River, between Accomac Co., Va., and Somerset Co., Md., and is about three or four miles wide by ten or twelve long. Near its centre lies Saxe's Island, having a sufficient population to make it one of the preaching places of Atlantic Circuit. Its inhabitants, in their mode of living and general habits, very much resemble the other islands herein described.

On the Somerset side of Pocomoke Sound is "Somer's Cove," the terminus of the projected E. Shore Railroad, the completion of which may be expected in a year or two, and which, when finished, will open a rapid communication between the cities of Philadelphia and Norfolk, Va.

CHAPTER II.

Birth of Joshua Thomas—"76"—Potato Neck—Father and mother of Joshua
—His Grandfather a Patriot—Death of his father—Removal to Tangier
Island—His stepfather—Love for his mother—Address to children—He
learns to pray—A drunkard's home—Neglect, poverty, and sorrow—No
bread—"Remember the poor"—Success in fishing—The Canoe—Death
of his stepfather—The bottle of brandy—Anecdote—He hears Lorenzo
Dow—"The Lord is here"—Last days and happy death of his mother.

"I was born," says Joshua Thomas, "in Somerset
County, Maryland, on the 30th day of August, 1776."

The stirring life which the following pages are designed to unfold, it will be observed, began in stirring
times. In the memorable year of the nation's nativity,
and close upon the day of its immortal "Declaration,"
may be found the date of Joshua's birth. He lived to
witness over "three score and ten" of its returning
anniversaries, and gave evidence in numerous ways of
that trait, which was not the least excellent and remarkable in his character,—a love for his country.

It may not be regarded as unimportant, to state the
exact locality of his birth. To ascertain this, required
considerable investigation. Most persons intimate with
him, supposed he had been born, as well as raised on
Tangier Island. He simply designates "Somerset

County," and leaves the particular neighborhood indefinite.

If the birth of an illustrious person reflects renown upon the locality where it occurred, and the good and great of earth are claimed with pardonable pride by those among whom they had their being, the credit belongs to Potato Neck, and to its worthy inhabitants the honor of this event.

"Potato Neck" embraces one of the most intelligent, enterprising, and populous communities in Somerset County, or on the eastern shore of Maryland. It has been termed the "garden spot" of Methodism, and by at least one minister well acquainted with the place, "The Land of Beulah!"

Here on the day specified, the man, whose biography we attempt to write, was born.

His parents were John and Martha Thomas. His mother's maiden name was Hall, a lady of striking personal beauty, and greatly beloved by all who knew her.

The grandfather of Joshua had espoused the American cause, in his country's struggle for freedom, and was at this time a soldier in one of the Virginia battalions, where he shortly afterwards died, amid the perils and privations of camp life; bequeathing to his posterity the memory of his patriotism, and that only. His services were never recognized or remunerated by Government, in any way that benefited his family. This may have been the result of neglect in application.

John Thomas, the father of Joshua, had been formerly a school teacher. This was an occupation of considera-

ble importance at that time. He afterwards joined a
'brother, named William, who was captain of a vessel, and
became a sea-faring man. His family lived during this
period in Potato Neck, where he also resided in the intervals of his voyages.

He died suddenly during one of these visits, and the
occasion of this deplorable event, it is said, was somewhat as follows : " He was about leaving home, and
after his vessel had been made ready to sail, went ashore
to take leave of his family and friends. Being barefoot,
he was bitten by a small dog belonging to a Miss Waters.
The wound was trivial, and did not threaten any serious
consequences. He committed his wife and children to
the care of Divine Providence, and, leaving them in the
society of their friends, proceeded on his voyage.
Reaching Tangier Island where his relations lived, he
and his brother went ashore, as was their custom, to pay
them a short visit before going to sea. By this time the
wound on his foot, or ankle, had become painful, and
from this insignificant cause, mortification set in, and
death speedily ensued."

The doleful news was borne across the sound to his
bereaved widow, with the last loving message of her departed husband: " I am going to heaven, bring the
children up to fear and serve God."

This charge the stricken mother now addressed her
energies to fulfill. She removed to the island, where a
comfortable subsistence had been provided for her, and
by untiring industry and economy for three years, was
doing well, until a dark shadow fell upon, and blighted
her being, in the person of a second husband, who,

though at first a "clever sort of a man," standing fair in the community, and "well to do," in a worldly sense, became dissipated and neglectful, ending in habitual and reckless drunkenness.

The manuscript of Mr. Prettyman contains, in his own words the main story of Brother Thomas' childhood and youth :—

"My mother," says Joshua, "was a hard-working woman, and tenderly loved her children. She did all she could to make them comfortable. I loved that mother with devoted fondness, and as I became able, I took delight in doing all I could to help her; for the Lord put it into my heart to be a thoughtful child, and to obey her in every thing."

The recollection of those days remained distinct with him, down to old age; and often, when addressing large congregations, and noticing children in the assembly, he would awaken their attention by a well-timed anecdote of his boyhood, and then speak to them, thus :—

"Now, dear children, let an old man, and a father, who has seen a great many days, and experienced a great many changes, exhort you to be good. Love your parents and obey them, as the Good Book tells you. Think how they love you, and how much they have done and suffered for you. Consider with what tenderness and care your mothers watched over you, when you were little babes in their arms. When you were sick, they could not sleep, but sat by your pillow night and day. Some of your fathers may be dead, as mine was, and you may be little fatherless children as I was. Oh! pity your poor sorrowing mothers, who have the double burden of father and mother upon them. How happy will your mother feel when she finds you willing to help her and please her! God will smile on you too, and bless you, and cause you to be happy and prosperous in the world: don't forget this."

Narrating the incidents following his mother's second marriage, he would say of his stepfather :—

" He used us very well for a time, and having some property of his own added to mother's, he appeared to have good management, and was steady and kind. But the refugees came along and burned our house down, and destroyed nearly everything we had in the world. This had such a bad effect on him, that he became harsh to us, and took to hard drinking, and never done much for us afterward."

Joshua was then about five or six years of age, and through all the successive years of his youth, until he was grown up, he had the misfortune to be in contact with that dissolute stepfather. Their home was a miserable little cabin, their clothing scanty, their food scarce, and the desolation which intemperance brings, had darkened all their previous joys. His poor mother, with an increasing family to care for, and her husband often away on his drunken frolics for weeks at a time ; or, if at home, treating her with rude indignities, had her cup of sorrow full. Yet she taught her children the fear of the Lord, and that trust in him, which formed their only stay and comfort.

Many a touching reminiscence of those days of want and woe, he took occasion to tell, in the ear of listening thousands in the brighter days of his after life.

"We suffered more than tongue can utter, and only for our kind neighbors we should have been still worse; for though they were poor, they were some better off than we were, and they pitied my poor dear mother and her ragged little boys, and brought her meal and other things, to keep us from perishing."

One of those neighbors used to tell an instance of the endurance and spirit of the little boy "Joshua." He said, one cold snowy day his wife looked out and saw a small moving object approaching the house. As nearer it came she discovered that it was the boy Joshua, without a cap, and feet bare; besides being but very thinly clad. He had tracked his weary way against the storm that morning, to say that they had no bread at home. For several days they lived on oysters and crabs, which the boys would pick up around the shore, at low water. Now the snow and ice cut off that resource, and he had come to look for something for his sick and sad mother. Tears came into the good woman's eyes when she saw the little fellow, and heard his artless story.

"Are you not almost perished?" she said, as she urged him to come in.

"Oh no," said he, "I am quite warm."

"But your feet must be nearly frozen?"

"No indeed, I don't feel the cold at all."

It is needless to say, his visit resulted in timely relief.

The infatuated stepfather became more and more negligent of his family, and was a perpetual source of annoyance to them, and the entire neighborhood. He made way with everything he could turn into money, to

purchase rum ; and became such a fearful specimen of
what intoxication would make a man, that the example
stood out like a flaming beacon, before his children, and
happily none of them chose the same course; but rather
avoided all contact with the destroying liquid. He had
been rescued from drowning repeatedly, by his neighbors or his own sons, and at length bought his last
bottle full.

He had a curious kind of flask, left by some of the
British, and with this, and a dollar he had by some
means obtained, he crossed the Pocomoke Sound to
Accomac ; there he bought his dollar's worth of brandy,
drank half of it at once, and started in his canoe back to
the island. He never reached it. His craft was found
drifting along the shore, and his body was subsequently
recovered, and buried in a lone grave on the sandy beach
of Accomac.

Connected with this, there is a curious combination
of circumstances. He had been mourned at home, but
not forgotten by his widow and children. They often
talked of him. Joshua one night had a peculiar dream,
and prepared in the morning to go across the Sound, expecting some tidings of his body. He met an acquaintance near the Pungoteague, who told him he had seen
his father floating past that day. Joshua landed, and
on inquiry found that the body had drifted ashore. He
assisted in the sad burial, and turning homeward he
picked up the veritable bottle his stepfather had in his
canoe, with the brandy still in it. This he carried up to
the house of the gentleman on whose premises Prouit
had been buried, and placing it on the mantel, requested

him to inform every person visiting him, whose it was, and how it came there, "and," said he, "perhaps in that way it may do some good."

The merchant who took the dollar for brandy, when he heard that the unfortunate man was drowned, became troubled about it, and wished Joshua to take the money back. This he indignantly refused, and the money was given to some poor person, who had no knowledge of its history.

Joshua and his little brothers became, at a very early age, expert fishermen, and could bring home a good supply of wild fowl in their season. In this way actual want was kept at bay, and the mother, comforted in the industry of her children, endeavored to make her lot as pleasant for them as possible. It was, however, a stern discipline, a rugged road, the path in which Joshua Thomas learned to advocate the cause of the poor; and in his ministrations, and in his own family, ever inculcate a sympathy with suffering ones, and an unmitigated loathing for intemperance. The iron that entered his mother's soul, wounded his also, and made him a weighty advocate for total abstinence.

"Train up the children that God may bless you with," he would say to his own sons and daughters, as they became married, and about to depart from his roof; "train them up, as I have tried to raise you, and never allow them to go to frolics, or to touch liquor !"

Those who delightedly listened to his camp meeting exhortations, will remember how frequently he was wont to advert to his early days. While the wealthy crowded around to hear, he would recall the days when pinching poverty was the incentive to his late and early toils, and address them thus :

"Dear friends, you have abundance of this world's blessings, and it may be that there is a poor starving family in your neighborhood. Oh, be kind to the poor! If you would know the purest pleasure a human heart can enjoy, be good to the poor. If you would have the benefit of prayers that reach the ear of Jesus soonest, and put gladness in the cup, where want and sorrow has left nothing but bitter dregs;—if you would make mothers such as mine tell their children when they say the Lord's prayer at night, to ask God on your behalf; —and if you want something comfortable against your own times of pain and death ; don't forget the poor."

"It may be," he would add, "that there is some poor unfortunate drunkard near where you live; do you ever think of his wife ? She is worse than a widow, and may not have a bit of bread to keep her and her children from crying themselves to sleep at night. God bless you ! don't turn a cold look on her, and refuse her some little help in time of need."

In the Prettyman narrative, we find the following: "I must tell you of a particular case of suffering: At one time we were many days without bread, and my little brother, Joshua, and myself went along the shore and picked up something to satisfy our hunger. I soon became sick, having no bread to eat, and my mother was much concerned about me. She gave me some medicine, which helped me a little, but the sort of medicine I wanted most was bread. When my step-father came home from the main, he brought some meal with him, and we were all so glad to see such a thing again.

"Mother quickly had some dumplings made and boiled, and I never tasted anything so sweet and good as those Indian dumplings did then. In a few days I was restored to good health.

"I desire to exhort a little here.

" Children, you who may read what I have told of my sufferings, how thankful you ought to be to your heavenly Father, that he has always given you bread, and to spare. Oh! be grateful for your daily bread, and pity poor children who may sometimes have none. Take your little basket, dear young friends, and ask your parents for bread, that you may carry some to the poor. You cannot conceive, understand, how they and their mothers will love you and bless you for it."

On the islands where his boyhood was spent, the canoe is an indispensable convenience in every family. The land is so interwoven with creeks, and cut up with water courses, that in many places a visit to one's next door neighbor can not be paid without the necessary canoe. Neither can the people attend Divine worship, or perform their ordinary business and intercourse without it. What the cart or carriage is to residents on the main, the canoe is to the islander. Great taste is shown in the model, rig, and annual painting of this kind of craft, and from infancy almost, the people become adapted to their management under sail, or with the paddle. A landsman would be amazed to see one of these small boys out in a gale, perched on the windward side, and almost blown out of water, riding the rolling billows, and looking as unconcerned as if on his accustomed cricket in the chimney corner.

Joshua became a skillful canoe navigator, and also a successful fisherman. The neighbors would take him under their protection, as they went off to their fishing grounds, and instruct him in all the arts and mysteries of hooking the crocus or trout that abounds in these waters. Sometimes he would "strike" a drum fish, so large that he could not lift it into his boat without assistance. When able to go out alone, he never failed in securing a good supply of fish, and was regarded by all who knew him, as a surprising boy, for industry and good luck.

Here is a notable incident, revealing that trait in his character, which may have been the great secret of his "good luck:"

"What I am going to relate now may appear strange to you, but it is a fact. Before I knew anything about experimental religion, I was in the habit of praying to God, to direct me where the fish might be found, that I might catch them.

"New fishing places would be presented to my mind, and I always went to them, and found my impressions had never deceived me. I generally obtained abundance of fish. When I caught one I always pulled off my hat, kneeled down in my canoe and thanked the Lord for it, and asked him to give me another; this practice I kept up continually. I often had all the fish I wanted when others caught none. I was ashamed to pull off my hat and kneel in the presence of others; therefore, I chose to go away from all the fishermen, that I might feel free to pray and give thanks. I followed the same plan to find and shoot wild fowl, praying first to be guided where they were, and when I shot and killed any, down, I went on my knees in the marshes and sometimes in the mud, and offered my thanks to the Lord. In this way by the blessing of God upon my labor, I was enabled to do a good part toward supporting the whole family."

A great change has come over the islands since the distant day we are now dwelling upon. Fishing and catching or killing wild fowl is still necessarily a branch of business followed by the provident; but there are so many new ways and means to make a living, and such facilities of trade have sprung up, that wealth has been realized as the reward of industry; and luxury, in many an instance, may be found, where, at that time, it took all a man's thrift and economy to procure the commonest necessaries of life. With the influx of trade and money, however, it is to be feared, there is not a corresponding recognition of the Author of all good, and a continuance of that simplicity and sincerity which characterized the people of *Anno Domini*, 1800.

They were by the force of circumstances deplorably ignorant of letters, and had very indistinct notions of the "truth as it is in Jesus," but they were morally honest, and lived, as a general thing, up to the light they had; a thing which can hardly be said of any community at the present day.

To show the indefiniteness of his early ideas about the nature of the Divine Being, Brother Thomas often related an anecdote which invariably made his hearers laugh; but his object was to magnify the grace that brought him and his neighbors out of darkness into marvellous light.

"Although I said the Lord's prayer regularly, and was in the habit of seeking guidance and good from his hand, I nevertheless had no correct knowledge of his nature or attributes. I could not read, never having gone to school in my life but two weeks, and grew up to manhood entirely unacquainted with the revelation of God in his word.

"I attended a religious meeting in Virginia when near 30 years of age. Lorenzo Dow was preaching very *powerful*, when a woman in the congregation became excited and happy; she started up shouting aloud. The preacher cried out, 'The Lord is here! He is with that sister.' I immediately jumped upon my feet to see the Lord, but I could not see him, and concluded within myself, 'This cannot be true; for I can see as well as he can, and I do not see him. That man must be one of these deceivers.'

"But God opened my eyes soon after, so that I could discern him in his Spirit's mighty presence and power."

Before concluding this chapter, let us follow the history of that "dear good mother," until we find her after a life of mingled *joy* and *sorrow*, sinking down in a peaceful and hopeful death, comforted in her last hours by her devoted son; and borne by him to a grave among her early kindred in Potato Neck.

She lived to the age of eighty, and spent her last days under his roof. When he removed from the Tangier

Island, she accompanied him and encouraged him in his work and labors of love. One Sabbath morning her death was expected. He seemed desirous of remaining with her, but she said no. "Go Joshua, honey, to your meeting, the people will expect you, and the Lord will watch over me. When you return I may be in heaven." He went to his appointment, told his classmates that his good old mother was going home to die no more, and on his way back, learned that her ransomed spirit had taken its flight to Abraham's bosom.

CHAPTER III.

Becomes a Waterman—Wants a wife—Prays for success—Is married—
Builds a house—Happiness at home—Baptism of his child—His attachment to the Episcopal Church—Parson Reese—Obtains a Prayer
book—Learns to read—Family worship—Prejudice against Methodism—
Troubled by its doctrines—Anecdotes—Wm. Miles—Mr. Gunby—Prayer
meetings started by Churchmen.

IN the present chapter we shall continue the narrative
of Brother Thomas, as given in the manuscript of Rev.
L. M. Prettyman, with such remarks and additions as
may be deemed necessary to a clearer insight into his
life and times, and the gradual formation of that character which made him afterwards so remarkable. He
says:

"When I became old enough to think of making my
living at some regular business, it was arranged that I
should go and live with David Tyler, and follow the vo-
cation of a waterman. He was one of our neighbors,
and was known to be a moral, good sort of a man, that
would take proper care of me, and bring me up right.

"To this man I am greatly indebted for the kindness
I received from him. He loved me as a father loves his
own child, and always treated me as a son. I fared well
as long as I lived with him, though I had many a day's

hardship in cold and storm; but I hardly minded such things at that time.

"My employer, though like all the Island people, a stranger to experimental religion then, was nevertheless a strictly moral man, and as far as he knew in what religion consisted, he practiced it, and taught it to me. I learned a great many good things from him."

Referring to this period of his life, he has stated that the first new suit of clothes he ever owned was bought for him in Baltimore, by this considerate Captain Tyler, and on receiving his new jacket, he pressed his old one upon the acceptance of a poor boy that happened to be passing at the moment.

His clothing up to this era had consisted entirely of contrivances, invented by his mother, and mostly constructed out of her own wardrobe. Boots were almost an unknown luxury among the islanders at that day, and even shoes were regarded as superfluous by those hardy and simple people. Nearly everybody went barefoot, so that, if cold pinched occasionally, corns never did, and health was generally of an excellent tone.

"In this way I lived until I was about twenty-three years of age, when I began to think to myself that I had rather have a good wife than anything else in the world besides. But then I came to the disheartening conclusion that I was not prepared to take this important step, having no-means to make a wife comfortable; and if I had, I thought surely no girl could love such an ignorant and awkward young fellow as I am.

"This did not allay my desire, however, and I kept meditating on the subject, until I began to pray to the

Lord that I might obtain a wife and some means to support her. I also promised if the Lord would bless me with a good wife I would begin to serve him better than I ever yet had done. I continued praying every day about this, and sometimes a hope would spring up that my way would become clear. In a short time I heard of a certain nice girl who gave some one to understand that she loved me! At this news my very soul was transported. I never was so glad to hear anything before. It made me feel like a man! But then would come the overshadowing reflection, I am so poor and destitute, what can I do? I dare not attempt to marry, for I have no means to keep house. In this state of perplexity I was often on my knees in prayer and tears; and finally concluded I would make sure of the good girl that loved me, and marry her, for fear I would not have such another favorable opportunity. We were consequently married."

This "good girl," was a Miss Rachel Evans, and became a very devoted wife and the mother of several children, of whom are now living John, Elisha, and Seymour Thomas, and Mrs. Hester Webster of Deal's Island. The minister who performed the ceremony was a Rev. John Evans, probably a clergyman of what was then termed the "old church."

"After I was married," continues the manuscript, "and looked calmly at my situation, I became very much scared, and did not know where to live or what to do; until my faithful friend, David Tyler, told me I might bring my wife and live with him, and he would still pay me for my services, until I could go to house-keeping.

This generous offer I gladly accepted, and for three years I had a home for my wife with his kind family, and with that of my father-in-law : keeping in view all that time the hope of building a house of my own, and setting up for ourselves.

" At length I built a small house on Tangier, and having saved some few necessary articles to begin the world with, I moved with great joy into my own home. Our entire stock of provisions consisted of three bushels of meal, and two little pigs. Of furniture we had barely enough to make out with.

" When settled in my own home, I was a happy man. I used to watch the smoke curl up my clay chimney from the fire, as I lay in my bed, and it looked beautiful. I thought I was the happiest man in all the world, with all I wanted round me,—a good healthy young wife and a nice little son,—my cup of bliss was full to overflowing. I thanked my God from the bottom of my heart, for all the good things he had given such an unworthy creature as I."

He envied no living being as we see him now; after the labors of the day were ended, he could turn his steps toward his own sweet home, meet at the threshold the glad welcome smile of his wife, and take to his breast the first-born of his house, his fine little prattling boy. He realized an ample reward for his previous self-denial in his youthful days, and had no anxieties about the future. His feelings at that time, found expression in his simple form of thanksgiving; subsequently it would have excited his shouting proclivities to an uncommon degree.

He had as yet no enlightenment as to his condition morally. He had never dreamed of the personal pleasures found in pardoned sin, and the abounding joys of experience in Christ Jesus.

His circumstances, however, had a mellowing tendency on his susceptible nature, and led him nearer, in sincere desire, and conscious duty, to the throne of grace. He longed to know and do the will of that Father, which he tried to acknowledge in all his ways, and who had mercifully led him on from infancy, to a healthy and hopeful manhood.

His industry had been blessed in providing daily bread, and adding to the comforts of his humble home.

The first important event of his domestic life, after he commenced housekeeping, was the baptism of his little son. The parents had a talk over this matter, and came to the conclusion that it was full time, and their religious duty to have this act performed.

Ministers of the P. E. Church had, at long intervals, visited and held service among the island people, while *they* occasionally spent a Sabbath on the Main, and frequented the church. In this way a decent regard was kept up, as to the ordinances and form of religion, and infant baptism was very generally practiced among them.

Hearing that a minister might be found at a certain place, he and his wife, with the babe, crossed the sound to Annamessex, and were directed to the house of a Mr. Henry Handy, where a Presbyterian minister was, for the time being, on a visit. He says :—

"I had inquired of my friends, who I thought knew

more about this matter than I did, as to the nature of the ordinance, and how I must do on the occasion. They told me the preacher would examine me closely about my religion. This puzzled me dreadfully, and set me to examine myself, and study out what it meant, and what I should say to him. When we came to Mr. Handy's, and they found out our business, the minister called me out, and we walked together, up and down the garden. When we were quite alone, he said to me, ' Do you believe in Jesus Christ,—that he died for us, rose from the dead, ascended into heaven, and will come at the last day to judge the world in righteousness ?' I was greatly agitated in his presence, but told him I did believe these things. He advised me how to live so as to be saved, and seemed much interested about me, and pleased with my open and simple answers. We then went into the house, and he baptized my child whom we called John. The ceremony was very solemn, and this whole matter made a very deep impression on my mind.

This " impression" accompanied him to the island, and moved him to talk with some of his neighbors, about their religious destitution and ignorance. They had no preaching, or regular worship of any kind on the islands, though they were all attached by early predilection to the service of the old Episcopal Church which they attended in Annamessex, and at Pongoteague, in Virginia.

Methodism about this time had begun to rouse the people in various neighborhoods, through its earnest and active agencies. The preachers had penetrated all along the eastern shore ; great revivals had occurred,—societies had been formed, prayer meetings started, and converts were multiplying on every hand. A few churches had been hastily erected in central localities, and were the rallying points of this new host, for Quarterly Meetings and Love Feasts; but from house to house the work was carried; and in Annamessex alone, the whole community, with but very few exceptions, were under awakening power. The islanders became aware of the state of things, but held themselves aloof from the meetings, and adopted the early prejudice that arrayed formalists against this new element of religious life. Believing that it might endanger their peace, and that it threatened destruction to the church of their fathers, they shunned the people called "Methodists," but were induced to fall in somewhat with the spirit of the times, and try to be more religious themselves.

A Parson Reese, still affectionately remembered by many, officiated then in Annamessex. He was sent for to preach on the islands, and went across several times at the instance of a few of the more intelligent and zealous church-men there. Joshua Thomas was generally delegated to bring the parson over, and this duty was very agreeable to his serious mind. Being so much in his company, it attached him very strongly to both the minister and the church. He had a good opportunity for conversation during these excursions, and improved it by asking questions, which the good parson very kindly answered, telling him how to be a good man.

This was his great concern at that time, and when informed that he must be "upright and honest, keep the Sabbath day holy, and attend church as often as he could"—he set himself to fulfill this outline of duty to the best of his ability. The parson also advised him to get a prayer-book, and have prayer in his family, which he soon did, having by patient and painful application, learned to read a little. He had to send to Baltimore to purchase the book, then set up his family altar, and tells us "he thought he was all right."

A contribution was raised for the minister, every time he came over to the islands to pay him for his services. The amount was from five to eight, and ten dollars a trip.

Mr. Thomas was a regular attendant after this at the old chapel which formerly stood near the head of Colburn's Creek, and of which the St. Paul's Church at Quindoqua, Rev. John Crossdale, Rector, is a modern and thrifty successor.

He and his neighbors, when on the way to their church, generally landed in the vicinity of the old St. Peter's Methodist Church, which was one of the first erected in that part of the country.

Mr. Wm. Miles who resided there, and was a prominent member of the new denomination, related an incident, showing the prejudice existing in the mind of Mr. Thomas against Methodism.

"The first time I ever remember to have met with him," said Father Miles, "was on a Sabbath morning near St. Peters. He was dressed in waterman's clothes, with a little round hat, a light striped jacket, pants rolled up half way to his knees, and his shoes under his arm.

"'Well, sir,' said he, accosting Mr. Miles, 'can you

tell me if Mr. Reese is going to preach to-day at the church?'

"He will not, sir; for he is gone from home and will not return for some time.'

"'Then I may as well turn about and go home.'

"He and Mr. Miles walked on together until they came opposite the Methodist Church, when Mr. M. said, 'We have meeting here to-day, and as you are disappointed in service at your own church, suppose you step in and worship with us.'

"At this invitation the countenance of Mr. Thomas expressed what he did not choose to utter with his lips. With a look of disdain, he seemed to say that he would not degrade himself so much as to enter the dreaded and despised place. He hurriedly started on, as if there was contamination in the neighborhood, and reaching the landing, spread his sails, and was off quickly for home."

Not very many years after the occurrence related above, there was a great gathering at this same St. Peters, of itinerant preachers, official members, and new converts to methodism from a circle of ten to twenty miles around. The eloquent Lawrenson was present. Local preachers, exhorters, circuit stewards, and class leaders, had met to deliberate, and recount the wonderful work of God in them, and through the instrumentalities he was was using to spread a knowledge of salvation by the remission of sins.

An Islander took his place among this band of brethren that morning, and was introduced by Brother Lawrenson as "Joshua Thomas, an exhorter in the society at Tangier Island!"

In the Sunday love feast, Brother Thomas told in burning words, the story of his conviction for sin, his search after a pardoning Saviour, his emancipation from pride, prejudice, and unbelief, and his glorious hope of immortality and eternal life. He shouted a little too, while recounting the great things the Lord had done for him.

An announcement from the Presiding Elder occasioned some surprise and much curiosity. It was in these words, "A stranger will preach here to-night."

Who this stranger was, soon became the topic of inquiry, and at the hour for worship, who should he be but Joshua Thomas! He was a very timid man, and invariably refused to announce a text when ministers were present. On this particular occasion, however, it is said Lawrenson rose and announced a text for brother Thomas, and he proceeded to preach a memorable discourse, the main substance of which was his own experience, before and after he obtained salvation by faith in our Lord Jesus Christ.

This was, indeed, a wonderful transformation and a somewhat singular coincidence. The first sermon our "Parson of the Islands" ever attempted to preach was on this quarterly occasion, and in St. Peters Methodist Church.

To return to the autobiography. He tells us: "When I and a few of my neighbors set up the family altar, and read the prayers which were pointed out as proper by our minister; it satisfied our conscience pretty well until we heard the Methodists preach, and talk about regeneration.

"I began to get troubled about something, I knew not what. I hated their new doctrines, but the more I thought on them the more I was torn to pieces and convinced that I yet lacked one thing, that my formal prayers and good works would avail nothing without real conversion, a change of heart from sin to holiness. These people said, 'I must be born again, and made a new creature in Christ Jesus,' I did not comprehend the meaning of this, and tried hard to think they were under a delusion about religion.

"I continued my prayers and duties, as *our* Church minister told me, and would sometimes wear off my troubles, until again and again the truth would open my eyes to a view of myself as a poor, lost sinner, destitute of the life, power, and comfort of that religion which others professed."

A gentleman residing in Annamessex at this period, a Mr. Gunby, gave the following statement:—He was well acquainted with Mr. Joshua Thomas, and always considered him a very sincere and honest man. He frequently lodged with him when he came from the island to attend church.

The Methodists were gaining ground very fast. Great revivals had swept through Accomac and many parts of Somerset. Camp meetings had been started, and produced a wonderful effect on the popular mind and heart. The people would crowd to the meetings, full of prejudice, fall under the word, and start into new life. Converts were accustomed to go from one house to another, holding meetings for prayer and singing, and sometimes whole families were powerfully converted.

Under these circumstances Parson Reese, the Episcopal minister, advised him (Mr. Gunby) and others of his church to hold prayer-meetings too, which they attempted to do, but were not very successful. When Mr. Reese came round again, he inquired how the people liked the prayer-meetings. Mr. G. replied, " Our folks say they do not want such meetings, they resemble too much these d—d methodist revivals, and must stop."

This Mr. Reese was a God fearing man in some good degree, and said he believed the Methodists were partly right, and wished his people to be like them. He could not prevail on them, however, to keep up prayer-meetings, and with tears in his eyes expressed himself to Mr. G. thus: "I know that this way is right, but what can I do? I am a poor man, and have no other means of support. I am dependent on these careless rich men, and I can do nothing with them that would induce them to forsake their practices and become humble inquirers after spiritual religion."

"Mr. Thomas was with us," continued Mr. Gunby, and attended some of our prayer-meetings, but merely sat and looked on without taking any active interest in the exercises, farther than that he seemed desirous of obtaining instruction and religious benefit."

In this state of uncertainty he continued for some years, until God, by the strivings of his Spirit brought him "by a way which he knew not," into enlarged enjoyment, and true gospel liberty, and prepared him to be an instrument in his hands of signal good to others.

CHAPTER IV.

Revivals on the Eastern Shore of Virginia—Rev. Thomas Smith—Dr.
Chandler—Pungoteague Camp Meeting—Joshua Thomas attends—His
sensations—Hears Lorenzo Dow—"An Earthquake" feared—Disturbance
at the meeting—Arrest of the wrong person—Mob raised—Managers arrested—Fined two thousand dollars—Rules and regulations for Camp
Meetings adopted—Effect of Methodist influence on Joshua—He prepares
to attend another meeting.

THE memory of those wonderful seasons of revival
that attended the first camp meetings held along the
eastern shore of Maryland and Virginia, and which followed the labors of Methodist preachers about the beginning of the present century, is growing indistinct,
and will soon have passed into oblivion, unless a historian
be found who may choose this fertile field, and rescue the
remarkable scenes of those days from fading out of the
mind of the Church.

One aid is left us in the "Life of Rev. Thomas
Smith," by the late Rev. David Dailey, by which the
measure of that amazing power and influence which established Methodism in Virginia may be ascertained.
The brief record from Mr. Smith's own journals, of the
revival of 1800–1, in Accomac and Northampton, will
prepare our minds for certain events which properly be-

long to the period we have reached in the history of Joshua Thomas.

The opposition of "the world, the flesh, and the devil," to this astonishing work of grace, was inveterate; but infidelity, formality, and the most obstinate prejudices melted away before the earnest preaching of that gospel which was the "power of God unto salvation." Conversions are reported by hundreds; persecutors became fast friends and valiant defenders of the faith; and many families, of the first grade in society in that part of the "Old Dominion," avow themselves to be adherents and professors of the religion of the cross.

Camp meetings were established soon after Dr. Chandler took charge of the lower district, and were remarkable for good order for a time, and for great simplicity in diet, dress, and religious worship.

No place possessed such attractions for the pious of that period as the "tented grove;" and companies traveled far, in those days, to witness the displays of awakening and converting power which attended the preaching of the gospel, and to help in those efforts which availed to spread the holy influence of prayer and praise.

A camp meeting was appointed to be held near Pungoteague early in the month of August, 1807, and to this occasion we clearly trace the first thorough convictions of Joshua Thomas. He was present by accident, or rather, by that Providential guidance which marked all his movements. It was a very large and, generally, successful meeting, though greatly interrupted by an outbreak of disorder, and an unhappy sequel which has made it memorable.

Large numbers were in attendance from various points up and across the bay. Vessels were chartered from the Manoken, Annamessex, and other rivers; and companies, consisting mostly of recent converts, crowded their decks to visit the meeting.

We shall let Mr. Thomas describe the train of circumstances by which he was thrown into the genial society of these voyagers, and at length found himself a personal observer of the manners and usages of a people everywhere spoken against.

It will be discovered that he was brought in contact with Methodism under such a form and spirit, as was best calculated to break the force of his deeply rooted prejudices, and greatly increase his desire to be a partaker with them in "like precious faith."

He says:—

" I was out in the Sound, one day, in company with several of my neighbors engaged in fishing, when three vessels were seen approaching us. Each of them was crowded with people, but where they came from, what their business was, or whither they were bound, none of us at that time knew. They laid their course close by the fishing grounds, and hailed us to buy our fish. We disposed of all we had to spare, and they engaged a Mr. Crockett and me to pilot them into Pungoteague creek.

" I went on board one of the vessels, and never in my life met with such affectionate and clever people. They had everything that was good to eat, and each began to invite me to partake with them. One said, ' Come and eat with me,' and another said, ' You must eat with me.' One very nice looking lady said, ' You shall sit right

down here, my victuals are all ready, so help yourself.'
So I sat down and she sat by my side and began to help
me to everything that was nice and good. It was the
best eating I ever enjoyed before. This lady was so
kind and loving in her manner that I began to watch
her closely, for I thought such familiarity in a stranger
did not seem exactly right. But I soon discovered
plainly that she was a pious, good woman, and then I
was not so shy, but felt quite comfortable and free among
them.

"After eating and drinking, I went ashore to prepare
for a trip with them next morning as pilot. They all
came to anchor just opposite my house, which was quite
near the water, and about sundown they began to sing,
and then to pray, and kept on singing and praying until
sometime in the night. All our men, and the women,
and children came down to the shore to listen to this
strange and most delightful music. It was the most
charming we had ever heard. The sounds seemed to
fill the whole air, and we thought it heaven on earth.

"Our people could have staid there all night long,
listening to the sweet hymns and wonderful prayers
which resounded over the waters.

"In the morning John Crockett and I went on board,
and they up anchor, and stood down for Pungoteague.
We piloted them up the creek where a lot of vessels had
already arrived, and then went up with them to a large
grove, where we found what appeared to be a wonderful
sight to us.

"There were a great many tents in a circle round, and
seats made for people to sit on. There was a place built

up with boards for the preacher to stand when he preached, and a great crowd of people moving about and talking together, while some were sitting in tents singing like the people on board the vessels.

"Every one appeared to be glad to see us, and shook hands with us, inviting us to stay with them during the meeting. Pretty soon they had preaching, and the most singular looking man I ever saw was the preacher that time. His name was Lorenzo Dow, and it was while he was preaching as I told you before, the woman became happy and shouted aloud, when he said, 'The Lord is here! *He is with that sister*,' and I jumped up to see him, if he was there; but could not see anything extraordinary, except the woman clapping her hands and saying 'Glory! glory!' A good many people commenced crying, and some fell on the ground, others were talking to them, and telling them to look to Jesus, and it was very soon a time of great confusion.

"After a while neighbor Crockett came to me and said he wanted to leave there and go home, I told him I did not want to leave yet awhile, for I began to *feel very strange*, and loved the people who had been so kind to us. I continued to watch the meetings, and saw several profess to be converted. Another preacher, Dr. Chandler, preached a great sermon. His text was, 'Awake to righteousness and sin not; for many have not the knowledge of God; I speak this to your shame.'

"The word took effect on my mind somewhat, and convinced me that I had not the knowledge of God, and with all my good resolves, I knew I often fell into sin. I do not know but that I might have learned the way of salvation had I remained, but Crockett kept at me to go home. Said I, 'Let us stay and hear and see more of it.' 'No,' said he, 'we must go; for if we stay here much longer, there will be *an earthquake, or something awful,* and we shall all be destroyed.'

"He appeared to be in such distress and alarm about the shouting, and singing, and people falling all around us, that I consented to go, and we went off together, and returned home to the island thinking about these things."

Happy for him—we think, that he did leave just at that juncture. Had he remained a little longer, the scene that transpired at that meeting would have revived his prejudices, and perhaps defeated the new emotions which were awakened in his mind about personal religion.

The scene we refer to was an unhappy disturbance of the camp, by a gang of wild and wilful persons, who would not be persuaded to leave the place, and who greatly interrupted the order.

Dr. Chandler was a strict, and very systematic man, and had his rules always obeyed to the letter. The managers of this meeting, acting under his orders, arrested the ringleader of the lawless ones, (as they supposed,) and proceeded to tie this person and imprison him in a temporary gaol, they had constructed for evil doers. Here they kept him under guard all night, while his friends were mustering their excited forces around, and threatening a general attack on the encampment with the avowed purpose of breaking it up.

Much anxiety prevailed while this state of things ex-

isted. Several scuffles took place, and a preacher named
Chambers from Baltimore received a blow on the head
or face that made the blood flow. He immediately took
his stand on the outside of the circle, and with the blood
running down his face, preached a powerful sermon,
which had the effect to restrain the religious persons
present from all violence in their contact with the infuriated mob who assailed them.

It was ascertained meanwhile that some mistake had
been made in the person who had been put in "durance
vile," and he was released. This partially restored
order, and the meeting went regularly forward. Next
day the sheriff of the county with a large posse arrived
on the ground, and placed Dr. Chandler and several
others under arrest for a breach of the peace, or false
imprisonment; and they were bound over to a future
adjudication of the case. This business resulted in a
fine of two thousand dollars, which the preachers and
their friends had to pay.

That some considerable injury was done to the cause
of religion we cannot but suppose, yet this affair had a
tendency to define the position of the friends and foes
of Methodism not only in Accomac but throughout the
peninsula, and resulted in a more judicious management
'of camp meetings in the future.

In the old journal for Annamessex Circuit we find
the following resolutions passed this year (1807), viz.:

"That the Quarterly Conference systematize a plan
by which all our meetings in the woods are to be hereafter regulated.

" That the regulations be printed and entered on the journal, and labels printed for the managers and guard.

" That the Conference preceding each religious meeting in the woods, appoint five managers, one of whom may be appointed chief, who shall attach to themselves, as occasion may require in their judgment, as many additional managers as may be necessary; said appointments to be made from members of society or otherwise, and the managers shall control the temporalities of the meeting."

The first office, many who are now our oldest and most honored men in the Church ever remember to have received, was that of either manager, guard, or "dog whipper," at these woods meetings, and the printed label attached to the hat or coat breast, was, in their young days, regarded as a badge of great distinction.

We have an account of four great woods meetings this memorable year. One in Potato Neck, one in Annamessex, one at Pungoteague, and one at Todd's Chapel. The Church militant retains several of the converts of those meetings, while hundreds have joined "the general assembly and church of the first born" in heaven.

The managers of the Potato Neck meeting were Francis Waters, Senr., James Waters, Lazarus Maddux, Wm. Waters, Wm. Colbourn, Hance Lawson, Dr. Robertson, Samuel Smith, David Wallace, H. H. Curtis, Wm. Boggs, Jarvis Ballard, Isaac Handy, and James Benson.

We left Mr. Thomas at his home on Tangier Island, pondering seriously the new questions elicited in his mind by what he had observed and felt under the word, and in the prayer meetings at Pungoteague. His neighbor Crockett was troubled in spirit too. An undefinable sense of dread had taken possession of his soul; and, though he fled from the meeting, the Spirit still rested on him until the earthquake came sure enough and broke up the fallow ground of his heart.

He was soundly converted shortly afterwards, as we shall find in the course of this narrative.

The religious movement had now commenced, and, like rising waters, it rolled in on the inhabitants of the islands until their own meetings became as remarkable as any that had preceded them.

Some of the inhabitants had been over to the Potato Neck meeting in the early part of the summer, others were preparing to attend the Annamessex meeting, now drawing nigh;—and to this meeting we must take our readers in the next chapter. The spot where it was held was, at that time, called "Williams' Woods," near the place now known as Roachville. The old woods have long since been cut down, the ground cleared up, and the spot is now a cornfield, where so many seeking souls could sing :—

> "How happy every child of grace,
>   The soul that's filled with joy and peace,
>   That bears the fruit of righteousness,
>   And kept by Jesus' power ;
>   Their trespasses are all forgiven,
>   They antedate the joys of heaven ;
>   In rapturous lays
>   Shout the praise
>   Of Jesus' grace
>   To a lost race
>   Of sinners, brought to happiness
>   Through th' atoning blood of Jesus."

Numerous camp meetings were held there subsequently, and greatly aided in building up the Church and bringing into the fold many of those who were "afar off," in "trespasses and sins." Several prominent adherents of the "old Church" were about this time converted, and joined the communion of the Methodists, in which they lived and died.

CHAPTER V.

Camp Meeting in Annamessex—Mr. Thomas resolves to attend—His uncle
Levi's warning—Arrives at the meeting—Cautious against imposition—
Will not have religion in the Methodist way—Great display of power—
He takes to the woods—Prays alone—Falls down—Becomes discouraged
—Mr. Wiltbank—" Behold the man !"—Goes to the mourners' bench in
the right spirit—Believes—Feels a mighty change—" Loves everybody"—
Begins to " cry out and shout"—Exhorts all night—Sorrow at breaking
up of the Camp—Returns home happy—Shouts through the corn—Prays
without a book—Tells his joy to all around.

" IT was much on my mind from this camp meeting,"
says Mr. Thomas, "to go to the next one, which, we understood, would be in a few weeks on the Main in Annamessex, lower part of Somerset County, Md."

Several motives prompted this desire. He had an intensely craving mind for information, and the stirring
exercises of the meeting he had just reluctantly left,
haunted his memory night and day. How people could
pray without a book, or preach without a sermon written
out before them, or exhort with words unstudied and in-
telligible, that thrilled him in a manner to which he was,
up to that time, an entire stranger; and, especially, how
people became as happy as they seemed, there in the
woods, with hundreds looking on, and listening to their

exclamations of hope and joy—this was, to the man Joshua, a phenomenon, an unaccountable mystery.

Then, again, his heart was won to this loving people. Despite his prejudices, their cordial Christian spirit disarmed him; their singing left sweet echoes sounding through his soul, and brought him into spiritual contact with higher and holier orders of intelligence. He had heard of angels, but now he seemed to apprehend something of their nature and service. His dreams revelled in companionships with those "round about the throne," and their kindred, as he felt assured those were, who sang so beautifully and praised God so heartily on earth.

But his chief reason for going to the next camp meeting was to learn the way of salvation more perfectly. The spirit said " Come," in its direct influences. God's eye was on the ardent, simple-hearted Islander, and without apprehending the importance of this step, or its vast results to himself and others, he set out for the " next camp meeting."

Not, however, until he had tried to influence some of his immediate friends and neighbors to accompany him. When the time drew near, he says :

" I wanted them to go with me, but could not prevail on them to do so. So, after my wife had prepared me something to eat, and some provision to take along with me, I set off alone. On the way I had to pass the house where my uncle lived (Levi Thomas). He was in the door, and as I was going by, he said, " Well, nephew, where are you going ?'

" 'I am going to camp meeting, uncle.'

" 'Have you nothing to do at home ?' said he.

" 'Yes, sir,' I replied, ' I have plenty to do.'

" 'Well, you had better go back and do it. If you go there, they will have you down to worship them. They are nothing but a parcel of Irishmen, who have run away from their own country to keep from being hanged. They have great *larning*, and know no other way to get a living but going about raising the devil by their preaching, and carrying on ; and then make people worship them and give them money !'

" I said, 'No, uncle, they will not get *me* down to worship them.'

" 'Now, nephew, let me tell you—stop a moment—when I lived up yonder in Dorchester, there was as nice a little church and congregation as you ever saw, and a nice minister too ;—and one Sunday morning, just as the Parson was commencing his service, one of these men rode up and hitched his horse under a great oak tree before the church door, and halloo'd,—you might have heard him a mile—" Choose ye this day whom ye will serve !" This so frightened the people, that some of them ran out of the church, and the Parson was so disturbed, he could not go on with his prayers, and he went out to the man and begged him to be still and not disturb the worship. He promised he would, and staid under the oak till the Parson finished the service ; and just as the people were coming out of the church door, he roared out again, like a lion, " *Choose ye this day whom ye will serve !*" One old woman cried out, "I will serve the living God !" " Come on then," said the preacher, and they all went and stood round him. He preached and halloo'd there for nearly an hour, and you might have heard him a mile off. You never heard the like! He tore the Church all to *shivers*, and they could never get a congregation there again, for he went into converting the people, and our Church went entirely down.'

" 'Well, uncle,' I said, 'I am not going for any harm, and I don't think they will do me any injury.'

" So I traveled on to where my canoe was, thinking over what I had heard. I did not like the thought of having my Church tore to pieces by these fellows, and it made me more cautious than ever."

That *caution* assumed the form of incredulity, and greatly retarded the operations of the Spirit on his mind, when he found himself within the circle of influence at the meeting. He began, as a critic, determined not to be imposed upon, but to investigate the whole procedure of conversion; and, if possible, remodel the arrangement for his own particular case. But hear him:

" It was on Friday that I reached the camp. Every thing was arranged in fine order about the ground. The number in attendance was very large, and the worship was going on in a very solemn and impressive manner. I listened to everything they said with great care and attention, and watched very closely all that was going on in the meeting. I was determined not to be deceived, and that none of them should put a *spell* on me, to make me fall down and pretend to be converted.

" Several sermons were preached, and exhortations delivered, to all of which I paid good attention; for I really desired, if there was such a thing as conversion, to have my heart converted. I was opposed to having this done in their way, that was, at the mourners' bench, or altar, in public, where the eyes of so many people would be fixed upon me. I wanted the blessing in secret.

"And now I know this pride and bashfulness hinder many from seeking and being saved. They are convinced, and feel their need, and they sincerely desire to be converted; but being unwilling to confess Christ before men, they grieve the Holy Spirit; he leaves them, and they are lost!

"My dear young reader, I beg you will never give way to that temptation, or allow bashfulness to hinder you from your duty. This is one of the most dangerous delusions of the enemy.

"During Saturday some were converted; one of my neighbors,—who came after I started,—among the rest. (John Parks.) I then began to feel very uneasy, and much concerned about being changed in heart. I went into the woods alone, and prayed that God would convert my heart, but felt no better. I returned again into the camp, still praying secretly to be converted.

"I felt so bad on Saturday night that I concluded I would go and kneel down with them at the mourners' seat, and try it once, determined that I would not fall nor cry out, as I had heard and seen others do. When praying persons came to talk with me, I would not let them, but rudely elbowed them off. I staid there some time, trying to pray secretly, until I became discouraged, and concluded there was no reality in being converted; and so I arose and went away.

"On Sunday morning there was a great meeting, and many professed to be born from above. They shouted all over the ground, and many fell, and lay as dead on the earth; when they recovered they began to praise God wonderfully. I watched all this, and thought much upon the scenes I witnessed.

"I went away into the woods again, a great way from the camp, the crowd, and noise, and tried harder than ever to pray, and get the blessing of a new heart there alone. After struggling a long time in prayer, and receiving no answer, I concluded I would try what virtue there was in *falling!* So I looked me out a smooth place that was free from roots and sticks, that I might not hurt myself in the fall, and kept my eye a little over one shoulder to see how to fall and not hurt myself: I then came down full length on the earth. I lay about ten minutes, praying to God to convert me there; and receiving no answer, I arose completely discouraged, and very impatient besides.

"I felt almost ready to declare, 'I do not believe in their way of being converted, and I will try no more.' I was sullen, and stubborn, and gave way to a wicked feeling of discontent, but all this time my wretchedness was increasing.

"Many a time since that memorable Sabbath have I thought over the blind perversity of my will, and the utter ignorance I was in, with reference to the gospel plan of salvation by faith. I never see a poor mourner in Zion, without feeling my heart melt in love and sympathy for him. Oh brethren! you who labor with poor seeking ones, to point them to the Lamb of God, don't get impatient with them because they do not seem to go right, as you know the way, to the cross. The old enemy holds a fierce contention over and with them, and it is hard sometimes to dislodge him from the heart in which he has long reigned. Step by step the sinner must grope his way, until he feels entirely humbled and lost. Then Jesus comes, and the glimmering light begins to break, when his soul believes firmly, and trusts fully in the merits of the Saviour. In a moment the heavy burden is gone, and the soul is filled with joy.

"But I must go on and tell you how it was with me. A Mr. Wiltbank preached in the evening, which was to be the last sermon. I did not like his looks very well at first; he had a rather hard looking face, and was given to speak very loud and broad. As he went on in his discourse I began to like him better. He put it on the Methodists pretty hard. I was pleased with that, and thought he was candid and honest, and had the right spirit.

"As he became more and more animated in his sermon toward the close, I felt something rise up within me, and say to me, 'Behold the man! see how he is moved by the Holy Spirit!' While he was preaching there, I obtained faith that I should be converted. I gave up all my whims and notions about having it done in secret, and made up my mind fully to have it in the Methodist way, if the Lord would forgive and convert me.

"The confidence *that He would*, became strong and unwavering. I felt something drawing me right to the feet of Jesus. Immediately on the invitation being given, I went to the altar, and kneeled down and began to lift up my voice in earnest prayer, that God would then convert my heart, and set me at liberty.

"Blessed be his name! I did not wait long before I felt a gracious change run through my whole being. I did not say a word about what I felt then to those about me, nor rise from my knees, but continued kneeling and wondering at the mercy and goodness of God. While thus engaged in the midst of the mourners, and silently adoring my loving Saviour, my half-brother came forward and kneeled close by me, bathed in tears. Something said to me, 'Do you love your brother?' I said, 'Yes, I do;' and I never felt such love before. I reached out, and took him by the hand to speak to him, but that moment I was so filled with the Spirit of life and love, I could not help shouting to the glory of God with all my might. It struck me in a moment, as quick as a flash of lightning, and my soul was filled unutterably with heavenly transport.

This was the first time I ever cried out in prayer or praise, in a congregation, but it was not the last. No, thank God; I have felt a heart to praise him, and have done it since that night, more times than I can number.

"'Hosanna to Jesus! my soul feels him precious;
    In bright beams of glory he comes from above.
My heart is now glowing, I feel his love flowing,
    I'm sure, that my Jesus I really do love.'

"As soon as this transport was somewhat abated, I rose up and began to tell all the unconverted I met, what God had done for me, and to exhort them to go and seek the Lord; for he would have mercy upon them.

"I went all over the camp ground in this way, telling everybody what a happy change I had experienced, and

urging them to pray for it immediately. The whole
night I spent in this manner, and sinners fell in heaps,
in different parts of the camp, crying to God for deliverance.
A great many were converted that night, some of whom
have gone home happy, and others are on the way with
' their faces thitherward.'

" On Monday morning the camp was broken up, and
we were all about to depart to our respective homes.
Here was a new scene, and a new sensation to me. I
came with curiosity, fear, and cautiousness, lest these
people should deceive me. I fortified myself against
what I imagined was their wild or wicked delusions; but
oh what a change! Sorrow now filled my heart at the
thoughts of parting. I cried like a child that had been
whipped. Some passed by, and said, ' What makes you
cry so?' I answered, 'I want to die here, I love the
very ground, and cannot bear the pangs of parting with
these loving brethren and sisters!'

" With a heart full of love and sorrow,—love because
God had pardoned my sins and converted my heart,—and
sorrow because I had to part with my new found brethren in
the Lord, and go to dwell among unconverted men,—I
left that dear spot, that precious place, where from above,
I first received the pledge of love, and started on my
journey home.

" I went to Mr. H. Handy's to spend the night. During the silent hours, I was up several times and prayed,
and was very happy all night. In the morning I prayed
with the family in my stammering way, as well as I
could—telling them what the Lord had done for my
soul. I then bid them farewell, and crossed the Sound

to Tangiers. I found my wife and children well, and prayed with them for the first time without a book, and praised God some time for the wonderful things I had felt and seen."

The friends of Brother Thomas, who were familiar with him in his active days of labor in the cause of the Redeemer, will be glad to find the preceding narrative in his own words, although they will miss many items from his account as given here, that they have heard from his own lips. The story of his conversion was the ground-work of all his public ministrations, and like the Apostle Paul, he made it telling, in the conviction of careless sinners, and to the consolation of sincere inquirers after God.

He sometimes intimated, while referring to his blunders when seeking religion, that it was the devil who baffled him, and at one particular juncture hurled a knot of pine wood at his head which he barely escaped.

There is an account of his meeting with his family, after his conversion, that goes farther in detail than his own brief allusion. It is said, when he met his wondering wife out on the path, and told her the glad news of his change, he began to shout, and shouted on until he traversed the lot in which some very luxuriant corn was growing. His wife became concerned to see him act so "singular," and alarmed lest he might break down all the corn. A neighbor came running over to see what was the matter, and finding him still at it, among the corn, called on him to desist or he would ruin his crop.

When they came to examine the damage, it was ascertained that he had not trodden down a single hill, or broken one stalk, although he had been nearly all over the patch, "leaping and praising God."

It will be observed that he began to pray in private—several times during the night after leaving the camp meeting; and also that he took up the cross next morning in the family where he lodged, and held family prayer.

These two duties marked all his Christian life in an eminent degree. His great power with God and with men was gained in secret at the mercy-seat, and in social life around the home altar. He lived by prayer and humble faith, and rarely, in all his travels, if ever, crossed a threshold, without commending the family with all its members, connections, and interests in prayer to God.

CHAPTER VI.

Brother Thomas begins to hold meetings on the island—Thomas Crockett—
First prayer meeting—All day at it—Conversion of neighbor Crockett
—Souls saved in the absence of a minister—Seymour and Lee—Tent
meeting—The revival on Smith's Island—Solomon and Richard Evans
—Great meeting at Richard's—Sinners quake and run—The devil after
them—Rev. Wm. Evans—Anecdote—The dance displaced by prayer meetings—The old orchard—Aunt Charity's dream—A church organized.

As soon as Brother Thomas returned from the meeting where he had found "the pearl of great price," he
felt moved to exhort his neighbors to "flee the wrath
to come." His soul was in a constant ecstasy. He
literally

—"Praised the Lord both night and day,
And went from house to house to pray,
And if he met one on the way—
He always something found to say,
About this heavenly union."

From this time dates the religious awakening which
spread from Kedge's Straits to Tangier Beach, and visited
every home and heart on the islands, with the call, in
the language of the apostle, "Awake thou that sleepest,
and arise from the dead, and Christ shall give thee
light."

Referring to his own narrative again, we find Brother Thomas inaugurating prayer meetings among his own immediate neighbors, which were successful in a great degree, in "preparing the way of the Lord," and leading the minds of both young and old to a clearer apprehension of true religion than they had previously entertained. Such was the respect paid this man by those who knew him, that the people implicitly follow his directions.

"Thomas Crockett, my neighbor, had always been a good moral man, and for some years read prayers daily in his family. All his neighbors thought well of him. I called at his house and said—'Brother Crockett, you and I always went together: now I have been to the camp meeting and God has—*understand*—converted my soul. I never was so happy in all my life before.' He said he believed, and commenced crying, and his wife cried, and said they were sorry they did not go to the meeting with me.

"I told him we must have our neighbors called together, and commence worship with them—that he must read, and I would pray and talk to them about religion. He said he was willing to do what he could, and we agreed to have meeting the next Sunday, and gave notice to all the people to meet early on Sunday morning. When Sabbath came, all the people turned out—men, women, and children, and T. Crockett read a chapter, and I called on my cousin J. P. to pray first, as he was converted before me; while he was praying, I fell down on my face and lay there weeping, and asking God to save the people, and help us to feel more for their souls, and be instrumental in leading them to the "ark of safety."

When the first prayer was over, I told them all to sing, and this they tried to do, every one of them; men and women, boys and girls, all joined in, and sung with all their might—the hymn was one most of them had lately learned and it went off well; then Brother Crockett and I prayed one after the other, and we continued praying and singing for *more than six hours!*

"I told them the next Sunday they must take a light breakfast, and do without dinner; for it would do them good to fast, and spend the whole day in religious worship, and God would feed our souls."

Fasting became at this early period in his religious experience a regular duty, and one to which he attached great importance, as long as he lived. He would abstain from food, frequently a whole day, when under concern about some personal matter of difficulty in his perception of truth or duty, or when he had an appointment of more than ordinary importance to fill.

During the long series of years he ministered at Rock Creek, stately on Sabbath mornings, it is said he never took anything to eat until after his labors were ended, which often occupied the entire day.

Rev. L. W. Nottingham of Northampton Co., Virginia, in a letter to the compiler, containing a number of interesting reminiscences, states that he heard him, in an exhortation on Deal's Island, advise the people, if they wanted a revival of pure religion, *to fast* as well as *pray* for it. "He said the Devil delighted in *full* Christians. If he could only induce them to *eat* a great deal, he knew they would not *work much!* or exercise that faith that was necessary to please God. Devils were cast out by prayer and fasting; and a *certain kind* by that means alone."

His Sunday meetings progressed until the third one; an account of which we will let himself narrate .

"The third Sunday we all assembled as usual, and when brother Thomas Crockett began to read, he was struck with such powerful conviction that he could hardly see for the big tears which began to flow from his eyes. He soon fell down on his knees, and prayed and wept so bitterly that his friends began to pity him; for they thought he was good enough. So he was, you understand, as far as the '*form* of godliness' went; but *now the power came*, and his blind eyes were opened. He told them to look to themselves, for he felt that he must be converted or he could not be saved. He continued to cry for converting grace, and did not seek in vain, for God came down among us, and set him at perfect liberty that day. This meeting closed about the going down of the sun, and was powerful to convict careless sinners, many of whom went away praying."

The converts now began to multiply, and it was a subject of new astonishment to Joshua, that souls should be saved, in the absence of the regular preachers, and under such circumstances as then surrounded them. He thought a minister of the gospel, a necessary instrument in saving souls, and none were likely to be converted, unless in this legitimate way. It now occurred to him, however, that God could use, and would bless any and every instrumentality employed for this end, and do the work when, and wherever sinners *believed in the Lord Jesus Christ.*

Two local preachers from Accomac, Va., Rev. Wm. Seymour, and Rev. Wm. Lee, hearing of the meetings, among the Tangier people, came off from the Main, one Saturday, bringing a tent, which they set up in a little hammock of trees near the house of Thomas Crockett. Word was quickly sent up to Smith's Island, and the people of that vicinity invited down to the Tangier tent meeting. Many of them came on Sabbath, which was "as one of the days of the Son of Man."

Brother Thomas describes it:—"Brothers Seymour and Lee, preached and exhorted both day and night, and the power of the Lord was there displayed, to wound and heal;—to kill and make alive; and eight or nine persons were happily converted.

"This was the most glorious day the island people had ever seen! Indeed, it was like a paradise below— a heaven on earth."

This brother Seymour was a most estimable man— widely known in the church as a zealous and devoted laborer; as was also his colleague, on that, and many a similar and subsequent trip,—brother Lee. One of brother Thomas' sons, born soon after, was named William Seymour, to perpetuate the recollection and love which his father cherished for the good man after whom he was named. The name of William Lee, also, is still familiar, through a similar means. Among the many who bear it as their Christian appellative, is the Rev. Wm. Lee Dalby, now and for many years a prominent member of the Virginia Annual Conference of the M. E. Church South.

These good local preachers repeated their visits several

times, and never without some seal's to their ministry, which was "*in demonstration of the Spirit, and with power.*"

The effect of the tent meeting on the upper end of the island range, was not less striking and salutary. Solomon Evans had been to a camp meeting in Potato Neck the year previous, and there "*tasted of the good word of life,*" under a sermon by the Rev. Solomon Sharp. Richard, his brother, had always favored the Methodists, and had attended a number of the great meetings in Annamessex and Accomac; these two men took a prominent and leading part in the revival on Smith's Island. At the house of "King" Richard, a prayer meeting was appointed. The people had assembled from every part of the island.

A local preacher named David Wallace, "a large corpulent man with a voice like thunder, and a zeal which nothing could intimidate or turn aside from its purpose; was invited down from his home on Deal's Island, to attend the meeting. Hance Lawson, another valiant soldier of the cross, from lower Annamessex, and an exhorter of great power, was also there.

The meeting was opened by the latter, with an account of what God was then doing among the people, and an exposition and defence of Methodist doctrine. Wallace followed, and while he exhorted, the house was shaken, a cry was raised in doors, and the panic spread among the crowd outside, until sinners were stricken down as by lightning.

Brother Thomas, and some of his converted neighbors

had come up, expecting to have a great time; and they were not disappointed. The Lord of Hosts was there.

Under the exhortation Richard's wife was convicted, and fell, crying aloud for mercy. At this there was a great alarm, some tried to get out at the door, but the pressure of the crowd outside prevented them; several women escaped through a window, and ran about, believing, as did many others, we are told, *that the devil was there and hard after them!*

Some of the men took to their heels; and one, Zachariah Crockett, ran about two miles, when he suddenly stopped, remembering he had forgot his hat and his wife! and retraced his steps, still in a run. When he arrived, old Mrs. Evans had obtained the blessing, and was shouting, while her daughter, Zach.'s forgotten wife, was down praying. He " *gave in,*" and tumbled on the floor a conquered sinner. This same man became afterwards a good Christian, and lived and died an exemplary member of the church.

Rev. Wm. Evans, long a resident of Smith's Island, and a companion in travels and labors with Brother Thomas,—now residing in Northumberland County, Va., —was at that time quite young, but remembers the day distinctly. In a conversation recently with the writer he said—" I shall never forget the first and the second time I saw Brother Thomas, and the contrast between these two occasions. The first time I ever laid eyes on him, he was engaged dancing at a great ball or frolic held at my father's (' King' Richard Evans') house. The second was in the marsh grass alone praying!

" At the dance referred to, he outstripped all his competitors among the young people of the islands, in agility, gaiety, and general good humor. He was dressed in a roundabout, and had moccasins on his feet, made of raw-hide, and laced tight, to enable him to dance. He had the name of being in his young days the best dancer on the island, and was the soul of every gathering for that kind of amusement.

"The next time I saw him was several years afterward, on the eve of the great meeting, where the ball formerly was held. I was going across the marsh, and came upon him praying there, without a soul near him. I was much startled at first, and greatly astonished at the contrast in his appearance. He looked at me very kindly, and asked me whose son I was. I told him, and he exhorted me to be a good boy, and obey my parents."

This was soon after his conversion, and during a visit from the Tangiers, to help in the meeting referred to. We can account for the unusual agency of the Spirit accompanying the word in those days, when men came together *praying along the way* for the salvation of their friends and neighbors.

A few of the good old church folks remained skeptical, and attributed all this to a delusion of the devil. "We thought so," said they, when word came that the brother Evans' Pungy, which had been sent with the preachers to their homes, after the meeting, was capsized on her return, in the Sound. "We told you this was the devil's doings, and now you see how it has turned out; this sort of religion won't do, it will break us up and ruin us."

This state of prejudice and alarm, however, did not continue long. "The devil and all his works" on that

island, had reigned with undisputed sway so long, that
many were blinded, until the light of truth revealed
their true condition. The onset of gospel artillery speedily put the foe to flight, and gained the day for Jesus, to
whom be glory, and dominion, "from sea to sea, and
from the river unto the ends of the earth."

The next meeting of note, on the upper end of the
island, was held at a place called the "old orchard,"
where Severn Bradshaw now resides, and in the immediate vicinity of the neat, commodious Methodist Church,
where the people have ever since statedly worshiped God.

At that early day there was a pine forest there, and
as the location was eligible and central, it was pitched
upon as a place for a "three days' meeting," and the
people again assembled, this time in larger numbers; for
they came from Holland's Island, Tangier, and several
places on the Main.

The laborers were Hance Lawson, Ephraim Price, the
father of Methodism on Holland's Island, Richard and
Solomon Evans, and Joshua Thomas, of course.

He was in the work soul and body. "It was curious
to watch him," said an old lady who remembered all
these occurrences distinctly, (Mrs. Denard Evans of
Deal's Island,) to the writer, "he was so happy that he
did not know what to do with himself, or to keep a limb
of him still!"

Before this meeting closed, a dream of one "Aunt
Charaty Thomas," related before it began, was remarkably verified. She dreamed "the tops of the trees were
all white as down, and glistening like silver, and that
she saw them covered over with sheep and lambs!"

"Break forth into singing, ye trees of the wood,
For Jesus is bringing lost sinners to God."

The sensations of a soul, after its transition from darkness and doubt, into the light of God's reconciled face, —when it looks out on nature,—the trees, and fields, the stars above reflected in the dancing water, and the objects of a diversified landscape,—all are new, peculiar, and glorious! Every leaf seems to convey a lesson of love; every flower, a fresh ingredient in the flowing cup of joy; and sea and sky seem to be in happy harmony with the disenthralled spirit while it sings:—

"Oh, the rapturous height
Of that holy delight,
    Which I *feel* in the life-giving blood,
Of my Saviour possessed,
I *am* perfectly blessed,
    As if filled with the fullness of God."

So *felt* many at the close of that meeting.

In this locality the Ark seemed to rest. A house was purchased and prepared for worship on the site consecrated by the conversion of souls, and a society formed, which is still in existence, and is in a highly prosperous condition.

The old house was afterwards remodeled into the more sightly and convenient style of a church. This building was burned down by accident, and replaced by the present edifice, which was dedicated by the Circuit Preacher, Rev. V. Smith, in 1855.

The brothers, Richard and Solomon Evans, were forward in every good word and work, from the time they espoused the cause of Christ until they finished their course, respectively, at, or near the age of one hundred years. We shall treat the reader to a few of their traditions of the Revolutionary and last war with Great Britain, in a subsequent chapter. Their devotedness to God brought them a rich inheritance in personal consolation through a protracted life, —in the piety of their children, and their children's children, to the third and fourth generation, and in the glorious prospect, which, dying, they realized of a "better country, *that is, a heavenly*," beyond this vale of tears. Their memory is blessed, and their works and prayers, in the influence their sons and daughters are exerting on the community, (who were converted early through their example,) do follow them on to their rest on high. Rev. William Evans, a local preacher, already referred to, is a son of Richard, and is a man of extraordinary power and pathos in the pulpit; he has moved thousands, in past days, to flee for refuge and lay hold on the hope set before them. He is still largely instrumental in well-doing, where he has chosen his home and sphere of labor on the western shore. We will often meet his name in the following pages. Denard Evans, a son of Solomon, a wealthy and worthy citizen of Deal's Island, sustains well *his* father's honored name.

CHAPTER VII.

First Camp Meetings on Tangier Beach—Thrilling scenes—Ten thousand present—"Sinners falling all around"—Brother Thomas a Manager— Liberal collections—He exhorts on the shore—Pedlars awakened—Rum traffic—A drunkard put to sleep—Fight prevented—A Camp Meeting without preachers—Remarkable providence—A Presiding Elder befogged —He preaches with power—Signal results—The "Parson" happy.

THE first camp meeting ever held on Tangier Island was in the summer of the year 1808. This was but a temporary affair, projected by Brothers Seymour and Lee of Accomac, who had taken a lively interest in the religious welfare of the people scattered over that locality. By this time a society had been organized, and the converts of the previous year were being trained in doctrine, discipline, and experience, by the faithful men whom God had raised up among them to direct them to Christ, and lead them on in holiness.

The appointment of a camp meeting at their own door, and for their own exclusive benefit, was a joyful era in the monotonous history of these islanders; an era, too, in the general history of Methodism on the lower portion of the Peninsula. Who has not heard of the Tangier camp meetings—even before the day of "Martha's Vineyard" monster gatherings; and long prior to the celebrated "Red Lion," or more recently, the annual "Camden Union" feast of tabernacles?

The place suddenly assumed an attractiveness and importance which belonged to no other mustering ground for the armies of Israel, scattered along the eastern and western shores of the magnificent Chesapeake, and from the interior of both Maryland and Virginia.

Even before the war, its fame had become wide spread, and its popularity as a place of resort for all classes of people established. But who can write its stirring history? who tell its tremendous moral results?—or enumerate the thousands who were born for glory there; and the tens of thousands who were edified, sanctified, and established in the faith of the gospel, as years rolled on, for full half a century, on the famous beach at Tangier?

Never until the last trump shall sound, and the sea give back, with every earthly grave, its dead, and the Books are opened, will be known the full measure of good accomplished by the powerful sermons, the earnest exhortations, the pious prayers, and all the combined appliances of camp week, for fifty years on this consecrated sand. How many of the ministers, whose preaching moved masses at this place, have gone up

> —" with joy the shining way,
> To see and praise their Lord?"

How many of the people, who frequented this place for good, and found it, in repeated baptisms of the Spirit, are now numbered with the glorified?

And, not oblivious to the other side of the question—

how many of the wild, untoward, and reckless, who grieved the Spirit, slighted grace, and wickedly rejected salvation, have gone the way of all the earth—the way of the transgressor—downward to *his* irreparable and eternal doom ?

But thousands are still among the living; who enjoyed the privilege of worship around this camp meeting altar, where so many warm hearts, glowing with holy ardor, oft knelt to pledge each other, and "vow unto the Lord" fidelity to the great Captain of salvation. Would that we were able to bring even faintly, and feebly, the light of other days across these pages, reviving the gradually growing indistinct memories of the fitful past, to stir them up by way of remembrance, in reference to the mighty works which God wrought in their days—and in many of their hearts; that they may tell it to the generations following, and not forget the works of the Lord or the wonders of his arm, on Tangier Island.

In following up the personal adventures of the subject which occupies the foreground in these memoirs, we shall lay before the reader a variety of facts, names, and incidents, which naturally intermingle in the design of our book, and which have been gleaned in a wide range of correspondence, relating to the camps held on Tangier; their sermons, visiting ministers, anecdotes, experience meetings, and remarkable conversions.

To begin with the first, which, as we have stated, was held in 1808, Brother Thomas says :

"We had a *wonderful meeting*. Some came from the Main and joined us; helping greatly to sing and pray. Believing souls were blest in an uncommon degree ; some were soundly converted, and our two good preachers (Lee and Seymour) rejoiced together, in the love of their Lord, and the progress of the work in this part of his vineyard."

The following year, 1809, he goes on to say: "The news of our first camp had spread up and down the bay, on both sides; and even to Norfolk and Baltimore, and we had a general camp meeting under the charge of the regular traveling preachers, a goodly number of whom were present. (Perhaps Solomon Sharp, the Presiding Elder of the lower district, was there and had charge.)

"The people came from every quarter, until large numbers were regularly tented on the island, and it was estimated at one time that there were ten thousand souls under the sound of the gospel. More than two hundred sail of vessels, of every conceivable class, size, and rig, besides steam-boats, were frequently in the harbor at the same time.

"At some of these meetings, there were such wonderful manifestations of the divine power and goodness to save sinners, that they would be seen in groups, all over the encampment, inside the circle and often without; praying, '*Lord, save or I perish,*' '*God, be merciful to me a sinner,*' while persons who knew them, and even strangers who never saw them before, would gather round to sing a hymn, and encourage their faith. No scene in this sinful world could surpass, in moral grandeur, that meeting, on some occasions of the outpouring of the Holy Spirit; when everybody you saw would be either singing joyfully the songs of Zion, or shouting

over their children and friends, newly born of God.   The
beloved preachers used to labor very hard; but a good
many of them by this time have gained their crown of
righteousness ; and do not regret the tears and toils they
spent for their Redeemer, and precious souls for whom
he died.''

The camp ground, before the war, was said to be a
not uncomfortable, or unattractive place.   There was a
fine grove of wild cherry, cedar, and pine trees, on the
spot so barren and bald in later years.   These were cut
down by the British to aid in the construction of their forts
and camp in 1814.   Every vestige of a tree was likely
to be removed at that time, and would have been, as we
shall see, but for the intercession of the man they respectfully called '' The Parson of the Islands.''

A few pine trees were left standing, and a remnant
of them are there yet, as a land mark to the coaster,
and as silent sentinels over the scene of many a thrilling
conversion.

Brother Thomas became an official member of the
circuit which included Tangier Island, shortly after his
conversion, as a licensed exhorter, which office he both
magnified and fulfilled in an unusual manner.   He never
aspired to be more than an exhorter, though at the
instance of his brethren and the preachers, Rev. L.
Lawrenson particularly, he was made a local preacher
about the year 1814.

The chief management of the Tangier camp meeting
was generally conceded to him.   No man could raise a
larger hat collection, on Sabbath morning, than he, when
announced, as was invariably the case, for '' outside the

tents and along shore." He came in from these incursions on the liberality of outsiders, toward supporting
the gospel, almost loaded with the essential specie.

As the meetings enlarged, and began to embrace multitudes whose object was pleasure or gain, the preservation of order became a matter of grave moment. While
Methodists and their friends and families came to the
beach for an uninterrupted week of religious enjoyment,
and generally came singing, continued instant in prayer,
and went away happy after the final farewell was said
and sung; others came with pleasure for their pursuit,
or a vain curiosity to gratify, in witnessing, with feelings
unaffected, the progress of the meeting; and not a few
each year were found on the shore with their wares to
sell, intent on driving good trade, and making gain their
god.

Articles that were in demand for the support of the
visitors and strangers at the meeting, such as bread,
cakes, cheese, &c., were not prohibited; but soon the
stock of merchandize became as various as the ordinary
wants of the people, and many did their shopping, in
the way of cedar ware, tin ware, hardware, dry goods,
groceries, and even millinery, in the booths on the beach.

These hucksters were from the large towns and cities,
and became regular frequenters of the meeting.

The difficulty now was to regulate this traffic, so as not
to allow of its encroachments on the worship and spirituality of the encampment.

Booths and stalls would attract to their array of wares
a crowd, who began to evince inattention to the sound
of the trumpets; and were very laggard in taking their

seats for preaching. This perplexed a certain preacher in charge, and led him to speak disparagingly of the signs of the times, and the opportunities for good amid so much worldliness as appeared to be flooding in on the meetings. Brother Thomas became uneasy at this state of things, lest the preachers should cease appointing them, and resolved he would be responsible for the outside department himself.

When the horns sounded for preaching, one day, and it was perceived that a large number remained beyond the circle, he told the preacher to commence service at the stand, and he would take care of the "shore folks." Out he walked, and mounted a vacant table in the midst of the traders and their customers—blew a sharp blast on a tin horn, and then told those who preferred hearing a *fine discourse* to go inside, for he himself was going to preach to all that remained. They gathered round him immediately and helped him to sing a hymn, then, after a melting prayer for all hands, Jew and Gentile, he commenced to preach or exhort; before he was done, three sinners were on the sand under conviction; soon others began to pray; and there he staid, until several backsliders were cut to the heart, and some penitents were converted.

Before concluding his exercises on shore, he exacted a pledge, and took the hand of every person engaged in selling commodities there, that as soon as the hours for worship were announced, they would close their curtains, and come up to preaching—a promise they all rigidly adhered to during the meeting.

The abomination of liquor could not be kept away

from the camp. They brought it and sold it despite the utmost vigilance on the part of the managers to prevent such desecration. Sometimes an inebriate would cause trouble among the order-loving and religious.

Brother Thomas would undertake the most unreasonable case, and kindly approach his better nature, win his confidence, and obtain such an ascendency over him that he could lead him wherever he wished.

On one occasion a young man, the son of a respectable and influential father, became intoxicated and very troublesome. Several of the managers surrounded him, and were about to handle him roughly, and commit him to jail, when Brother Thomas became aware of the difficulty. He interfered in the young man's behalf, became responsible for his good conduct, and parleyed with him there, until he succeeded in getting him round to his own tent. He then prepared him a place to lie down, and soothed his chafed spirit by gentleness, until he fell into a sound sleep. He then induced his good wife to sit near and fan him while he slept, "for," said he, "the poor, dear man is burning up with the wretched stuff he has drank." Shortly after, a company of wild young men came up, swearing, and looking for their comrade. They heard that the managers had him; and, all ready for fight, they approached, asking, "Where is Mr. —— ?" "Brother Thomas took him away," was the reply. On they came to the rescue. Meeting the man whom they were after (Brother Thomas), they demanded the release of their boon companion. "Where is he?" "Come," said Brother Thomas, "and I will show you." He led them to his tent door, and pointed in. There was their

friend, snoring on a clean, soft pillow, and Mrs. Thomas
with a large wing of a wild goose patiently fanning him,
as if he *was her own child!* The scene broke down their
fierce and reckless spirits in a moment, and not a man
of the crowd but felt that Brother Thomas had entire
victory over him. He had the pleasure to see some of
those same young men converted in a short time, and
received from the mortified and sobered youth, whom he
befriended, expressions of the most unfeigned thanks,
and promises of amendment in morals and life. He gave
him a parting exhortation, which, it is likely, he has
never forgotten.

Instances like the foregoing, showing his great tact,
and wonderful influence over men, might be indefinitely
muitiplied.

From some cause, one year, it was decided in the
Quarterly Meeting to hold no camp meeting that summer
on Tangier Island. Perhaps the preachers and members
on the circuit had taken exceptions to the growing custom
of traffic that it engendered. Brother Thomas was not
present at this decision, and had no knowledge of the
matter at the time. He had been making arrangements
as usual, and had circulated the announcement of a
meeting, and invitations to people near and far, to be
present. When he learned what action had been taken,
he was utterly overwhelmed. A greater trial of his
faith and patience had never beset him. He betook
himself to prayer; then followed up the Presiding Elder,
Rev. James Smith, to secure a favorable notice from
him, but he was informed, the people had decided the
question and he could not interfere. "Well then," said

Brother T., "will you come and preach, if we go on and have a meeting?" That he could not agree to. Greatly disheartened, he tried the circuit preachers next, but met with no encouragement. "Good Lord," said he, "what will I do? Thou hast never failed me yet— tell me what I must do—give up our camp meeting where thy word is preached, the people made happy, and poor wandering souls, whom thou delightest to save, converted?"

This thought decided the case. "It came to him" to go right on and hold the meeting, but it cost him fastings, perplexity, and great tribulation lest he might displease his ministers by insubordination. He again appealed to them, but none would agree to aid him. The time rolled on. The Sound began to whiten with the sails of spreading vessels, with their hopeful freight on board, bound for Tangiers. The day arrived, and there he was "alone," but not "in his glory!" *He was a scared man.*

Several clever Virginia gentlemen rallied around him and cheered him up, by saying, "You can preach and exhort, and we will take the management." Col. Thoroughgood Taylor of Accomac—now of Petersburg, Va., was made head manager, took command of the forces, and adopted his rules. A local preacher from some quarter arrived, and to all human calculation, he and Mr. Thomas would have to do the Sabbath preaching. It was Saturday night, and the anxious mind of Brother T. had no repose. "Lord, send us a preacher," he would plead as he continued in agonizing prayer.

Sabbath morning dawned, and with it the glad sight,

to our frightened parson, of a portly minister landing on the beach, and heading for the ground.

Who could it be? Why no less a personage than *the Presiding Elder himself*, who had refused to attend. And how came he here? You see, he took passage up the bay, and Saturday night fell calm and foggy, so that his captain made a harbor and came to anchor. What harbor should it be but Tangiers! And there was the encampment right before his eyes, as he reached the deck that Sabbath morning! Had the Lord, to whom Brother Thomas cried in his trouble, any hand in this matter? The preacher thought so at once, went ashore in haste, and reported himself for duty.

The occurrence made considerable talk during the morning interval, and when the hour for preaching arrived, Mr. Smith took the stand, and according to his own admission, never felt such light and life from God, and such liberty and power in preaching the gospel as he enjoyed that morning. Salvation rolled over the congregation like a mighty billow, and a large number entered into liberty under the living word.

Wasn't Joshua a happy soul that Sabbath day?—His faith confirmed—his fears dispelled—his prayers answered, and a multitude of souls rejoicing in the God of their salvation! His cup ran over, and he could, and *did* sing:—

> " I'll praise the Lord, I'll praise the Lord,
>   I'll praise the Lord wherever I go.
> And now my happy soul can tell,
>   I'll praise the Lord wherever I go.
> That Jesus hath done all things well,
>   I'll praise the Lord wherever I go."

CHAPTER VIII.

Extension of Methodism—Appointments formed—Comparing notes—Love
for the Church—The hymn book—Tangier Church—Meeting day—Early
contemporaries—The Crocketts—Baptism by immersion—His sickness—
Anointing—"Goose grease"—Health restored in answer to prayer—
Health of the islanders—Doctors dreaded—Mrs. Lovey Evans—Dr. Williams.

DURING the interval between 1808—the period when
camp meetings were commenced on Tangier Beach—and
the breaking out of the war, we find Brother Thomas
"in labors abundant," and have gleaned a few facts and
anecdotes relating to this period of his history.

He became the acknowledged leader in that religious
movement which spread over the islands, and firmly established Methodism as *the system* best adapted and most
useful to that people. Societies were organized, and
taken in charge by the circuit preachers, who, about this
time, began to visit the islands regularly in their itinerant rounds. The Accomac preachers included the lower
islands in their preaching plan, and the brethren laboring on Annamessex circuit took charge of Smith's and
Holland's Islands.

Before churches were erected, the ministers preached
in private houses, or in the open air, and always with

success, in building up believers, and directing the inquiring soul to a present Saviour. Their own souls were abundantly watered from on high, during these visits, and their hearts greatly rejoiced in this work, which, though it cost them time and much exposure, amply repaid them for their labors of love.

Brother Thomas gave himself almost wholly to the service of the church, in conveying the preachers to and from their island appointments, and attending meetings, not only in the vicinity of his own residence, but at distant places, where his labors were much blessed to the people.

The circle of his acquaintance widened every year, by intercourse with persons attending the annual reunion at camp meeting. In this way he became known to thousands, as an exemplary Christian, a powerful exhorter, and a successful manager of the meetings. Among the objects of interest to all strangers who visited that celebrated place, and chief among the subjects of conversation on their return home, was this ardently devoted, and widely useful man. The anecdotes he related were repeated in social circles far away, and it became a marked day in the experience of many, when, obedient to their pressing invitations, the island preacher favored his friends with a call, and "held meeting" in neighborhoods where his services were in demand.

He began a system of itinerant labors, about this period, embracing all the islands, and several places on the adjacent main, which was kept up during his whole after life. His popularity never waned, nor did he become weary in these gratuitous toils, to feed the flock, and follow the wandering, in imitation of the Master whom it was his desire and delight to serve and honor.

He took particular pleasure in comparing notes with his brethren of the regular ministry, to ascertain whether any exceeded him in the number of meetings attended, sermons preached, or distance traveled, in the performance of his duties. He considered himself under obligations to do his utmost for the advancement of that branch of the church to which he owed everything. Few, with greater truthfulness than he, could say or sing:

> " For her my tears shall fall,
>   For her my prayers ascend;
>   To her my toils and cares be given,
>   Till toil and cares shall end.
>   Beyond my highest joy,
>   I prize her heavenly ways;
>   Her sweet communion, solemn vows,
>   Her hymns of love and praise."

" Her hymns" were a source of the greatest pleasure to him. Like thousands who have been gathered into the fold of Methodism, and have become the best theologians of the day, from learning the stanzas of the Wesleys, he made the hymn book his standard on "systematic divinity," and gathered his best conceptions of religion from its attractive pages; not that he overlooked his Bible, or failed to search diligently this record of Divine wisdom and grace, that he might be "thoroughly furnished unto every good word and work;" but his hymn book, as the companion of God's revelation, he found to be its clearest and most comprehensive expositor.

That his Bible justified a redeemed sinner in "walking, leaping, and praising God," and exclaimed, "O clap your hands;" and that his hymn book corroborated the authority, in many of its exultant strains, was to his mind conclusive, not only as it regarded the privilege, but a positive duty, to shout!

He was a literalist in the fullest sense, in his understanding of the Scriptures. What they said, he did, and their omnipresent Author honored his simple credence and unreserved obedience in many remarkable instances, as will hereafter be shown.

The precise date of the erection of the Methodist Church on Tangier Island, we have not been able to ascertain, but here it is, with its familiar surroundings, its gathering congregation, and its devoted minister—Rev. J. A. Massey, who at present exercises pastoral care over its interests and its members.

Our Artist has aimed to represent the scene as it appears on "meeting day." The signal flag has given notice far and wide that the preacher has arrived. Canoes are stretching across the waters toward the landing. Some are drawn up to the shore, and made fast there, while the people hurry into the place of prayer, soon to make its walls vocal with their hearty hymns and fervent supplications.

The friends of Brother Massey will be able to distinguish some resemblance between him and the likeness intended for him in the fore-ground. The book he carries, may be a favorite volume selected to beguile the tedium of his voyage across the Sound, or may be designed for one of the islanders who wishes to study divinity. He appears to be in excellent trim for a sermon, and will, doubtless, rightly divide the word of truth, when in the pulpit, and his hearers will, as is their custom, receive it with meekness and many earnest responses.

In the distance may be seen the residence of Brother John Thomas, oldest son of the man whose influence and efforts mainly contributed to the erection of this church, and who, in the person of his son John, is still ably represented in the neighborhood of his early residence. John is engaged in merchandizing, and is a valuable citizen, and a devoted member of the church, which stands as a memorial of the active zeal of his honored father.

The principal contemporaries of Brother Thomas, when the church was built, were brethren named Crockett, who had been converted, and were fellow helpers with him in the work. The person of this name who accompanied him to Pungoteague, and fled from the camp, fearing an earthquake, had been followed by the Spirit, until constrained in deep conviction to say :—

> ———" I yield, I yield,—
> I can hold out no more ;
> I sink, by dying love compelled,
> And own *Thee* conqueror."

Another, as we have seen,—the impetuous Zachariah Crockett,—was " conquered," at the great prayer meeting on Smith's Island, and came out on " the Lord's side." A third was he who fell, while reading the Bible to his neighbors on a Sabbath-day some years be-

MEETING DAY ON TANGIER ISLAND.—REV. J. A. MASSEY.

fore, and there surrounded by the amazed people, wrestled in prayer, until he was made a partaker of saving grace.

The descendants of these good men are at this day the pillars of the church, and in their happy meetings often sing with unusual emphasis :—

> " We are travelling home to God ;
> In the way our fathers trod ;
> They are happy now, and we
> Soon their happiness shall see."

It was through the persuasions of some of these good brethren that Brother Thomas was induced to submit to baptism by immersion. The circumstance is alluded to by Mr. Massey in his Introduction. This was also a subject of very frequent remark in after years, by himself, when he learned the fallacy and folly of the assumption pressed upon his susceptible mind at that juncture —that " he could not be saved without being baptized after this mode."

It appears he was satisfied after having immersed himself, until a minister named Layfield from Virginia came over, and " led in" several of his immediate friends, while a hymn was being sung on the shore ; then did Brother T. consent to be " buried in baptism," that he might secure whatever grace or good belonged to the performance, and gratify those who in this manner aimed to follow Christ.

The spot where the ceremony occurred, was thereafter, and is still known as " Baptist Point." It was a memorable day to Brother Thomas ; for in the excitement of the moment, he " went down into the water," forgetting to leave his Hymn Book and Testament behind. The result was a disaster that greatly *dampened* his joy; his precious books, when extracted from his saturated clothing, were found to be nearly ruined!

No amount of persuasion, however, could induce him to cast in his lot with the zealous denomination which had for the time being assumed his spiritual guidance. His affection for that church which brought light to his benighted mind, and peace to his troubled conscience,— which followed him with the overtures of saving mercy, and won him to her warm embrace—which laid her strong, loving arms around him, and opened before him "a great and effectual door" of usefulness,—was too strong to abandon her communion and forsake her associations for another.

He would have been "one among a thousand," in any denomination, but in no sphere could he have been so extensively useful, or have fulfilled the mission of Divine providence, as in that which made him the Methodist "Parson of the Islands."

The Baptists failed in establishing their tenets to any great extent on the island, and, it is said, never succeeded in organizing a church there.

It was during the period of which we now write, that Brother Thomas was restored to health from a protracted and dangerous spell of sickness, by a mode resorted to but rarely, if at all, at the present day. Various remedies had been applied, and no favorable indications of returning health appearing, he became restive under confinement, and troubled by the cares of the church and the exigencies of his family which pressed upon him, and greatly longed for deliverance. Reading the pages of his Testament, he happened on some advice directly bearing on his condition. It was contained in the practical Epistle of James, as follows :

"*Is any sick among you ? let him call in the elders of the church ; and let them pray over him, anointing him with oil in the name of the Lord : And the prayer of faith shall save the sick, and the Lord shall raise him up.*"

This, thought he, is a safe guide, and *cannot fail* to effect a speedy cure. "Elders," he supposed to be *elderly persons*, of good report in the church. His mind fixed immediately on Brother John Crockett, and his brother Zachariah, as answering the requirement. He sent for John in haste. On his arrival the matter was fully explained, and the passage repeated. "Now, Brother John," said the sick man, "you must do exactly as the good Book directs. I have no oil, but yonder is *plenty of excellent goose grease !* which I suppose will do as well; use some of it, and then pray in faith."

"Brother John" was taken somewhat aback by this proposal, and confessed he had but little confidence that a cure could be effected in this way. He proceeded, however, with the anointing, and offered a fervent prayer for his beloved friend. There was no apparent relief obtained, and both agreed that the reason of failure was probably their weakness of faith.

"Go," said Brother Thomas, "and tell Brother Zachariah to come and try it. "Zach." soon arrived, and, after learning the particulars, "goose grease" and all, clapped his hands in a very decided and earnest manner, and exclaimed, "Why Brother Joshua, that is the very thing, I believe it will do you good, for it is the good Lord's plan."

"Go on then," said the other, "and let us believe for a certain and speedy answer."

Brother Z. was of an ardent, impulsive temperament, and entered into this procedure with great zest. After an unctuous application of the "goose grease," he knelt down and began to pray, telling the Lord what had been done according to His own word, and how sick his "poor brother" was; "and now, Lord," said he, "raise him up!—send down the power!"

The "power" came, first upon Zach. himself, so that he became very happy, and began to shout; then upon Brother T. who leaped from his weary bed—cured in body, and filled with the Holy Ghost—and joined in the rejoicing of his friend, praising God for the signal answer given, and the verification of His holy word, which thereafter, more than ever, was believed by both as an unfailing foundation.

As a general thing, sickness in its complicated forms was rare among the hardy, temperate people who inhabited the islands in those days. Persons have lived to the age of 104, and, it is said, never in all that time experienced the sensations produced by swallowing "doctor's stuff!"

Most of the ailments peculiar to their situation and climate yielded to simple treatment, and were easily subdued by good nursing, a healthy constitution, and religious hope! For fevers of all kinds, and from all causes, cool water was the only and effectual specific; for prostration and weakness, some rare delicacy to tempt the appetite was sought out, and applied with salutary results.

Among those whose names are remembered with affectionate regard, as gentle and skillful attendants to the wants of the sick, none is cherished more than a Mrs. Lovey Evans, who gave unremitting efforts to relieve the ills to which her island neighbors were subject. Her far seeing sympathy hoarded the fruits of autumn, for some exigency in the following seasons, when a good apple became a desirable luxury; and her skill and economy provided the products of midwinter, to meet a possible longing during the languor of summer. She was never known to be at fault, where a sick person expressed a desire for some particular kind of fish, fowl, or fruit. Her stores were always available, and her resources equal to every emergency. In this respect, she was an angel of mercy, ministering to the wants and wishes of others. For this she seemed to live, and her life was both useful and happy. A quiet conscience, she maintained, was the best opiate in pain, and faith in God, the most infallible remedy, in the day of trouble. With the measure she meted, it was returned to her own bosom. When age and infirmity began to wear her system down, she lacked nothing. Her friends were numerous, and her necessities, as far as human aid could reach, were promptly met. In a very remarkable manner, we are informed, did she sometimes receive what she conceived a liking for. In sickness she desired to have a certain kind of fish. It was not the season for "Drum"—the peculiar species she wanted,—but she was gratified notwithstanding. One of the boatmen coming in, captured a "Drum," which unexpectedly came in his way, and brought it to "Aunt Lovey."

After this, she wanted a slice of some particular fowl of the wild duck species, that frequented the adjacent waters. This, though entirely out of the season, was accidentally procured, and the good old lady remarked that she knew God could furnish her, in or out of season, with all she asked: "for," said she, "it is written, '*No good thing will He withhold from them that walk uprightly.*'"

The dreaded doctor, in more recent times, is found to be necessary, when disease of an obstinate type prevails. Those who enjoy the acquaintance of Dr. R. W. Williams, formerly of Virginia, and at present pursuing his professional duties near Cambridge, Md., may draw on his resources of anecdote, to an almost unlimited extent, for reminiscences of his visits to the islands, and his intercourse with Brother Thomas, with whom he was on very intimate terms, and the inhabitants at large, among whom he is remembered respectfully, as a model practitioner— not only in the preparation of "powders and pills," but in his habit of holding family prayer with his patients ; and when all human skill becomes fruitless, in pointing the sinking one to Jesus, the Great Physician, and in assuring the dying that "this is a faithful saying and worthy of all acceptation, that Jesus Christ came into the world, to save sinners."

CHAPTER IX.

Arrival of the British fleet in the Chesapeake Bay—Rendezvous at Tangier
—The Islanders made prisoners of war—Talk with the admiral—The
camp meeting trees spared—Forts erected—Remarkable phenomenon—
—Holy ground—Religious soldiers—A sailor's narrative—" Methodist re-
ligion"—Conversion of a captain and mate—Skirmish—Death of a young
English soldier—The Parson on board the flag ship—Exhorts in the ward
room—Stammering—The doctor—A close question—Death of his wife—
Sustaining power of faith—Second marriage—A wife from the Lord.

THE waters of the Chesapeake Bay, in the vicinity of
the group of islands which form the principal scene of
our narrative, have been the theatre of many stirring
incidents in the days of the revolution; and also subsequently during the war of 1812.   The British fleet made
Tangier harbor and Island the centre of their operations
while the bay was being ravaged, the capitol burned,
and the City of Baltimore bombarded.

We have already given a few recollections of the days of
" 76," and now in the course of our history find ourselves
brought down to the period when the island became a
rendezvous of the British forces.   This was during the
years 1813–14.   A large reinforcement came over from
the English shores; and a squadron of about fifty or
sixty sail entered the Chesapeake Bay.   We have some

brief memoranda of this period in the manuscript so often quoted from; where, in Brother Thomas' own words we read as follows :

" As the troubles and horrors of war have happily passed away, never more, I hope and pray, to revisit these shores ; and the present generation know but little of the many afflictions and trials of their fathers and mothers, I will tell them something of those days.

" The first we knew of the British being nigh us, was the report of their guns firing down the bay.   The same day some of their shipping came up abreast of my house and anchored.   Soon after we saw about fifty men in full uniform, with their weapons of war, land on the beach, and proceed in marching order towards Z. Crockett's house.   Our women and children were dreadfully scared ; but I told them not to be alarmed, as the Lord would undertake for us, and prove our refuge and defence—'a present help in the time of trouble.'

"I hardly knew how to act in this case, but finally concluded to go out and meet them.   When I came near the officer, I pulled off my hat and he pulled off his; which I thought was very gentleman-like.   I then approached him, and he held out his hand kindly, which I took, and we shook hands in a friendly manner.

"We walked on together until we arrived at Zachariah Crockett's house; he told the women he wanted that house to lodge in, and they must put it in order for him. I informed him he could not have it : at this he seemed to get angry, and replied he would not ask my leave, that *we were all his prisoners.*   I told him there was a house not far off, that would suit him better, and it was unoccupied; so that he would not compel poor women and children to go out of doors. At this he cooled down, and, after a little, said, 'Come go with me, and we will look at that house you speak of.' They remained on shore that night; and, after breakfast in the morning, went on board their ships; taking a lot of our cattle, sheep, and hogs with them, for which they paid such prices as they saw proper. They next landed on Watts' Island, and examined it, after which they sailed away out of sight, and we saw no more of them for several days.

"In a short time we heard their firing again and four large ships appeared coming in. They cast anchor in Tangier harbor, and landed about two hundred men on the lower beach, where they pitched their tents, and immediately went to work with all their might, clearing off the ground and building forts.

"We watched their movements, as they continued their work, and I discovered that they were cutting down all the timber before them—wild cherry trees, pines, and cedars without distinction. Our beautiful camp ground, where we held our great meetings, was likely to share the same fate. I felt so uneasy at this, that I could not rest.

"*It came to me,* that I must go and see the Admiral about this matter, and beg him to spare our camp ground. The next day I resolved to go and try, when I saw his flag streaming at the top of the staff; for by that sign we always knew when he was on shore. I went to the sentinel that was stationed near, and told him I wished to see the Admiral; he raised his little flag, and the Admiral came that way, and asked me what I wanted. I answered, 'Sir, I have a request to make of you.' 'Well, what is it?' said he. 'Why, sir, it is this:— if you can spare any of these trees, I am very anxious you will keep your men from cutting just round here; for this is the grove in which we worship, and where our camp meetings were held before the war; and if we ever have peace again, I hope we shall want to continue these meetings; for in this place we have felt "it *was the very gate of heaven.*"'

"I then went with him around the ground, and pointed out to him where the circles of tents stood, and where the preaching stand was, and the spot of ground before it where we held our prayer-meetings for mourners.

"'*Mourners,*' said he, 'how is that?' I went on in my stammering way to inform him that when sinners heard the gospel preached, and felt their need of Christ, they came in crowds to this spot, and knelt down to pray, and cry for mercy, and we prayed with and for them; and hundreds of souls have been converted right here.

"While I was telling and showing him these things, he looked at me with great sharpness, and when I was through, he said, '*And who are you?*' I told him, with my hat in my hand, that I was 'a sinner saved by grace.' I could see an air of solemnity on his countenance, and he told me the grove should be spared. He gave orders immediately to the whole army that they should not cut *so much as a limb* off that grove; which orders were so strictly executed that a man came very near being punished severely for cutting something that happened to be in his way.

"They all, after this, reverenced that ground, and would not desecrate it in any way, or pitch a tent in it, but on the outside of the sacred grove.

"They still went on with their buildings and walks; and when they were finished, it was a most beautiful place. The two forts were erected a little to the south of the camp ground, east and west from each other, and about three hundred yards apart. The tents of the army were pitched in a semicircular form, extending about half round on the north side, and a very pleasant summer house was built in the centre.

"In hot weather, this was a most lovely place. The fresh breeze would come in from the salt water, and breathe through the grove, giving life and pleasure to the languid, while in other places the people were suffering greatly from the heat.

"The circumstance I am now going to relate," continues Brother Thomas, "may not be believed, but I will give a statement of the facts, and leave every one to follow his own judgment as to their credibility.

"On one of those very calm summer evenings, about the close of the day, the officers and men first heard a *strange noise,* as if sounds were floating in the air; then, after a little space, the sweetest and most melodious singing was distinctly heard. They went out of their tents to ascertain where it was, and followed the sound until they found it lingering directly over the preaching stand, and the place in front of it where the prayer-meetings were held. It appeared to them to be about the

tops of the trees. The singing continued near half an
hour, and struck the army with such surprise and awe,
that all conversation ceased for that night.

"The next morning, when John Crockett came into
camp, they told him about this singing, and remarked
that there must have been a great deal of preaching and
praying in that place to make it as holy as they believed
it to be. They confessed that they were too wicked and
bad to occupy a spot so near heaven, that they could
hear the angels sing as they lingered around it. They
never polluted the place after that."

Among these wicked and ungodly soldiers and sailors,
Brother Thomas found several praying men, who professed to have been converted in the Methodist way in
England, and seemed desirous to "hold fast the profession of their faith without wavering."

Many an interesting chat took place between him and
those who sought his acquaintance, believing him to be
a good, holy man. They put themselves often in his
way to have a talk about Jesus, and a short season of
prayer for mutual strength to bear the cross and honor
their God and King.

He was greatly delighted to hear from their lips the
story of their conversion, which tallied so nearly with
his own experience; and through them obtain some information of the state of religion in the foreign countries
where they had been.

Wesleyan Methodism had turned thousands of the
standing army of Great Britain to the standard of Immanuel, and enlisted them to do battle for the Lord of
Hosts. Strange providence! that men who mourned for

sin, among Cornwall miners, and who at provincial revivals were made happy in believing, should here find sweet fellowship with those of like precious faith, and realize the blessed truth, that the children of the kingdom, wherever found, sweetly agree in the bonds of that threefold cord that cannot be broken.

Brother Thomas treasured up many of the experiences he heard from these, his brethren in Christ, and well beloved; and was greatly confirmed in his Christian confidence by their communion.

"Oh!" thought he, "if we could hold a camp meeting now, and get all these soldiers and sailors converted to God, and have them to carry across the seas traversed by their mighty fleets, and the islands and countries frequented by their powerful armies, the experience of justification by faith, and the testimony of Christ, as *'the Saviour of all men, especially of them that believe!'* "

But the turn affairs speedily took interrupted his longings for a "regular camp meeting," and gave him unexpected favor with rank and file, and access to all, as a minister of the gospel of the grace of God. The following narrative he had carefully taken down, and preserved as a memorial of the power of grace:

"A pious soldier, in conversation with me, became very happy, and informed me of an adventure he had on board a ship in which he was bound to the continent of America. 'On board our ship there was nothing going on but swearing and wickedness. This grieved me every day so much that I was in the habit of retiring to an unfrequented place to pray alone, as I had none to sympathize with me in religious faith and hope. I spent many happy hours thus, with my Bible and Jesus. One day I became so much engaged that I forgot the time, and was not on deck at the usual muster, and roll call of my company.

"'The Captain inquired for me, but none of my comrades knew where I was. After a while I remembered where I was, hastened on deck, and reported myself to my Captain. He asked me where I had been. I informed him I had been down in the sail room. "What have you been doing there?" said he. I told him I had been praying. "Praying to what?" "Praying to my God," said I. "To your God? what kind of a God is he—black or white?" To this I made no reply; for his reckless profanity hurt me to the soul.

"'They called a court martial immediately, and condemned me to be flogged.

"'I was ordered to strip, and did so. They then tied my hands, and swung them to the halliards so high, that I could barely stand on my feet. While the boatswain was about commencing to "lay on" my bare back, I began to sing with my whole soul:

> " Behold the Saviour of mankind,
> Nailed to the shameful tree :
> How vast the love that him inclined,
> To bleed and die for me!"

"'The Captain cried out, "Boatswain, hold on! don't strike!" He stepped forward in front of me, and saw my face covered with tears. After a short pause, he inquired, "What sort of religion is this of yours?" I replied, "Sir, I am a Methodist."

" ' Do you want to pray ?'

" ' Yes, sir, I must pray as long as I live. I cannot do without praying.'

" ' Well, my man, how would you like to pray in my cabin ?'

" ' I would feel it a privilege, sir, to pray anywhere.'

" ' Well,'' said he, turning away, " Whenever you are off duty, you may go into my cabin and pray as much as you please. Guard, untie this man.'

" ' I was then liberated, and all those standing near appeared silent and serious. I noticed tears on some of their faces.

" ' I went soon after, full of love to God and man, down into the Captain's cabin, and knelt down to pour out my soul before the Lord in thankfulness, and ask him to convict and convert my poor wicked companions.

" ' The Mate came in while I was at prayer, and fell down beside me, saying, " Pray for me." He appeared to be under deep conviction. I prayed for him until the Lord converted his soul, and filled him with joy and peace. The Captain coming down about that time, was met by his Mate at the companion way, who cried out, " Oh ! Captain, Captain ! This religion is so good, you must have it ! you must have it !''

" ' He laid his hands on the Captain's shoulders, and, while the big tears were rolling down his face, drew him, unresistingly, into the cabin, where we both prayed for him. He began to weep and pray for himself, and not long after, was powerfully blessed.

" ' The lion was turned into a lamb, and we all rejoiced greatly in the mercy of God. We then held meetings regularly every day, to which the crew were invited, and some of them were awakened to a sense of their lost condition, and sought pardon in the wounds of a crucified Redeemer. Seven were converted when we reached port; which was in one of the West India Islands. The captain gave me permission to go on shore and hold meetings, and we had a happy time there. I formed a society before I left, and hope they are going on to perfection, and increasing more and more."

Rev. Mr. Kemp communicates another anecdote, showing the intimacy Brother Thomas enjoyed with this people, and the estimate they put upon his character:—

"A noble looking young man, the son of religious parents in England, who had been carefully reared, and designed for a religious life, threw off all restraint, forsook his home and friends, and enlisted as a soldier. He was with the army on Tangiers, and attracted the notice of Brother T. particularly. Through the influence of his friends at home his discharge was obtained, and liberty given him to return to his parents. Before leaving, however, he wished to distinguish himself, in some expedition of danger, and went with a company of soldiers to the Virginia shore. There, in a skirmish with the militia, he was severely wounded, and brought back to the island to die.

"Brother Thomas was almost constantly at his side, as life ebbed away, pointing him to the 'Lamb of God;' and before the young soldier breathed his last, he felt his sins forgiven, and left an assurance behind that he was saved through the all-atoning blood, and hoped for eternal life."

Brother Thomas obtained favor with the officers and soldiers of the army, and sought every means to do good among them.   It will be noticed that there was much high-toned honor and generosity evinced in their treatment of the island people.   What they needed in the way of provision, they paid for, and generally restored vessels that had been captured, where the owners were poor, and made application to the Admiral commanding. We could fill a volume with the incidents of those days, handed down to the present generation, or repeated by eye-witnesses, who retain a vivid recollection of the events of that year.

We continue to quote :—

"The next circumstance I wish to relate, is this : The Admiral sent his steward, and took whatever he liked out of my garden, telling me I must go on board and he would give me my pay.   When I went on board, I was amazed at everything I saw.   The man took me away down into the bottom of the ship, and filled my bag with rice, and the 'Parson of the Islands,' (for so they all called me,) had to lug it up three pair of stairs; and as I came to each deck, the officers would roar out, 'What have you got there, Parson?'   I began to feel ashamed, and would have given all that my garden contained, rather than be mortified by their talk.   When I reached the gangway, I let my bag of rice down into my canoe, and was about leaving as fast as I could, when an officer tapped me on the shoulder, and said my presence was required in the ward-room.   This was the place where the chief officers were collected together. I thought, 'Now, what shall I do?   Must I go among those officers barefoot, and in the rags I had on!' But no time was given me to parley; so I off cap and put it under my arm, and followed the officer who came after me with the message. The moment I entered the ward-room, they all roared out laughing to see 'The Parson of the Islands' in such a rig as he presented. At this I felt *my old nature rise,* and said to one I knew to be the doctor, 'Have you called me in here, sir, to make fun of me?' 'Upon my honor, Parson, I have not, sir,' said he, and he gave the other fellows such a look as shut them up in a moment.

"'Well, Parson,' said the doctor, 'I understand you were to exhort last Sunday after our chaplain; why did you not do it?'

"'Because he did not ask me, sir,' said I.

"'Well,' said he, 'we want you to preach to us here in the ward-room; come, give us a good sermon.'

"'I will, if you get permission from the Admiral.'

"'Oh, he will not hear you,' said the doctor.

"'Indeed he will, sir,' said I, 'for if I get at it, and the power comes on me, every one aboard this ship will hear me.'

"'Well, Parson Thomas, I have heard that before you were converted you had a great impediment in your speech, but since your conversion you are clear of it.'

"'Yes,' said I, 'while talking about spiritual things, exhorting and praying, it is taken away.'

"'Well,' said the doctor, 'we will now turn our conversation, and talk about temporal things.'

"It then came to me—if you force a stammering, you will never be able to talk clearly again; and I thought if I did not stammer, he would think I had told a lie.' But the same spirit whispered, 'Leave that to me; I will see to that.'

"The doctor then commenced talking about the affairs of the country and government. He asked me,

"'Did your President, Mr. Madison, do right in declaring war against Great Britain?'

"I said, 'You have asked me a very uncivil question; for how should I know about things done in Washington or England, seeing I live on this little island, so far from those places; and how can I know about the king's business, and Mr. Madison's business?' I stammered very badly while making this reply, and I could not help it. He then said to me, 'You have given a better answer than Mr. Madison himself could have given, and I will reward you well for it.'

"The doctor then inquired of me what disease my wife had, as she had been sick for some time. I told him as well as I could, and he prepared some medicine, with directions how to take it, and it done her a great deal of good, though it failed to cure her, and she died soon after.

"They would not let me away until I gave them an exhortation, which they listened to with respectful attention, and then gathered round to shake hands with me as I was leaving. I was truly glad to get off, and determined in my own mind to give the ward-room a 'wide berth,' ever afterwards."

His visits to the fleet, however, were frequent, and his acquaintance with the Admiral and high officers of the ships was intimate and pleasant.

The incidental allusion above, to the death of his beloved wife, Rachel, which occurred while the army was still encamped in his neighborhood, and while the excitements and distress of the existing war prevailed, added greatly to his perplexity, and filled his cup of domestic joy with bitterness. She had been the sympathizing partner of his early struggles for a home, and comparative independence. She shared the domestic incidents and ills peculiar to their lot, with a true womanly fortitude; and with a cheerful and happy disposition. She had seen her devoted husband in all the vicissitudes of his darker days of doubt and perplexity on the subject of his personal salvation, and largely partook of his new-found joy in Christ Jesus. She lived to see him an uncompromising Christian, and a widely influential man. Her children, of whom she left four or five living, were growing hearty and happy in her smiles, and repeating their simple prayers at morn and eve, around her knee. A new claimant on her maternal love, had just gladdened her heart and home; the infant named after his father's friend, Seymour; and, just as life was opening hopefully before her, she drooped and died. Desolation mantled that humble, but, hitherto, happy abode, and fell upon the hearth, which had been so bright with her presence and love. The bereaved husband bowed to this adverse blast, and meekly said in his Christian faith and resignation, " *The Lord gave, and the Lord hath taken away; blessed be the name of the Lord.*" He found hope in her death, and sorrowed not as those who have no expectations beyond the grave. His constant attention and care was now needed for his little motherless children, and suitable provision made for the helpless infant.

He had recourse to prayer, and daily looked to God for help and direction in this time of distress. The promises of his Bible assured him strength according to his day, and grace sufficient, in the severest conflict. His hymn book, too, furnished many a sweet lesson of patience and hope. He read over, and rejoiced in such precious sentiments as the following:

> " In every condition, in sickness, and health,
> In poverty's vale, or abounding in wealth;
> At home or abroad, on the land, on the sea,
> 'As thy days may demand shall thy strength ever be.'

> " Fear not, I am with thee, O be not dismay'd,
> I, I am thy God, and will still give thee aid;
> I'll strengthen thee, help thee, and cause thee to stand,
> Upheld by my righteous, omnipotent hand.

> " When through the deep waters I call thee to go,
> The rivers of wo shall not thee overflow;
> For I will be with thee thy troubles to bless,
> And sanctify to thee thy deepest distress.

> " When through fiery trials thy pathway shall lie,
> My grace all-sufficient shall be thy supply;
> The flame shall not hurt thee, I only design
> Thy dross to consume, and thy gold to refine.

> " E'en down to old age, all my people shall prove
> My sovereign, eternal, unchangeable love;
> And when hoary hairs shall their temples adorn,
> Like lambs they shall still on my bosom be borne.

> " The soul that on Jesus doth lean for repose,
> I will not, I will not, desert to his foes;
> That soul, though all hell should endeavor to shake,
> I'll never, no never, no never forsake."

For one of the most interesting anecdotes of his life, which should be recalled in this connection, as the event took place about this period, we turn to the sketch furnished by Rev. Brother Massey in his introduction.

Brother Thomas, through all the subsequent years of his pilgrimage, looked back on this circumstance, as the most marked evidence of his Heavenly Father's loving kindness. The delicacy of his position, the exigencies of his situation, and the wisdom of his (God appointed) choice, made such an impression on his heart, that with the weight of gathering cares and crowding years upon him, and under such bodily affliction as falls to the lot of but few on earth, he nevertheless rejoiced until his dying day in that deliverance, which, at this juncture, came opportunely to his relief.

He narrated the anecdote as given by Brother Massey, so frequently, in his public addresses, that it assumed, according to the peculiar color or temperament of the listener, a variety of hues; and is handed down to the compiler in diferent shapes; but of all the accounts given us, that referred to is most accurate and consistent.

CHAPTER X.

No event in the history of Rev. Joshua Thomas, gave
such a wide celebrity to his name, or was remembered by
himself with more interest than that which, in the course
of this narrative, we now proceed to record.

As the man, who in preaching to the enemies of his
country foretold their defeat, and warned them against
proceeding to Baltimore; who gained their respect for
his unflinching adherence to truth and right, and who
was instrumental in pointing many of them to the Saviour of sinners,—he earned a notoriety, and well mer-
ited distinction that will live through many generations.

The Prettyman Manuscript continues :—

" Towards the close of summer, in the year 1814, we
were made aware of some important movement among
the forces encamped on the island. Preparations began
both on shore and through the fleet in the harbor. Sig-

nals were exchanged, orders given, and all became bustle and activity.

" Some of the officers told me the cause of all this ;— they were going to take Baltimore. I told them they had better let it alone; they might be mistaken in their calculations; for the Baltimoreans would resist them, and would fight hard for their city and their homes.

" ' Oh!' said they, ' we can take it easily.' I told them it was a dangerous undertaking, in my opinion, for I believed God would fight for the good people in that city, and aid them in defeating their enemies.

" Before they left Tangier, they sent me word to be ready to hold a public meeting, and exhort the soldiers, on the camp ground. I did not like to refuse, and yet I was very unwilling to perform this duty. I thought and prayed over the matter, and *it came to me* that I must stand up for Jesus as a good soldier, in the fight of faith; and as some of these men might be killed in the battle, and never have another opportunity of worship, that it was my duty and privilege to obey their order, and hold the meeting. It was arranged to be on the last Sunday they were in camp. Early that morning, the flags were hoisted, the drums beat, and every preparation was made for a full turn out.

" Boats were plying from the ships to the shore, and bands of music were playing on board.

" At the hour appointed, the soldiers were all drawn up in solid columns, about twelve thousand men, under the pines of the old camp ground, which formed the open space in the centre of their tents.

" I stood on a little platform erected at the end of the

REV. JOSHUA THOMAS PREACHING TO THE BRITISH ARMY ON TANGIER ISLAND, 1814.

camp nearest the shore, all the men facing me with their hats off, and held by the right hand under the left arm. An officer stood on my right and one on my left, and sentries were stationed a little distance to the rear.

"As I looked around on my congregation, I never had such feelings in my life; but I felt determined to give them a faithful warning, even if those officers with their keen glittering swords, *would cut me in pieces* for speaking the truth.

"After singing and prayer, I began to feel better in mind, and more at liberty. Soon all fear and embarrassment were taken away from me, and I proceeded in my exhortation as freely as ever I did, in any place, or before any people.

"I told them in the commencement what caused war, and fighting among nations and men;—what made this once good, happy world, so full of evil and misery as it now is; and what brings ruin on men, soul and body. *Sin*, I said, done all this; but ' *It is a faithful saying and worthy of all acceptation, that Jesus Christ came into the world to save sinners.*'

"I told them what kind of a sinner I was, and how He *saved me from sin ;* also, many of my neighbors, and that He was ' able to save to the uttermost all them that come unto God by him.' I described some of the seasons of refreshing we had enjoyed in that spot, ' from the presence of the Lord,' and thanked them and their Admiral for the kindness they manifested to us ;—but I could not bid them God speed, in what I understood they were going to do.

"I warned them of the danger and distress they would

bring upon themselves and others by going to Baltimore
with the object they had in view. I told them of the
great wickedness of war, and that God said, ' *Thou shalt
not kill!*' If you do, he will judge you at the last day ;
or, before then, he will cause you to 'perish by the
sword.'

"I told them it was given me from the Almighty that
they *could not* take Baltimore, and *would not succeed in
their expedition.*

"I exhorted them to prepare for death, for many of
them would in all likelihood die soon, and I should see
them no more till we met at the sound of the great trumpet before our final Judge."

The service concluded, many stepped up to the intrepid parson, and thanked him for his faithful warnings,
and said they hoped it would not go so hard with them
as he had foretold. He shook his head, and said he felt
that many that day had received their last call.

In the bare outline of his exhortation which we have
been enabled to lay before the reader, it will be discovered that he touched on many points of fundamental
truth : the doctrine of the fall of man, the effects of sin,
and the only name given under heaven among men
whereby the consequences of this condition can be
averted, and the sinner saved. At that period in his
discourse, he took occasion, as usual with him, to tell his
own experience, which we may well suppose was a simple
and living illustration of the power and preciousness of
saving faith.

Delicately he acknowledged their consideration and
generosity to him and his people, and with unflinching

fortitude held up before them the wickedness of that career in which they were all engaged. God's absolute command on the "mount that burned with fire," is hurled in among the ranks, and we can imagine the interesting exposition that was founded on the words : his description of scenery, as the "thunderings and lightnings" attested the dread presence, and fearfully indicated the majesty and might of the God of Abraham, and Isaac, and Jacob; whose word endureth for ever. He appeals to the last judgment too, and draws a startling contrast between the " righteous saved, and wicked damned," and closes with a prayer that his strangely interested auditory may be dissuaded from sin, and find mercy at the cross.

The most remarkable thing about his address, however, was the steady persistence with which he predicted the defeat of their intended expedition to Baltimore. The army had hitherto met with but feeble resistance at any point up or down the Bay. Bladensburg had proved the weakness of our defence, Washington was a heap of smoking ruins, Alexandria capitulated without resistance, and now with concentrated force, the whole squadron pours its flushed and confident thousands on Baltimore.

Under these circumstances it might well be supposed that this city was doomed to destruction ; yet in the face of all the probabilities of the case, Joshua Thomas expressed a conviction " that came to him" of the result, which subsequent events proved to be correct. Was this on his part a mere wish,—a whim, or peradventure ? " *You cannot take it !*" he reiterated that day. Perhaps he remembered that thousands in that city were on their knees, morning, noon, and night, interceding with God! That some of his acquaintances from "Light Lane Meeting house," who had, by their success in prayer and labor at camp meeting there on that beach, displayed "power with God," were in the city, and formed its rampart and defence, in unseen agency with the Lord Jehovah! That Divine being was *his* strength and song, at all events, and had become his "salvation."

The proud fleet weighed anchor, and with pennants streaming, and decks bristling with the machinery of war, stood up the Bay, and left the anxious islanders awaiting the issue.

The booming of heavy ordnance was wafted o'er the waters day after day, and night after night—gun answering to gun, until silence told the people of Tangier that the fight was over. But was it gained or lost by the assailants? For tidings that might settle this question they waited with sleepless eagerness. Brother Thomas showed no concern, except for the slain in battle, of which he expected to hear. He says:

"When the battle was over, we saw them coming, and I went down to meet the first that landed. I felt great distress, for fear many of those I knew had been killed, and also lest some of *our own people*, (the citizens of Baltimore,) had met their death. My worst fears were far short of the reality!

"The first officers I met, I asked them if they had taken Baltimore? They looked at me and said, 'No, but hundreds of our brave men have been slain, and our best General is killed. It turned out just as you told us the Sunday before we left: we have had a bloody battle,

and all the time we were fighting *we thought of you*, and
what you told us.   You seemed to be standing right before us, still warning us against our attempt to take Baltimore.' "

A few messages were conveyed to him, of a deeply
affecting character.   One sought him out, and informed
him of a comrade who was mortally wounded at North
Point, and who, before he breathed his last, said, " God
bless Parson Thomas.   He showed me the way to Christ
and now, though I die, I hope for mercy and salvation
through the name of Jesus, and expect to meet that good
man in heaven."

A poor wounded grenadier returned, and in a conversation with the " Parson," said ; " I never felt my
sinfulness before God until that Sunday you preached
to us ; and while the bullets were flying, and my comrades falling on every hand, the other day, I cast myself
on the merits of the Lamb of God, and now feel at
peace."

Another told him he should carry the recollection of
that exhortation home with him to England, and not
forget it while he lived.

Thus was " bread cast upon the waters," and saving
truth scattered over the wide seas, by a man whose only
boast, was, that which we find marked and emphasized,
in his well-thumbed hymn book, as the great motto of
his religious life :

> " Nothing less will I require,
> Nothing more can I desire ;
> None but Christ to me be given ;
> None but Christ in earth or heaven.

O that I might now decrease!
O that all I am might cease!
Let me into nothing fall!
LET MY LORD BE ALL IN ALL!'

After their protracted imprisonment, (for the island
people were all this time *prisoners of war,*) the news of
peace was joyful to them beyond all expression. They
were among the very first on the continent to receive the
welcome tidings. "In the month of January, 1815,"
says Brother Thomas, "we perceived a mighty stir in
the camp one day; and witnessed signals flying, and
great commotion on ships and shore. We could not tell
what it meant for some time. By and by, one of the
officers came riding up to my house as hard as he could
gallop, crying out, 'Oh! Parson Thomas! Parson
Thomas! *there's peace!* THERE'S PEACE!!' I inquired,
'How do you know?' 'Oh!' said he, 'yonder is the
ship,' pointing down the bay to where a large vessel
was seen coming up, 'and she has a *white flag* at her
mast head. That signal means peace, and now we know
the war is over!' I became as joyful as he appeared to
be when I saw the white emblem, and heard the salutes
fired, my heart leaped within me as the noble ship steered
on to Washington, where the treaty of peace was soon
after agreed to, and ratified by our President.

"The news flew, like lightning, over the United States,
and everywhere there was great rejoicing."

With one more paragraph, the manuscript, which,
though worn with age, has been found so interesting and
serviceable, closes: and thereafter we must depend on
the somewhat disconnected, but abundant, memoranda

supplied by those who have come to our aid with commendable alacrity, and with contributions which will be found interesting and accurate in relation to "The Parson," during his subsequent, and more public ministry.

"As the ponderous men of war piped to weigh anchor for the last time, we all were gathered on the beach to return their waving farewell. We had some blessed meetings together before they struck their tents, and many tears were shed between us, as we took the parting hand; for though in general they were enemies to our beloved country, we found many of them friends of Jesus, and fellow citizens with the saints, in the household of faith, and hope to meet some of them among the saved at last."

When the camp meeting season rolled round that same year, the active spirit of the good Parson had made every arrangement for a great gathering of the armies of the Lord on the old ground at Tangier. Hundreds who had never visited the place before, were in attendance, and wonderingly listened while Brother Thomas recounted the history of the past few years, on that remarkable spot. The mounds which were constructed as forts were there, and the graves along the shore to the south, where many of their dead had been buried, were also to be seen, with other traces of the history of the occupancy of the island by the British army.

The preachers at that meeting, drew many forcible illustrations of divine truth from the incidents of the war. Rev. L. Lawrenson, who about this time began to be known as one of the most mighty and eloquent preachers Methodism had ever owned on the Peninsula, instructed and electrified thousands by his great sermon on the text, "*Now then we are ambassadors for Christ, &c.,*"—referring to the war, its ravages, its end; and the treaty of Ghent, made by ambassadors for their respective governments; and forcibly applying this text, as the authority of God's ambassadors to make a treaty with sinful men, "beseeching them, in Christ's stead, to be *reconciled* to God." "Oh! that the white flag of peace may be hung out to-day!" he exclaimed, "as the symbol of reconciliation between you, rebel sinners, and your long suffering and forbearing God!"

It was not long before the depression occasioned by the war, and the general stagnation of business resulting from the presence of a powerful enemy, almost at the doors of the people living near the Chesapeake waters, yielded to prosperity with the return of peace. In this present year of grace, 1860, the visitor to almost any family residence in the lower counties of the eastern shore, may, on inquiry, gain abundant information about those trying years of invasion and anxiety; and hear of vessels captured and burned or sunk, of dwellings plundered, and the names of persons among the militia companies, who met, at every point, and repelled, in every encounter, the advance of the foe.

It is not within our scope, or the province of these memoirs—to dwell upon the engagements that took place at various points along the rivers and bay shore, in which signal bravery was displayed by the citizens, in defence of their homes and property: or we might pursue this theme to almost any extent. One circumstance may be recalled and corroborated before we close this chapter.

It will be remembered that we gave an account of a skirmish which took place in Accomac, in which a very promising young British soldier was fatally wounded and afterwards died in camp at Tangier, hoping in Christ through Parson Thomas' prayers and religious instruction. That engagement is well remembered by many still living. Brother Garrison Burton, a prominent member and friend of the Methodist Church in Accomac Co., Virginia, was in the engagement referred to, and gave the writer, some years since, a vivid description of what he termed "this *brush* with the enemy," causing him to beat a precipitate retreat, before repeated volleys of musketry, with which the valiant Virginians repelled him from their shores.

We do not know how far religion really lost ground from 1812 to 1815, in this region of country. The preachers attended regularly to their work. Revivals are mentioned, as having taken place at intervals, churches were erected, and local preachers and exhorters were commissioned every year, to swell the official host of this aggressive branch of the church which seems to have continued steadily advancing in successes and resources, "leaning on the arm of her beloved; *clear as the sun, fair as the moon,* and terrible as an army with banners!"

Camp meetings, as we have intimated, were resumed on the beach with increased zest and energy ; and as we have incidentally introduced the name of Rev. Lawrence Lawrenson, in connection with these mighty convocations of the Methodist people, it may be interesting to many who loved that man of God, as perhaps they loved but few men—particularly as little, if anything, has been published relating to his ministry, character, and success, while in this part of the Lord's vineyard,—to present the result of some extended research for memorials of his life and labors, in the form of a separate chapter.

CHAPTER XI.

Mr. Lawrenson on the Peninsula—Acquaintance and intimacy with Mr. Thomas—His social habits—Appearance—Cause of despondency—Pulpit efforts—Favorite texts—Incidents—The sheep and lambs—As much right to preach as Paul had—Hypocrites—Curtis' chapel—The lawyers—Charade—Adventures with Mr. Thomas—Preach like Lawrenson—A sign to stop—Preaching in bed—Amusing scene—Shouting in a fog—. Elijah's mantle—Death of Lawrenson—Memoir—Last experience joyful.

THE history of our "Parson of the Islands," would be incomplete without some allusion to a man for whom he cherished the most unbounded admiration, and in whom he was almost bound up by a sense of obligation and a respectful deference that filled his heart and strongly marked his future life.

That man was the REV. LAWRENCE LAWRENSON.

Mr. Lawrenson became a member of the Philadelphia Conference in 1810. After four years of toil and travel we find him on the Annamessex Circuit, and learn that he became at once a prominent and popular minister of the gospel. His name stands connected with this particular field of labor during the year 1814, and again in 1816, and 1817. The two following years he traveled the Accomac Circuit, and was, by earnest request, returned to Annamessex in 1820.

He was appointed Presiding Elder of what was at that time called the "Chesapeake," or Lower District, in 1822, and in this capacity, served the church the full term of four years. His district included the fields of labor he had formerly occupied, and where his hold on the affections of the people was so strong and mutual.

During all this time—ten years—he and Mr. Thomas were intimate friends, and traveled much in company; the one amused and cheered up by the other's simplicity, quaintness, inexhaustible humor, and lively religious temperament; while *he* was profoundly impressed, and daily edified, by contact with a man surpassed by none who have sustained the character of a Methodist preacher, on the lower part of the Peninsula.

He gave a character and position to the denomination, with the interests of which he was identified, which it has maintained, through evil and good report, until the present time. Of all the itinerant preachers who have traveled this circuit, for the last fifty years, none are remembered more distinctly and affectionately than he. The texts he used, the sermons he preached, even his manner, tones, and features, are present to the minds, and still warm up the hearts of those who knew him; and who, under his powerful appeals from the pulpit, were drawn to the cross, and led into the fold of Christ.

He was almost an idol with the early Methodists in various localities, where most of his leisure hours were passed, and so commanded the regard of persons of other denominations, or of no particular church affinity, as to make for himself a cordial welcome to their homes. He gained such an ascendency over their minds, as to "prepare the way," for his successors, to an almost universal acceptability among all ranks and classes of the people.

As a feeble memorial to his honored name, we have gleaned a number of facts and incidents, which will recall the "former times," lingered over by many in the church, as the bright days of their own past history and experience.

His quick discernment detected in the character of Brother Thomas certain traits, which endeared this good man to his heart. At his instance the island exhorter was authorized to preach, and under his persuasions, as we have intimated in a former chapter, the first effort at preaching was attempted at St. Peter's church, in Annamessex.

In the same way did he encourage others, in whom he discovered adaptation to the work, to assume positions of prominence in the church, and was generally successful in putting "the right man in the right place."

One of the most notable peculiarities about him was the depression and melancholy which at intervals seemed to prey upon his mind. He would at intervals sit silent for hours, and sometimes for days, among his friends, without evincing any desire for conversation, never speaking except spoken to, and then would merely answer, "yes," or "no." At such times it was remarked, he drank water almost incessantly, and if alone would walk the floor in abstraction and deep study. He never shunned society, or avoided his acquaintances under such circumstances. At other times he was partial to young society, and in the company of ladies, would exert himself to show attention and be agreeable. He was not a misanthrope, as some conjectured, from the reserve they observed in him at times; nor was he haughty or proud, though he eschewed the cut-a-way style in his coat, and dressed unlike the fathers and his brethren in the itinerancy at that day.   His portly person, florid face, bristling hair, and general carriage, may have been mistaken for indifference to the usages of the times when it is often declared, " you could identify a Methodist preacher as far as you could see him," and when members, like their ministers, " put on meekness" in the form of a strait breasted coat, or a broad brim hat!   Mr. Lawrenson dressed in the finest material, though he never seemed particular as to how his apparel was adjusted on his person, or whether his respectable broad cloth was on wrong or right side out.

He spent much of his leisure time in Potato Neck, at the residence of his friend, Francis Waters, or that of Mr. Sudler, for the families of whom he manifested a special regard.   At Brother Waters' he found a congenial spirit in the person of Mr. Francis Waters, Junior, who about that time became a preacher, and is still a highly talented and useful minister.

With Miss Susan Waters he enjoyed an acquaintance which materially contributed to his happiness.   She is said to have been one of the most amiable, accomplished, and devotedly pious ladies of her day.

In her early, and lamented death, it was supposed, died the hope, and in her grave was buried the love, of Lawrenson.

If this conjecture is correct, it may account for much

of the apparent desolation of his social feelings at times, and justify the subsequent indifference he exhibited, when approached on the subject of marriage by some who took that liberty, from the desire they felt that he might adopt a more settled life.

His refuge from despondency was the pulpit. This indeed was his true sphere. In class meeting he rarely became animated, or said more than a few words, after his unvariable question, "Tell us the state of your mind?" had been answered with fluency and feeling by the members.

As a preacher, he soared, oftentimes, to the third heaven of ecstatic joy and triumph. With a crowded house, and a warm-hearted few to sustain him by prayer, he seemed imbued with "the unction of the Holy One."

His efforts were "in demonstration of the Spirit and with power;" and the fruits of his mighty outpourings of burning eloquence were gathered, in converted hundreds, into the church. So vivid were his representations of divine truth, that men under the influence of worldly pride, or denominational prejudice, trembled as he portrayed a "trembling Felix," and were *altogether* persuaded to espouse Christ, as he depicted the beauty and glory of an immediate surrender to the claims of the gospel, in contrast with the temporising and soul-destroying policy of him who said, "Go thy way for *this* time." On this text "his word was with power."

When he announced that stirring appeal from Isaiah, "Come now and let us reason together, saith the Lord; though your sins be as scarlet, they shall be white as snow; though they be red like crimson, they shall be as

wool!" and told the merciful condescension of a long
suffering God, as revealed in his providence, and the plan
of redemption; even the children of his congregations
were thrilled and impressed to that degree, that, at their
firesides to day, they speak to *their* children "the words
of this salvation as they heard them from his lips.

A lady informed the writer, a short time since, that
she never forgot the following verses after hearing him
quote them in one of his sermons :—

"Suppose the sea with ink was filled,
    And parchment all the land ;
And every single stick a quill,—
    A scribe each ready hand.

"To write thy love, O gracious God !
    Would run the ocean dry ;
Nor could the scroll contain the whole,
    Though stretched from sky to sky."

"I shall never forget," says another, "the sermon he
preached, and the meeting which followed, the night I
was, with several others, converted. The service was
held at Brother Jones', in Rock Creek, near the Thoroughfare. He went down there to preach for the accommodation of the old people who were too infirm to
attend church. His text was John xxi. 15, 16, 17. He
walked the floor while preaching, and on the point of
'Love to Jesus,' was more than ordinarily animated and
eloquent. 'Peter's language,' he said, 'was the language
and settled sentiment of his own heart, "*Yea, Lord, thou
knowest all things—thou knowest that I love thee!*"'

"'And now,' said he, 'I have the lambs of the flock

to feed. These dear little children. Children, I want to win you to Christ; little lambs, come into his blessed fold. Oh gentle Shepherd! loving Jesus! take them now in thine arms, and seal them for thine own!' This prayer was answered in a most signal manner that night." The lady who gave me this account was then a small girl, and was, with others, then and there so filled with Divine love, that they still hear their Shepherd's voice; and, as members of the Church, "go in and out, and find pasture," none since that hour having been able to pluck them out of his hand.

The preacher, also, had much to say to, and about, the sheep, and the diligent pastor's duty. He was so happy that he clapped his hands joyfully, saying, "Glory to God,"—dwelling with full, round emphasis on the "GLORY," and always pronouncing the sacred name in a short, rapid, and energetic manner,—"Glory to God" —as he walked through the crowded rooms of weeping and happy people—"I am feeding my Lord's sheep, *hallelujah!*"

It appears he often went out of his ordinary way to visit and preach to the aged and infirm.

The house of Lazarus Maddux in Potato Neck, was the spiritual birth-place of many precious souls. There the first society was formed and nurtured, which has now expanded into the "Fairmount Station." Father Maddux was one of the most holy, useful, and highly respected men of his day. He was an exhorter, and, though once recommended and elected as a licensed preacher, to his credit, it is on the old journal recorded,

"He refused the honor," and preferred the more humble office of a hard-working exhorter in the Church.

To the house of this "Father in Israel," Mr. Sudler once accompanied Brother Lawrenson, on a similar mission to that at old Mr. Jones' in Rock Creek.

He preached from the passage in Acts, "And the disciples were called Christians, first at Antioch."

He had been low spirited for some days, and was, at first, somewhat "dry" in his remarks, as he reviewed the conversion, travels, sufferings, and successes of the Apostle Paul—the revival at Antioch, and the characteristics of a true Christian. In the course of his remarks he became happy, and bounding off the second step of the stairway, where he stood, he walked the floor in great exultation of soul, exclaiming, "Glory to God! I feel that I am commissioned from on high, and have *just as much right to preach as Paul had!*"

A text well remembered as the foundation of one of his masterly discourses was, "Buy the truth, sell it not."

Another of his telling sermons was based upon our Lord's words, "The Queen of the South," &c., and exhibited in grand proportion the character and claims of the Son of God.

Salisbury was one of his appointments at that period, being connected until many years afterwards with the Annamessex circuit.

At this place he is remembered as one of the most eloquent and effective preachers the older people have ever known. Many of the prominent citizens of the town were attracted to hear him, and though strongly attached to church forms, and opposed to some of the stirring doctrines he advanced, were finally induced to seek regenerating grace, and a knowledge of sin forgiven, and pardon sealed on their own hearts, under his ministry.

He was in the habit of leaving the pulpit toward the close of his sermons, and stepping down on a bench in front, which he walked to and fro, appealing to and exhorting sinners to seek a present salvation.

When stopping at Brother Riders, he fell into one of his gloomy periods, a man named Levin Hitch, who was chief singer in the church, and noted for his liveliness in conversation, and his resources in anecdote, visited him, and greatly cheered him by his welcome company.

A brother on Deal's Island, who had left the church for some cause, was induced to seek readmission after listening to one of his powerful sermons at Rock Creek. Mr. Lawrenson, in closing the discourse, exclaimed, "What more can I say? What else can I do to win you to my God? I will go down on my knees and there plead with you." Down he went, into the altar, fell on his knees, and continued his entreaties, until the power of the Spirit came upon the people.

"That sort of preaching knocked me over," said this man to a neighbor, as they were repairing to their homes.

He took his congregation by surprise once at Rock Creek, while preaching on the parable of the marriage supper. After an able exposition of doctrinal truth in relation to the character and extent of the gospel provision to meet the world's want, he began to apply the subject, and expose the cavilings and pretexts which men employ to evade the direct call of Divine grace, and continue in the pursuits and pleasures of sin.

"And now," said he, with an intense earnestness, and a soul on fire, "it may be that there are some under the sound of my voice, who are sincerely desirous of an interest in the promises, and long for fellowship with the people of God: but they look around them and raise the question, 'To whom shall I go; with what body of professing Christians shall I cast in my lot, and identify my interests and hopes for eternity? There is a church, but its standard of personal piety is low, and its doctrines indefinite or unintelligible. I cannot venture there. But here is another denomination, its creed is consistent, its ritual excellent, and its history respectable, yet there does not seem to be vitality in its teachings, or that which may meet and satisfy the need of my craving soul in its formula. I want power to save. Well, there is another church, full of life, fire, and zeal. Its ministers appear honest, its members in earnest, but there are hypocrites among them, and loathing hypocrisy. I keep myself away from their communion. What shall I do?'

"I'll tell you what *I* would do," said the preacher. "If I was to-day in such a case, without church connection, and seeking one which I thought would best promote my present and eternal salvation. Between the church said to have no hypocrites and one that was charged with having many, which do you suppose I would prefer?"

Everybody supposed he would, and knew *they* would prefer the one without these blots on the name of Christ, these pests to true piety, and expected to hear him announce this preference in his next breath: but no; he avowed his choice of the church that was accused of having plenty in its fold.   This declaration was startling to many, but he proceeded to assign a reason in vindication of his choice.   "Where hypocrisy exists," he maintained, "there is evidence even in this fact, that the good and true are there: but in that denomination where not a case of this kind appears, there must arise a suspicion that there is nothing there worth counterfeiting; no sound saving religion at all!"

To illustrate this position, he added, "I have been many years traveling about in this country, and have been well acquainted with the status of your Somerset County Bank, but I have never yet seen or heard of a counterfeit on its currency; and why? because its money is *below par!*   Counterfeits flood the land, but they are all on sound banks, safe institutions, and no other.   He would be a silly fool as well as a great knave, who would devote his misdirected genius to the task of counterfeiting a worthless bank.   So that this objection, which I have heard over and over again against the Methodist Church, has no real force in it, but rather proves, if there *are* miserable counterfeits and hypocrites among us, that *we are not below par;* that we stand fair before a gainsaying world.   I give glory to God for this, that there is in the doctrines, experience, and practical holiness of our beloved church, a vitality that commands the reluctant, but emphatic commendation of her enemies.   *Let me be a Methodist!*"

There were "amens," we may well suppose, to that,

and, while hypocrisy was unmasked, the faith of sincere Christians was greatly confirmed by this mode of illustrating the subject in hand.

He had a habit when fully aroused in the pulpit of stepping back, and then surging foward to give emphasis to his utterance. Whenever the people noticed this movement they knew his soul was free, and the "Spirit of the Lord God rested upon" him.

Curtis' Chapel has often resounded with the tones of his voice. To this place, the people for many miles around repaired on the occasion of his visits. The families of Captain Cottman, and Colonel Jones, also that of Z. Long, Esq., attended his ministry, and made him a welcome guest at their homes, when he preached there.

The supposed fact, that he had been educated for the bar, attracted legal gentlemen to his congregations, and many who regarded with contempt the name of "Methodist" before, after hearing him were led to respect the denomination he represented, and abandon the prejudices they had in ignorance formed against this people.

One Sabbath morning at Curtis', he had, to use a common expression, "the harness on," and wielded the "sword of the Spirit" with an irresistible effect. A Judge and several members of the profession from Princess Anne were present, and confessed themselves astonished at the power and pathos with which he urged home the truth. "He is a giant in intellect," said one, as they met outside after sermon. "And *good* as he is *great*," said another. "Come," said a third, "I have never paid a cent to help these fellows along, let us put something in the hat to-day."

The collector approached, and was astounded to see a number of notes, of respectable denomination, thrown in. His summing up for the "support of the gospel" that day, was comparatively enormous.

One instance is given, where his constitutional infirmity followed him to the pulpit, and so depressed his feelings that, although the congregation were as usual attentive and interested, he suddenly closed the Bible and turning to Brother Quinn who sat behind him said, "Brother, get up and finish the sermon, for I cannot."

His playfulness at rare intervals, when he could adapt himself to any company, without losing his habitual dignity, the following incident will show :

Meeting with Brother Pinto, who was then a young man and somewhat bashful, at the house of a mutual friend, he inquired if he could solve the following charade :

> " In olden time as Scripture doth record,
> Lived one who never did offend the Lord ;
> The truth he told and ne'er did sin commit ;
> Yet in Christ's kingdom he shall never sit."

"Who was that?" said he. Mr. P. happened to be posted and answered correctly, much to the amusement of both parties who had a pleasant laugh over it.

He then entered into familiar conversation with him about his conversion, and connection with the church, and exhorted him hold fast his profession—thus preaching in the parlor as well as in the pulpit.

Such was the man to whom Joshua Thomas felt drawn by an irresistible impulse, following him to learn re-

ligion from his lips, while *he* tried to cheer him by his
faith and prayers.

The history of those adventures in which the two men
Thomas and Lawrenson figured together, would fill
many a page. We have room but for a few, "from
grave to gay, from lively to severe."

When Brother Thomas became a local preacher, and
formed his preaching plan, he found his resources often
inadequate to the demand made upon him. Texts, he
had marked in great abundance, but of sermons, his
stock was very limited. He went off to Annamessex on
one occasion to hear Brother L. and while listening to
the sermon, "it came to him"—in the form of a temptation as he afterwards discovered, to model his style after
that of Brother Lawrenson, and a desire took possession
of him, to try and preach exactly like his preceptor. He
gave absorbing attention to the discourse—noted text—
introduction—argument—illustrations, and conclusion,
and avoided every thing that might have a tendency to
divert his burdened thoughts before his return home.
When he arrived, he made a special appointment, intending to astonish his unsophisticated neighbors, with such
a discourse as they never heard *him* deliver before.

"Won't they wonder," said he to himself, "when
they hear what I am going to say to-day?" The congregation assembled, the "Parson" took his position,
performed the introductory services, and proceeded, in
the dignified and forcible style of Brother L., to announce
his text. He proceeded with a few sounding sentences,
then stammered—finally stopped, in as tangled a thicket
as ever poor preacher was before. He saw his error,

confessed his fault to the people, and forever abandoned the idea of preaching like Brother Lawrenson or anybody else—" And brother," he would afterward say, " when I tried to go on again, *I could not even preach like Brother Thomas!*"

In this severe way he learned the homiletic law—without the aid of Simeon, Claude, or Dr. Clark. " *Be yourself!*" The memory of that hour, when in the ordinary parlance of the *species clericus*, he felt "in the bushes," or the "strait jacket," or, in his own more forcible if homely phrase, "in the gripes!" brought with it horror to his mind.

How far others may have had a similar experience, and trying to be *more*, have fallen below their own ordinary level, we do not feel free to investigate. Brother Thomas was ever afterwards emphatically *himself*.

He rated his abilities in comparison with the itinerant preachers, and especially with the eloquent and mighty Lawrenson, as very small; yet his brethren always put him forward whenever they could, as much for their own gratification, as in view of the fact, that his "talk" greatly interested and benefited the people.

On one occasion Brother L. requested him to fill his appointment, and preach in his place. This he declined doing, but the other insisted. "No," said Brother Thomas, "you preach, and let me exhort after you are through." "Better let me exhort after you," said Lawrenson, "for then, if you make any mistakes, I can correct them." This argument prevailed, and he proceeded to preach. The discourse was tedious and tiresome, the people wearied, and his friend out of patience when he wound up. When they had retired, and were alone, Brother L., in familiar pleasantry, alluded to the long sermon. "Why did you not stop me," said Brother T., "when you thought I ought to sit down?" "Oh," said the other, "I did not like to interrupt you." "Well now," said he, "next time I preach or exhort too long in your presence, give me a sign to stop when you think I have gone far enough."

This was agreed upon, and before long, Brother T. was again before the congregation, his friend and monitor sitting behind him. He was in good trim, and the people were all attention, as he began to tell an anecdote at the commencement of his exhortation. Brother Lawrenson had occasion, in the narrow pulpit, to change his position, and in doing so, touched the speaker with his foot. This was the concerted sign, and much to the astonishment of the people, as well as to the surprise of Brother L., he abruptly sat down without even finishing the sentence on his lips. "Go on, brother," said L., "You touched me," said T. "It was an accident," said L., "go on, go on." "Can't do it now, b-brother," said the discomfited T., "you have spoiled my exhortation, and now, *understand*, our bargain is broken, and hereafter I shall talk as long as I please." "Agreed," said the other, and so the misunderstanding was mutually settled.

The adventure at a camp meeting at Nanticoke Point, in which Mr. Lawrenson volunteered an apology for his friend Thomas,—how he managed the matter, and what came of it, will be given in a future chapter.

When they were thrown in each other's company, Brother Thomas generally improved the opportunity, in seeking information on the Scriptures, and direction how to preach from this and that passage. They were at a Quarterly Meeting on a certain occasion, and after retiring for the night, kept up conversation until a late hour. Brother Parks and one or two preachers were present, and all had a word to say, or an opinion to advance, on the plan, divisions, and doctrine of particular texts. Brother Thomas expressed a great partiality for a certain passage, and was asked by Brother Lawrenson to "try it," and give them a sermon right off. Brother T. began to "work" his text, and after a little, sat up in bed, his horizontal position being unfavorable to gesticulation and fluency. As he "warmed up" with this "trial sermon," and floated off into deeper soundings, he slid out of bed, and continued his discourse walking the floor. He preached up to shouting point very soon, and "went off," in a regular spell of rejoicing. This was too much for the excitable Brother John Parks. The fire caught, and he was speedily on the floor. The other preachers sat up in bed, and said "Amen," to the resounding "Glory." Meantime the family and friends who lodged below stairs, had been roused by the "big meeting" going on, and had come up to help, when some one suddenly struck a light !   *   *   *   *

The ludicrous spectacle upset all gravity in the mind of Lawrenson for many days, and was remembered for years afterward; he could never think on this scene, when "light was thrown upon it," without immoderate laughter.

Among the presents cherished by Brother Thomas,

were two elegant shirts from his friend Lawrenson, one of which he always put on, in after years, when he had an appointment of more than ordinary importance to fill, thinking that this arrangement approached the idea of " Elijah's mantle !"

Mr. Lawrenson occasionally preached on the Islands at the house of a good old churchman, there being no place of worship erected as yet, and it being the most commodious and central for the assembling of the people. Among these simple, loving people he enjoyed himself very much, and the voyage to and from the islands being invariably made in company with Brother Thomas, they had " glorious times." Once they were steering for old Brother Evans' on Kedges Straits, when it fell calm, and became densely foggy. Floating on with the tide, and not knowing whither, Brother T. offered a prayer, then sung a hymn, after which Brother L. addressed the throne of grace. When another hymn was started, Brother Thomas became happy, and commenced to shout, and shouted on until their craft touched the shore. The mist clearing away at the moment, revealed to them the bearings of their situation, and to their surprise, they were at the very landing, to which they were bound.

Stopping for dinner at a place in Annamessex after one of these trips, they were both hungry, but the repast was very plain, and very scanty. Their host remarked, " Brethren, help yourselves to what you see, (a couple of diminutive herrings,) if we are not good people, it is better than we deserve, and if we are God's children, we ought to be thankful for anything."

"Hold on, brother," said Mr. Thomas, "that sort of talk will do for such as you and I, but Brother Lawrenson here deserves the fattest chicken or the best turkey on your premises, and you would believe it, if you had heard him preach yesterday as I have."

The news of Mr. Lawrenson's sudden death came upon his Island friends, and the people generally among whom he was known and loved, as a heavy blow. None mourned him with a keener sorrow, a deeper sense of bereavement, than Brother Joshua Thomas—who, ever afterward, counted heaven all the dearer, and more desirable, since he hoped to meet there the friend of his soul, and spend an eternity with his redeemed spirit "before the throne."

He died on the 4th day of April, 1829, in the fiftieth year of his age. The immediate cause of his death was an inflammation of the throat; and the tidings brought great grief upon his brethren and friends.

His Memoir published in the Annual Minutes, though brief, is a fitting tribute to his memory. In it, the writer says: "In the various stations assigned him, he labored with distinguished acceptability and success. As Presiding Elder, he endeared himself to the preachers and people. He possessed a noble and generous mind; and although greatly subject to lowness of spirit, yet under the influence of a divine unction he often preached with an energy, eloquence, and effect equalled by few, and perhaps exceeded by none. He triumphantly soared above his constitutional infirmity, and poured forth the truths of the everlasting gospel, with an ardor that evinced his sincerity, and with an affection that gained the attention, and melted the hearts of his hearers.   And now he lives to die no more."

The inquiries made by some of his most intimate friends, as to how he died, and whether he gave evidence of possessing faith and consolation in his last hours, brought to them the welcome intelligence that his death was a triumph.   It is said that shortly before the fatal hour, he was heard to repeat with much fervor and emphasis, the following stanza :

> " His name yields the richest perfume,
> And sweeter than music His voice,
> *His presence disperses my gloom,*
> *And makes all within me rejoice.*"

CHAPTER XII.

Richard and Solomon Evans—The " Spanker,"—Mrs. Evans and the officer
—She gains the victory—A long married life—Second Marriage of Solomon—His record of preachers—Recollections of the Revolution—A
woman's curse—Grissom—Barge fight in Kedges Straits—Ghost stories—
A haunted man—A jacket demanded—Saulsbury's grave—Captain Weems
—Naval engagement—Effective broadside—Reminiscences—A renegade's
death—A barge pursued—A brand from the burning—" The fathers,
where are they ?"

BEFORE removing the scene of our narrative from the
lower islands where Brother Thomas continued to reside
until about the year 1820, we have a few sketches to
introduce in relation to men and things there. Our
readers will remember some allusion to the Evans'—
Richard called " king" from the fact of his possessing a
conceded ascendency in religion, politics, and general
business among the island people; and Solomon, called
by his neighbors " Uncle Sol," and by our parson
" Brother Sol." These two men from their great age—
having been personally conversant with the incidents of
the Revolutionary war—and from their sterling character
for honesty and devotedness to the church, were looked
up to as the chief men of Smith's Island. They lived
near Kedges Straits, and in the early days of the church,
provided a conveyance for all their neighbors who lived

above the great thoroughfare to attend the meetings. They had a large canoe on which they put a flat bottom, the easier to glide over the shoals at low water. She was called "*the Spanker*," and carried many a happy freight to the little church in days of yore.

In winter time, so great was the zeal of these men, that they would frequently break the ice, and work their way in this manner, to the place of prayer, which they could not reach except by going most of the way by water.

They have left as a legacy to the church sons and daughters, who have inherited all the Christian firmness and devotion of their honored parents.

The wife of Solomon Evans, in the days of British invasion, was an intrepid and fearless woman. Companies of the English were in the habit of "foraging," wherever resistance was not expected, and beyond the eye of their honorable head officers. Barges under the command of subalterns would come off, and ransack the houses around Kedges Straits.

On one of these incursions they visited Evans', and proceeded to help themselves. She watched them appropriating various articles which she prized,—among others, a beautiful china bowl, that had been handed down with a remarkable history, through several generations, from her ancestors. When the officer took it, she objected. and seizing it also, held on with a death-like grasp. " Let go," said he. " I *won't*," said she. " You must," he roared. " Never," said Mrs. Evans. He then swore he *would* have it. She using the same emphatic expletive, said *she would have it*, at the risk of her life.

He gave up his prize, remarking, " Well, it is a pity you were not made a soldier, you would conquer the d—l himself." She triumphed in the *scrimmage,* as it was called, and the bowl remains in the family, as a trophy of her victory, until the present day.

This remarkable woman and her husband lived together sixty years and six months. When she died, his loneliness became intolerable. At the age of four score and ten, he was left in his dreary dwelling without her companionship. The sight of a vacant chair that sat over against his place by the fireside, and the ever-present memory of her long and loved society, affected his strong nature to tears. His own health was still firm, and his activity wonderful, for a man of his years.

At the instance of some of his friends, he was led to the conclusion that he should replace his lost companion by another wife. After consulting the Circuit Preacher about the matter, and gaining his assent to the expediency of this step, he hoisted sail, and made a visit to Holland's Island, where lived an amiable woman, Mrs. Price, widow of the good Ephraim Price. She was then seventy-five, but compassionating the situation of her friend and gallant suitor, she consented, (bless her!) to take the vacant chair by his hearth, and they were married. He outlived her, and soon after her decease, went the way of all the earth, after she was " buried out of his sight."

With him there went down to the grave as varied and eventful a history as falls to the lot of but very few men. He voted at every Presidential Election down to 1850, and remembered distinctly the breaking out of the war for Independence.

When Rev. R. E. Kemp and the writer were on Princess Anne Circuit in 1850, we paid a visit to this venerable man, and found him in the enjoyment of his faculties and health, at the age of nearly one hundred years.

As soon as we had partaken of dinner at his table, he called on us to pray, after which, he reached up to a shelf, took down an old account book, and turning to a particular place, recorded both our names. We were curious to know the reason of this, when he informed us that he had kept a list of every preacher's name who had broken bread at his table, and offered prayer at his domestic altar. We scanned the column with deep interest, noted the marks which signified the sad mortality of the "Fathers," for, as he ascertained each minister's death, he made a record of the fact and date; there we communed with the spirits of many of our predecessors as he told us the traits of their character, the texts they had used, and the years they labored in his vicinity.

"I expect to meet them," said he, as his eye kindled, "I expect to meet them soon, in that glory world they told us of, and to which so many of them have ascended in holy triumph." "They will welcome you to their mansions, Uncle Solomon," said Brother Kemp, "when the good Lord calls for you." "Yes," said he, "I expect so."

Brother K. inquired as to his knowledge of the incidents connected with the terrible barge fight in the straits. "I remember it," said he, "as if it was yesterday. The engagement began just opposite my door,

I went down and climbed a tree to be out of danger, and witnessed the whole battle."

As to the traditions, ghost stories, and phenomena that were frequently repeated on the authority of "Uncle Solomon," we gathered all the particulars in his own language, and to correct the exaggerations prevalent on this subject, we give his "narratives extraordinary" a place among the annals of early times, which are gathered here.

"Grissom," said he, referring to one of the commanders at the barge fight, "Grissom was a brave but a bold and godless man. His death was remarkable. He oppressed poor people, as we thought, unnecessarily. The day before he encountered the British, one of the island women came to him, begging the return of her children's wearing apparel, which some of his men had, among other things, removed from the house. He was in a bad humor, and ordered her away. She persisted in her reasonable plea, and followed him, until he turned and struck her across the arm with his sword, and swore at her to be off. She fell on her knees and prayed the Almighty that a ball might go through his heart before that time next day. Meantime the encounter began. Grissom fought bravely but fell, and lost the fight, and when examined, it was found that he was shot through the heart, and instantly killed.

"The sound of oars, the collision of boats, the clash of steel, the booming of the guns, and the mingled oaths and entreaties of the contending forces," continued Uncle Sol, "were in my ears for months and years after that bloody day. I can almost distinguish these noises yet, in the dead of night." He saw twenty-two men stark and gory in death, hauled up on the shore after the battle, awaiting burial. It was an awful sight. Some days after, a man named Hopkins found a body along shore, and after removing some valuables and clothing, left it in the water. He was haunted afterward, it was said, by an apparition of this drowned soldier.

Once in his canoe fishing near a point of marsh, he heard a noise somewhat like "hah! hah!" and on looking that way, saw the apparition coming towards him, leaping like a frog, until it jumped clear over him into the water beyond! He frequently met the same appearance in lonely walks, and once saw it approaching his door. He called his family to look, but they could discern nothing.

After he had been haunted until almost beside himself with fright, and hearing the "hah! hah!" until the sound had become familiar, he went off to the main and consulted a Parson Adams, who told him a certain form of words to speak when he next saw it; and he would *lay* it. Thus fortified he returned, but forgot the formula in his fright at the next encounter.

The ghost however disappeared, his body having been recovered and buried by the brothers Richard and Solomon Evans.

He told us another case, and seemed to believe it as firmly as he believed anything. A man, named Lawson, found a body in the water, and took its jacket, which he began to wear. The jacket was demanded a short time after, in a very unusual manner. This man in company with another was out fishing: a storm came on and they pulled ashore, taking refuge under their canoe, which they had turned bottom upwards. Suddenly they felt an unaccountable dread falling upon them, and heard a thumping on the canoe, which was whirled over, and a voice said, " *Give me my jacket!*" Several times was this repeated, until Lawson took off and laid aside the garment in dispute, which he never wore afterwards.

While in this mood we shall give another " circumstance," told as sober fact. A person named Saulsbury, who made his home on the islands, proved unfaithful to a lady whom he had promised to marry, but whose confidence he had betrayed. She laid a fearful malediction on him, and from that hour he began to fail.

In company with Job Parks he went off one day on a gunning excursion. It was in the winter of 1780, the coldest ever remembered in that latitude. Night came on, and they turned homewards. Parks reached his house, but the other was found next day, dead and frozen in the ice. He was carried up, and buried in a certain orchard, where for some time afterwards a light was plainly seen, like a flame of fire lingering over his grave. This flame, by association with the curse he had become involved in, was shudderingly regarded as a signal of his fate.

We received at this time an account of a desperate naval engagement, during the days of the Revolution, which has found no previous historian, as far as we have, by considerable effort, ascertained.

A sloop of war, bearing the American ensign, was chased into the Pocomoke Sound, and there brought to bay, by an English brig, cruising in those waters. Both vessels opened fire, and continued to wage the fight until the red cross of St. George came down, and the brave Yankee conquered his proud foe. He had at the moment of victory but seven men of all his force, that were not either killed or wounded. With his prize he started for Annapolis, and on the voyage met another "Britisher," a rakish looking schooner, who bore down on him "like a hawk on a chicken."

The American Captain, (Weems was his honored name,) said to the daring remnant of his crew, "Now my brave fellows, this bunting never comes down, so prepare yourselves for another brush." The guns were shotted with their last round of ammunition, and a pair of "*steelyards*" crammed into one for which there was no death dealing ball. On came the enemy, blazing away at random. The hats and jackets of their comrades below in the sick bay, were ranged on deck to look like crowds of men. When the favorable time came, and our sloop which had been silent before, yawed a little, the Captain shouted, "*Now men, rake her!*" The whole available force of the broadside went banging and crashing into the other vessel, and the steelyards made a tangent through her mainsail, cutting away the halliards, and cowing the opposing craft—or her crew—to that degree that she struck at once, and Weems arrived in due time at his destination, with another trophy of his bravery.

From a budget of reminiscences furnished by Rev. Mr. Kemp, we select a few more particulars connected with "Uncle Solomon" and his times. He writes:

"Solomon Evans was one of the most remarkable men

I have met with in all my travels. As cotemporary, and a faithful fellow laborer, with Brother Thomas, he merits a prominent place in the regard of posterity. His name is as ointment poured forth, and his influence and Christian life will long be remembered, as one of the jewels, whom God has gathered home to adorn the living temple of the skies. While the blood-thirsty and cruel live not half their days, the righteous have the promise, "With long life will I satisfy him, and show *him* my salvation."

His recollection was remarkably distinct about the barge fight between the Americans under Captain Whaley and Lieutenant Handy, and the British, who numbered the infamous renegade and Tory, Jo. Whalon, among their forces. This Whalon was a desperate villain; doing unheard-of enormities, in crime and blood, in those trying times. He escaped the fate of several of his associates in crime, who were tried, condemned, and justly executed at Cambridge, Md., after the war. He ended his days on the marshes, with no companion but his guilty conscience, which gave him no rest day or night, but arrayed before him an avenging God. His groans and screams could be heard at a great distance, when dying there alone.

"The battle in Kedges Straits, appeared, for a time, to be in favor of the Americans, but a magazine exploded at the moment when victory was near, and this disaster turned the tide of success in favor of the British. One of the American barges which had been fitted out in Talbott county, under command of Captain

Hadaway, was pursued for more than fifty miles up the bay, as far as Sharp's Island, but fortunately escaped.

"While on Cambridge Circuit, in 1844, I met with a Mr. Cook, near Hills Point, who was in this engagement. I was also well acquainted with an old Mr. Porter, in Talbott, who was one of the bargemen on that memorable occasion, and was wounded in the fight. He received from his country an acknowledgment for his services, in the way of a pension, that helped him in his declining years.

"His was a singular case. He lived in sin over 70 years, and in his extreme old age, grounded the weapons of his rebellion, and became a subject of saving grace. ' *Was not this a brand plucked from the fire ?*' "

These " old men and fathers," *where are they?* They are removed to the realms of bliss, where war and wasting come no more.

> " No rude alarms of raging foes ;
> No cares to break the long repose ;
> No midnight shade, no clouded sun,
> But sacred, high, eternal noon."

CHAPTER XIII.

"BE sure to insert a sketch of Brother Parks in your book," writes one of our itinerant ministers, "for he was almost inseparable from the good 'Parson' in travels, adventures, and religious exercises during a great many years; and his name demands, and richly deserves a memorial among others renowned in the church, for their virtues, integrity, and disinterested devotion to the service of God, and the honor of Methodism."

JOHN PARKS was a cousin to Brother Thomas, and raised in the same neighborhood with him on the Tangier Island. He was converted at the same time and place, that witnessed the other's translation out of darkness into the light and liberty of the sons of God.

This change took place in his heart a day or two prior to the conversion of Brother Thomas, and made him at

once a worker in the vineyard of his Lord. He was at
the first prayer-meeting started on Tangier; and it will
be remembered, made the first extemporaneous prayer
on that occasion. The prayers he has offered, and the
exhortations he has delivered, since that wonderful September Sabbath in 1807, are only numbered in the record on high, and known to Him who is not unrighteous,
to forget his servants' work and labor of love.

His life has been hardly less eventful, if not so widely
useful, than that of Brother Thomas himself. The frosts
of over fourscore years have gathered on his brow, and
he is now calmly awaiting his change, in the attitude of
him of old who prayed, "Now, Lord, lettest thou thy
servant depart in peace, for mine eyes have seen thy salvation."

His brother, the estimable and pious Charles Parks,
finished his course at the age of 77, a few years ago, at
his residence on Deal's Island; where, in comparative
ease and affluence, he spent the latter years of his useful
life.

He had been a class leader in the church for very
many years, and was one of the most exemplary and
pious men of his day and time. The lot on which the new
church stands, was donated by him; and the adjoining
grove, in which camp meetings are now held, is year
after year placed at the disposal of the community for
this purpose by his son, Captain Jacob Parks, for whom
no better wish or prayer could be offered, than that he
may imitate the excellences, and enjoy at last the inheritance, his sainted father has gained " through riches
of grace in Christ Jesus."

The wife of Brother Charles Parks survived him, and but recently has gone to the blissful reunion of the skies. She was one of the oldest residents of the island, at the time of her decease, and was always known as one of the "excellent of the earth." Her patience in suffering, her prayerfulness in trouble, and her hope in God at all times, has left on the mind of all who knew Britania Parks, a bright illustration of the "beauty of holiness."

John and Charles were zealous in the cause, and prominent in the church from the time of their conversion. They had both, previously, been accomplished fiddlers, as were several of their contemporaries on Smith's and Tangier Islands. It cost them a severe struggle to give up the sweet strains of their catgut, so strongly were they wedded to this source of pleasure.

When, however, religion began to be the prevailing topic, and dancing was displaced by prayer meetings, no fellowship could be tolerated with "the unfruitful works of darkness." The fate of fiddles was sealed.

Conscience had decreed the incompatibility of this unwitting agent in levity and frolicking, with the new life, and sternly demanded a severance of the affections from every idol, and an eye single to higher and holier pursuits.

In the parley between inclination and the inward monitor, a sort of compromise was effected for the time being, and the *role* of music was entirely altered. Instead of the lively jig, or the popular reel, Brother Parks could almost make the strings intelligently, and with vibrating harmony sound the stanza:

> "Turn to the Lord and seek salvation !
> Sound the praise of Jesus' name !

> Glory, honor, and salvation!
>   Christ the Lord has come to reign!"

His new programme of tunes embraced all the populai melodies of Methodism at that day. It was a marked, and most agreeable improvement, they said, to assemble in the evenings at some neighbor's house after the labors of the day were ended, and, instead of the senseless exercises of a "hoe down" dance, have a violin accompaniment to such strains and choruses as:

> "Come friends, will you go?
>   Glory! glory! glory!
> Oh! come friends, will you go?
>   Glory! glory! glory!
> Come all the world, come sinner thou:
> All things in Christ are ready now!
> Ye need not one be left behind;
> For God hath bidden all mankind!
>   Glory! glory! glory!"

This progressed very well for a while, but the question was raised, and warmly argued, as to whether a follower of Christ should use this instrument in any religious service, since it revived recollections which were "not joyous but grievous," and by association with sin, had become discreditable? This opinion prevailed, *destruction fell upon the fiddles!* and their inspiring strains subsided into silence there forever.

At first the offending article was simply hung out of reach on the wall, then put out of sight in the family chest, for it was acknowledged that as long as the eye could rest on it, the elbow ached for exercise and the fingers itched for a trill on the threads. Nor was the difficulty obviated even then. "Pluck it out, and cast it from thee," was the uncompromising demand, and Brother John, after a season of solemn prayer, threw his fiddle into the fire—bow, rosin, and recollection together ! His brother Charley's soon followed, and with these two at least there was an end of what Wesley in one of his hymns of the Cornwall watch-meetings calls : " Reveling and frantic mirth."

With good Brother Bradshaw, the case was slightly different. He continued toying with his idol, the violin, after his conversion, against the advice of his brethren, and the upbraidings of the inward voice, until he was aroused to a sense of his danger by a dream. Starting one night from his restless bed, he seized the " unruly member," ran out to a fence corner, and with one fierce blow broke the instrument to shivers, and became at once happy in the consciousness of having " laid aside" this " weight," " and the sin which so easily beset" him, resolving henceforth to " run with patience the race that was set before him ; looking unto Jesus."

He has not reached the end of that " race" yet ; having now arrived at the age of 83, a sound, hearty man ; always at his place in the meeting house, to reach which, and return to his home, he has literally to " paddle his own canoe."

The mother of John and Charles Parks, remained " in Egypt," some time after they started for the goodly land. They made her case a constant subject of prayer, but she remained—in the language of John, " very *stubbid !* and hard set against the new religion." They succeeded in getting her across the sound to a camp meeting at the old ground, hallowed beyond all other places, as the scene of *their* "heavenly birth."

She looked on apparently unmoved, while the work of conviction and conversion was going gloriously forward.

"We prayed, and prayed," says John, "but there she stood with a frown on her face, looking at the mourners. Directly," he adds, "I obtained a little more faith. I 'hollered' across to her with all my might; 'Oh, mother! mother! "seek the Lord while he may be found." *Seek him now!*' With that the power of God struck her and *away she went!*"

Not away, dear reader, as you might suppose, from the place of prayer and penitent crying; but "*away*," in the sense of coming to the ground all in a heap, a convicted sinner! "Didn't we shout then," says her son, "when we saw her weeping and praying before the Lord at last?" This aged mother continued praying—went home seeking, and in a very short time, among her own children and neighbors, was made a partaker of peace in believing, and became an "Israelite indeed."

About the same time Richard Bradshaw, after an intense struggle, lasting for weeks and months, entered into life. This fine old Patriarch was a pillar in the church, and left a large family of sons and daughters, following him on to the place

> "Where saints of all ages in harmony meet,
> Their Saviour and brethren transported to greet,
> While anthems of rapture unceasingly roll,
> And the smile of the Lord is the feast of the soul."

Of these, we have Solomon Bradshaw, a resident of Annamessex, Haney, a valuable brother in the church on Smith's Island, Tyler, at the old homestead on Holland's Island, and Mrs. Capt. Wm. Price, and Mrs. Thomas, widow of the Rev. Joshua Thomas, living; others have "crossed over," and shall have a feeble tribute in our memorials hereafter.

Brother John Parks was the companion of Brother Thomas in visits to camp, and quarterly meetings near and far, and being of a more unsophisticated nature even than his fellow laborer, was led into numerous adventures of a somewhat humorous character.

Rev. Brother Kemp, when on the circuit, took a never failing delight in his company, and has furnished a number of anecdotes relating to the man, familiarly termed "Father Parks."

He narrates: On a certain occasion Brothers Thomas and Parks were in company across the bay, attending to some business. A warm-hearted Virginia gentleman invited them up to his house to spend the night, and accompany him on the morrow, which was Sabbath, to his usual place of worship. They gratefully accepted the invitation, and after a very pleasant night's rest, arose early on the following morning. Brother Parks, in dressing, could not find his shoes. A suspicion flashed across his mind that they had been stolen during the night, and this was strengthened by the fact that a "nigger boy" had softly entered the chamber, and "*rummaged* about there," after they had retired.

"What *shall* I do, Brother Thomas?" said John. "Look about, Brother John," said the other, "it can't be possible that any one would steal such an old pair of shoes as yours, in this fine house." "They are gone, brother," said John despairingly. "Why," said Brother Thomas, "are there no shoes here? What are those?" (pointing to a pair neatly polished, and laying at the bedside.) "Oh, brother," said he, "I have examined them; they are not mine." Brother Thomas took a glance at the shoes, and saw they were all right. The only difference was, a complete transformation by the "blacking" process, which was so unusual to John that he was completely bewildered in their identity.

Like his friend and companion Brother Thomas, he was once left a widower with several small children. He was afflicted by their helplessness, and felt it to be his religious duty to provide for their young and tender years a mother's presence and care, in the place of the one removed from them by death. "But," said he, "I waited, and waited, and *waited*, until some of my friends should propose this change for the better. Not one of them said a word to me about it. And I waited and waited, until at last I concluded I would wait no longer, and went right off and was married."

"How long *did* you wait, Brother Parks?" said Mr. K.

"Ah! brother," said he, "I waited *for the matter of three weeks !*" This might be regarded as but a short period—too short in the conventional usages of the world, but to him it was a weary age; and the act which might be regarded as savoring of indifference to the memory of her, who had gone, in his view of it, was a monument to her worth, and the best appreciation he knew how to evince, of the sex in general, and her value in particular.

He set about building a vessel of the "Pungy" class,

many years ago, but his funds were inadequate to supply
the drain upon them, in the process of finishing his boat.
He concluded to borrow some money, and went to Brother
R. B—— for that purpose. There he met a neighbor
on the same errand, and concluded within himself it was
no use to ask, as he could not give security, and the
other could.

To his surprise, however, the "moneyed man," ascertaining his business, volunteered to lend him the cash,
in preference to his more wealthy neighbor, on the
ground that he had no security, and would not be likely
to meet with accommodation elsewhere, while the other,
having "*strong backers*," could obtain what he wanted
almost anywhere. (Where could we find such men and
principles now-a-days?)

Brother Parks was not entirely out of the difficulty
yet. His bill of costs remained unsatisfied in part, and
he succeeded in obtaining $50 from a sister E. He
wanted more, and waited until this sister, who he knew
had money, received a great blessing at a certain meeting. While she was fervently praising the Lord, he
thought it the best time to put in his plea, and asked
her for the loan of $50 more. "Yes, Brother John,"
said she, "yes, *a hundred* if you want it, bless the Lord!"
John felt like praising too, his way had opened so fa-
vorably, and lest the dear sister should change her
mind, he went straight with her and received the money.

The vessel was finished, and in due time the borrowed
money was paid. Success followed his enterprise, and
he made a good living by the use of his new craft.

Being anxious to hear the result of the election in

1844, he and Capt. Jacob Barks sailed out together to
Hooper's Straits, to hear the news from some homeward
bound vessel.   While there, they employed the time
catching oysters.   At length a vessel came steering in,
and hailing her, they learned that Mr. Polk was elected
by a large majority over Mr. Clay.   "Ah! Brother,"
said he, "I cannot oyster any longer, Polk is elected,
and the country is ruined! come let us go home." It appears from this that he lacked philosophy enough to be
a politician.

He was "taken in and done for" a few years ago by
a rascally impostor who came to the island, and represented himself as a missionary.   With open heart and
arms, Brother Parks received the fellow to his house,
made appointments for him to preach and lecture, and
rejoiced that God had given him the privilege before he
died, of seeing a man connected with that work which
he conceived to be the grandest and most glorious of all
enterprises.   He had often, under missionary sermons,
and while reading his "Advocate," pictured to himself
the privations of the men who have gone to "Greenland's
icy mountains," or "India's coral strand," to tell the
story of the Redeemer to those who never heard his
name; and now to have a *Missionary* under his own
roof, was, he thought, the highest honor of his life.

Alas for him! *he harbored a scamp*, who was soon
discovered, and had to beat an ignominious retreat from
that neighborhood.

While treating of "Uncle John," we may add a few
more of the numerous anecdotes, which have caused the

laugh to be always against him, when they came up for review.

He had become addicted to the "popular vice" of using tobacco. The older Methodists paid great deference to the opinions and godly admonitions of their preachers. Brother Massey, a great many years ago, originated a movement looking to the total prohibition of drams, pipes, and tobacco.

In the former he succeeded to a good degree in raising the standard of temperance in the church throughout his District, and many a tippler " *on the sly*" was officially decapitated, or hopefully cured.

In the tobacco department he was less successful; but he "did what he could," in the way of preaching and ridicule, to break up the fraternity of smokers, snuffers, and those who chew.

At a camp meeting on Deal's Island he had publicly, and with affectionate earnestness, exhorted his brethren to "go and sin no more." Brother Parks walked out in the woods to meditate on the crisis, for he was a lover of cavendish, and he loved his minister. He met Brother James Lawson, "an old offender" at the pipe practice, who had wandered away also, in his perplexity, and was solacing himself with a private whiff. "Ah, brother," said John, "here you are, and smoking yet, what will become of us?" "Don't know," said Captain L., unless we quit."

"Agreed!" said Brother Parks; "let us bury here in the sand both pipe and tobacco." The bargain was, that as long as one held out the other would in like manner refrain. A grave was scooped in the clean sand,

and one laid down his "plug," the other his pipe, and a very respectable wedge of "Virginia" on top. The grave was covered, and "here," said Brother Parks, (making a cross on top with his toe,) "here let them lie." "Amen," said Brother• Lawson, and with hearts and pockets lighter, they walked back to camp and listened to a sermon. Before it was well through, one of these brethren became uncomfortable, then fidgety, and finally, remembering a peculiar mark in the sand, took a circuitous walk in a certain direction. The other seemed to be in mental perplexity, as he sat in a distant part of the congregation, and after preaching, made a bee line for the big pine which he remembered stood near the new made grave. He was too late ! As he came in sight, there was his "companion in distress" on all fours scratching down after the prize.

"Is that you, Brother Parks ?"

"Ah ! Brother, is that *you ?* I can't stand it !"

"Neither can I," said the other; "hand here my pipe !"

A short time after the anti-tobacco movement set in, a change of preachers was expected in course, and Brother Parks was very uneasy. He unbosomed himself to a friend, saying, "If our next preachers are 'down' on tobacco, what *will* we do ?" "Let us wait and see," was the reply. They waited, and soon the new preacher made his appearance at their appointment. In the warm welcome which Brother Park extended, he held on to his hand until he thought he discerned a faint streak about the corner of his mouth. "All right," thought he.

But the "old preacher." How stands the case with

him? Two weeks later, *he* came along, and preached; after the benediction had been pronounced, and the people retired, a few of the "old heads" gathered round the new incumbent, and engaged in conversation. Brother Parks began to fear he had a foe to tobacco in the person of his pastor; when, to his inexpressible delight, the preacher nudged him on the elbow, and, in an undertone, asked, "Do you chew?" "Yes, brother," said he, hastily feeling for his piece. "Give me a crumb," said the preacher; "I like a taste after preaching on warm afternoons." "Here, brother," said John, "here, *take all I've got!*"

Brother Parks, despite these eccentricities, has enjoyed the confidence of both the Church and "the world" through a long life, and is now the oldest exhorter on our circuit record, having been licensed nearly 50 years ago.

He lived on the larger Deal's Island many years, and held meetings in connection with Brother Thomas in his own house, before a church was erected there. We are informed that these meetings were crowned often with extraordinary power and grace; and, among many others converted there, were some of the children of the zealous men who thus were "instant in and out of season" to do good.

He subsequently bought a farm on the edge of the Wycomico river—a beautiful situation—and there, while these lines are being written, "In age and feebleness extreme," he is awaiting the summons that shall soon remove him to a better inheritance.

Some years ago his health was impaired, and his life

thought to be in jeopardy. The late Dr. Handy of Princess Anne, by skillful treatment, brought him through the crisis. About the same time he became involved in litigation, which threatened to overthrow his title to the property he held. Lawyer Waters (Wm. S. Waters, Esq., now of Baltimore) generously undertook the case, and gained the suit for his old Methodist friend. These circumstances altered his opinion of lawyers and doctors considerably. He had, in his simplicity, supposed that both professions were under the "wo" of his Bible, and looked upon them as a reprobated class of men. In his prayers subsequently, he remembered the estimable doctor who had saved his life, and the able lawyer who had saved his property, invoking upon them his blessing and the favor of God.

It has been the privilege of the writer, as his pastor, to visit him frequently since he was stricken with paralysis some months ago. From this attack it is hardly probable that he will recover, but his sky is clear, his mind is "calm as summer evenings be," and his hope is full of immortality and eternal life. He greatly enjoys a visit from "his beloved ministers;" and, though at other times wandering and dull in his faculties, rouses up when they are announced, and invariably becomes happy as they kneel by his side, and commend him to God, and sing, as was the case on our last visit, while his soul seemed on the wing for glory:

> "Friends fondly cherished have passed on before;
> Waiting, they watch me approaching the shore;
> Singing, to cheer me through death's chilling gloom,
> Joyfully, joyfully will I go home!"

CHAPTER XIV.

Thomas Barbon, a Portuguese—Educated for a priest—Runs away and becomes a sailor—The battle of Trafalgar—Deserts the ship and swims
ashore—Imprisoned in Spain—Arrives in America—Settles in Somerset—
Attends the Tangier camp meeting—" Catches a crab"—Is converted—
Temperance movement—Resolutions—Charles Barbon—Parson Wilmer
on rum—Liquor casks emptied—Pigs and poultry drunk—Last days of
Brother Barbon—Reflections—Experience meetings at Tangier—Contrasts.

THE Tangier camp meeting was sometimes the means of
conversions of more than ordinary interest. One very
remarkable case was that of Thomas Barbon, a Portuguese, in the year 1818.

His previous life was of a very eventful character.
" Stranger than fiction," had been his career from early
youth to manhood. At the suggestion of many who
knew him, we have gathered a few facts and incidents
which may not be deemed inappropriate here.

He was born in 1772, in a village on the river Dora,
about 30 miles from the coast of Portugal; and became,
at a very early age, attached to a Roman Catholic establishment, for the education of youth, and a church
where the rites of worship peculiar to that denomination
were performed. He was designed for the priestly office,

but took a decided dislike to the men in whose charge
he was placed, and the mockeries of their manner of
worship.   The character and morals of his spiritual ad-
visers were so bad that he became disgusted, and resolved
to run away rather than remain among them.

At the age of thirteen he fled, and determined to follow the fortunes of the sea.   He shipped at an adjacent
port in the relation of cabin boy, and for ever became
separated from the associations of his youth.

He made sundry voyages to distant places on the
coasts of continental Europe, and graduated to the position of a regular hand before the mast.

In the changes incidental to his mode of life, he found
himself in some place under control of the English government, and was seized by a press gang, and placed on
board a line of battle ship, in the fleet commanded by
Lord Nelson.

His hardship and maltreatment following this change,
were revolting and almost incredible.   The ship on which
he served was ordered into line at the memorable battle
of Trafalgar, and was stationed quite near that proud
vessel which bore on her deck the intrepid Nelson, and
at her peak, his broad pennant.

Mr. Barbon remembered as long as he lived the details
of that renowned engagement; and to the preachers,
who were ever welcome at his fireside, he could recount
all the manœuvres of both the contending fleets.   He
saw the watchword signal run up in a ball of bunting to
the mast head of the Admiral's ship, and unfold its appeal to the honor and bravery of British tars,—" *England expects every man to do his duty!*"   The ship on

which he was *compelled* to do duty, was, at one juncture of the action, ordered round to a certain position, with a view to pour a volley of "hot shot" into one of the most magnificent of the French frigates. The order was promptly executed, and thirty-two pounders, heated until flaming red, were hurled into the magazine of the doomed foe, and with an earthquake concussion, she exploded, and was blown to fragments over the surrounding waters. The ship and her contents were burst to atoms. Some of the fragments fell on the deck where he stood, and hundreds of the crew of this wrecked vessel sunk before his eyes in the briny deep.

So intolerable had become the suffering he endured, that he deserted his ship soon after the great battle of Trafalgar, and in the darkness of the night, swam ashore, a distance of three miles. In this he made a very narrow escape from drowning, but life was such a burden, that he preferred anything to a longer continuance on board.

Following the pursuit he had chosen, he next shipped on board an American vessel, somewhere up the Mediterranean, and was captured by his old enemy, while in the Straits of Gibraltar. The English cruisers had just begun to exercise their assumed right of search, which eventually led to the war with this country. As a deserter he was taken, and placed again on board a British ship, but disowning allegiance to her flag, and insisting on the protection of that under which he was found, he was taken to Spain, and endured the horrible sufferings which were inflicted on unfortunate prisoners of war, in the notorious dungeons of that country. His statement of the hunger, wretchedness, and abuse received while there, almost beggars description.

After a time he was released, in company with some of his fellow prisoners. He then shipped for New York, and shortly afterwards made his way to Baltimore, where he was married in 1806. After following the sea a short time, he came to the Eastern Shore, and settled in Somerset County, near White Haven, where he spent the balance of his days, a highly respected citizen.

In the summer of 1818, as we have stated, by a singular train of circumstances, he was at Tangiers.

Through all the years of his youth, and up to that time, he had felt no particular attachment to any form of religion. He was skeptically inclined, and indifferent to the subject of his salvation. He merely took shelter, when in contact with professors, under the wing of Popery, and avowed himself as of that persuasion, though he despised its empty forms, remembering the experiences of his early days.

The Tangier camp meeting, as we have elsewhere shown, usually attracted all classes of people, and about that time excursions were frequent to the beach from various points along the Rivers and Bay. Companies of men would charter a vessel, provide themselves with fishing apparatus, and take an excursion for pleasure and health, timing their trip to the week of the camp.

A party of whom Capt. Alexander Jones was the ac-acknowledged head, and including Mr. Barbon, set sail from White Haven, on a fishing trip to the beach. When their vessel arrived, the harbor was crowded, and the meeting under full headway. It was a novel sight to

Mr. B., but he seemed to be opposed to religion, and entirely bent on the species of sport, for which he had left home.

One Sabbath morning, his companions prepared to go ashore to attend the preaching, and invited him to go with them. This he refused at first to do, preferring, as he said, to spend the Sabbath "crabbing,"—that is catching crabs along the shore. Captain Jones, who was a friend to religion, and associated with the Episcopal church, insisted on Mr. Barbon's going up to hear a sermon. "No, Captain Sandy," said he, "I does not believes in dis sort of 'ligion, let me stay and catch crabs." "Oh come," said the captain, "a particular friend of mine, Dr. Waters, is going to preach, and I want you to hear the sermon for my sake." Thus prevailed upon, he came up to the camp, and took his place in the congregation. The minister referred to, (Dr. Francis Waters of Potato Neck, an associate of Lawrenson, and a very talented young man at that time ; now, and for a great many years back, President of the Chestertown college,) delivered a pointed and powerful sermon. The word reached the heart of the Portuguese sailor, and awakened him to see himself a lost sinner, and to cry, "Men and brethren, what shall I do to be saved?" He was taken in hand by good Brother Thomas and his fellow laborers around the altar, and after a tremendous struggle with doubts, prejudices, and self-condemnation, he obtained a "knowledge of salvation by the remission of his sins," and was made a partaker of that peace and joy, which enabled him to cry out, "*O Lord, I will praise thee ; for though thou wast angry with me, thine anger is turned away, and behold now thou comfortedst me !"*

In his experience afterwards, he loved to refer to that glorious Sabbath on Tangier beach, where "love divine first found him," conquered his rebel heart, and revealed to him the way of life.

" I wanted to catch some crabs," he would say, " and didn't I catch *one mighty big crab*, when I felt my sins all pardoned, and found a new heart, by the blessed Spirit which came on me as I prayed and cried to the Lord for mercy !"

He returned to his home *a new man*, and began at once to " *bring forth fruit unto holiness.*" He set up an " altar unto the Lord" in his family, and invariably afterwards acknowledged Him in all his ways. His wife was a woman of calm temperament, amiable disposition, and, though not a member of the church, was devout and holy in life and conversation.

He was afterwards appointed an official member of the church, and was punctual in the performance of all his duties. His house became a pleasant home for the itinerant preachers, and his place was hardly ever vacant at his own church, or at the quarterly meetings of the circuit. In company with Louis Phœbus of precious memory, he went to all the camp meetings within reach, and on every suitable occasion gave testimony in favor of the religion of Jesus Christ, of which he could say : " Her ways are ways of pleasantness, and all her paths are peace."

He kept a country store, and as was customary in those days, among the commodities of every such place of business, he usually laid in a supply of spirituous liquors. This article was regarded as a necessity almost everywhere, in former times; but in this respect who will say : " The former times were better than these ?"

He attributed the first movements of the great temperance reformation, to a species of unwarranted zeal, and fanatical folly. When in 1831, the following resolutions were adopted, he began to feel some trouble of mind in relation to the traffic and sale of ardent spirits, and fairly met the question, " Is it right ?" The resolutions, which we here introduce, are spread on the old journal of that year, and are no less forcible, important, and necessary, in these days, than at any former period :

" We, the members of the Quarterly Meeting Conference of Annamessex Circuit, being sensible of the great evils which result from the manufacture, sale, and use of ardent spirits, do hereby Resolve :

1. That we will not drink spirituous liquor ourselves, nor give it to our families, or laborers, except we are convinced it is absolutely necessary as a medicine.

2. That we will neither make nor sell it; for we consider that we should thereby encourage, and profit by the use and abuse of it by others.

3. That we will, by every fair and honorable means, discourage *treating*, in order to secure an election.

4. That we will deal with those merchants who will not sell it, in preference to others.

5. That our preachers be requested to give a copy of these resolutions to each class leader, desiring him to use his influence to obtain the signatures of his members and neighbors thereto."

The members present at this Quarterly Conference were Wm. C. Allen and James A. Massey, Circuit Preachers; Edward Larkins, Isaac R. Willet, Thomas Summers, Purnell Pusey, and Stephen Taylor, Local Preachers; Lazarus Maddux, Nathan D. Dougherty, William Dix, Lewis Phoebus, James Tyler, Daniel Ford, and William Miles, Exhorters; John Fontaine, David Lankford, Mitchell Phoebus, Ephraim Reese, John Stephenson, and some ten or fifteen others, as Class leaders and Stewards.

Brother Barbon was not at this time a member of the Conference, but the action of those brethren whom he loved, had to be respected, and the manner in which he "cleared out" his stock of the vile stuff is worthy of record.

He had a son, Charles Barbon, a promising and very amiable young man, who had professed religion at a camp meeting at Curtis' Chapel in 1827, and took at once a high and holy stand on the Lord's side. Charles attended the store in the absence of his father, and before the day of the resolutions, had taken a conscientious dislike to the traffic. He had been to Salisbury and heard an address by one of the earliest advocates of temperance there—Brother David Vance—and resolved to measure out no more. His father was not satisfied with such scruples, and became somewhat irritated when his son stoutly persisted in his course. A wretched, intemperate husband about this time, who resided across the river, killed his wife in a fit of drunkenness; and to add to the sum of evidence accumulating against his liquor business, the Rev. "Parson" Wilmer, of the Protes-

tant Episcopal Church, commenced a lecturing crusade
to help on the temperance cause. He delivered one of
his most pointed and convincing appeals, at the Hungary
Neck Methodist Meeting House, to a large congregation.

Brother Barbon was out, and heard the speech. The
arguments he had used to justify his course were torn
to fragments, and in the vivid view of that untold evil,
demoralization, poverty, and woe, which rum engenders
on society, he hastened home, deliberately rolled out his
barrels into the yard, procured an axe, and dashed in
the heads of every cask containing spirits, wine, or cider,
—letting the liquid poison flow over the ground. His
good wife stood in the door, and thought he had become
demented; but no, he said he "had just come to reason."

The pigs came along and began to investigate the pud-
dles caused by this strange proceeding, and soon became
"half seas over." His turkeys and chickens had a
peck or two at the liquid, and they were directly "drunk
as a fool." The geese next had a dram, and all became
tipsy, so that his liquor business ended in a general
"drunk," and his premises have been clear of even the
smell of it ever since. He "went in" heart and soul
for the resolutions, and was appointed leader of the
society soon after, which relation he held until age and
debility obtained for him release, in the appointment of
another.

His son Charles, it was expected, would have been one
of the brightest ornaments of the church, had he lived;
but death removed him early to his expected mansion in
the sky.

With Brother Thomas Barbon, the writer enjoyed very intimate friendship, when on the circuit in 1850. His narratives of other days, and foreign lands, possessed for the young preacher, himself an adventurer in the past, a romantic interest, and would make, could they have been written, a volume of thrilling incidents.

He has recently died at the advanced age of 86, full of faith, and blessed with the undimmed prospect, after all his privations and wanderings, of a "House not made with hands, eternal in the heavens."

From the contemplation of his dying hours, and that rest which he has gained among the glorified in the presence of his Lord, we cannot but turn our eye away back to the Tangier beach, the awakening sermon, the penitent cry, and the wondrous change that took place that day in 1818;—altering, as it did, the whole course of this man's aims and hopes, and quickening in him that principle of true piety that shone in all his actions, and made him a valued citizen, a useful Christian, and an heir of immortality. His was but one of unnumbered instances, in which the thoughtless mind has been impressed under similar circumstances, and the wandering waif of fortune, ungodly and afar off, has been brought nigh by the blood of Christ, and made a child of the covenant, a fellow heir of the promises, and a member of that family, which "in heaven and earth are one;" a trophy of grace, and an evidence of the utility of camp meetings.

Well might the "Parson of the Islands" stand up for his favorite means of grace, and plead for the continuance of such meetings, when views adverse to their

propriety, expediency, or necessity, began to steal into
the minds of order-loving people, or ease-loving preachers.
"If the Devil has learned the way to our camp meetings," he would argue, "let us raise the standard of
Immanuel in his face, and shout the war cry of our
Captain, as we assail his forces; then as the hymn
says:

"Great spoils we shall win,
From death, hell, and sin,
And 'midst outward afflictions shall feel Christ within."

One of the most thrilling features of the meeting at
Tangiers, was the experience meetings that were held as
a part of the exercises of every camp. During the
speaking and singing, on one of these occasions, few
stragglers could be found outside the tents, or along the
shore. Everybody was drawn to that centre of light
and power, where God's people "spake often to one
another."

Old veterans told the tireless story of their triumphs
through grace; young disciples, in glowing words, proclaimed what God had done for their souls. Ministers
of the gospel related the strange way in which the
Divine hand had led them, the conflicts and cares peculiar to their holy calling, and the love which *constrained*
them to tell His name, who died on the cross, and lives
to save sinners. Women, ripe in the graces of the Holy
Ghost, and fluent when religion became the theme, would
also pour out their tears of joy, while they faced the
listening throng, and commend their Lord to others!

"If all the world my Saviour knew,
All the world would love him too."

The most effective preaching was on the occasion of
the love feasts and experience meetings.   Then, words
were uttered that were as fire in dry stubble.   Skeptics
stood trembling like Belshazzar when he saw the handwriting on the wall; no sophistry could invalidate the
force and genuineness of a faith that made the feeble
mighty, the weak strong, and the convert of yesterday

> "Bold to take up, firm to maintain,
> The consecrated cross."

The interchange of feeling and experience, by persons
so widely separated in their residence and pursuits, gave
to these hours of holy intercourse, an increasing and
absorbing interest.   A Christian from the far south
would speak of his conversion, telling when and where
it occurred.   Then would follow an experience by some
one from the mountains of Pennsylvania, the City of
Baltimore, the fervent soil of Accomac, or the Islander
at home amid the very scenes of his spiritual birth, saying, "Whereas I was once blind, now I see," and, referring to the goodness and love of the God-man, proclaim, "*He hath opened mine eyes.*"

In these exercises Father Thomas took the greatest
possible delight.   His own simple and ever interesting
story, of the past and present in his life, and the kindling
hopes which filled his expanding soul, when the fire
burned around him, was related; and his usual shout, or,
indeed, several spells of shouting, attested the measure
of his religious joy.

Among those who frequently revisited the memorable
place where they first tasted the pardoning love of God,
was Mr. Barbon, and in these experience meetings,

added greatly to the general interest, by narrating the change wrought in his heart and hopes, and his prospect of a better world—encouraging both ministers and members, in the great work of preaching and prayer.

How often is it the case, in the crowded and excited congregation, that a stranger is passed by, or a poor anxious soul, newly awakened to seek religion, neglected, even after they approach the "mourners' " place, craving instruction, sympathy, and prayer; while the laborers, intent on some particular object of their regard—perhaps an acquaintance or relative—seem only concerned that *they* receive attention!

One of the best evidences of true Christian faith and love, is that principle within, that prompts a man or woman to kneel by the side of the stricken one, whoever or *whatever* that one may be, to pour into the ear of the "weary and heavy laden," tidings of Him who said, "Come unto me." The freezing formality that sometimes may be found right near the altar, and the miserable pride, that is detected in partialities and prejudices, among those who profess a religion that discards or abandons none in the hour of grief and tears, is a false feeling, unworthy a sincere Christian anywhere.

Well meaning persons, without considering the effect of what they do, will ask, " Who is *she?*" or " What and whence is *he?*" and with the spirit of a Pharisee, will stand off, disdaining contact with some, who, in this way, " come unto" Christ, and appeal to all around by their cries, " Pray for me—tell me the way to Jesus; *help me* to break the shackles of vice and sin, that gall, while they bind me!"

It may be, and to some extent *is* true, that individuals who are actuated by impulse alone, are found in the throng at our camp meetings; and that low characters under the stinging consciousness of sin and shame, will fall down in the dust, smiting on their breast and saying, " God be merciful to me a sinner." They give but little grouhd of hope to the pious, that they *mean* to forsake their ways, or that they will persevere in learning to do well. It is whispered of this one—" She has *professed* several times before;" and that one,—"He is not sufficiently in earnest to 'flee the wrath to come,' and be saved *from* his sins;" yet what are we to do in such perplexing cases? Let us suppose what the gentle Jesus would do! Let us think of what he did, and said, and suffered, until our souls become imbued with that pity which yearns over the fallen, that love which follows with beseechings the lost, and that constant remembrance of the "rock whence we were hewn, and the hole of the pit whence we have been digged," that will hide pride from us, and move us to take poor outcasts as we find them, and by all the appliances at our command, aid them, in even the semblance of an effort, to " break off their sins by righteousness, and their iniquities by turning to the Lord." What if we are often mortified, and disappointed, and imposed upon? Blessed be God! we are often, on the other hand, constrained to believe that he is better to us than all our fears; and that through the wonders of his grace, in its workings on the unregenerate and vicious, transitions occur, which reward most amply all the toil expended in aiding them to put their trust in God; and attest, beyond peradventure, the abil-

ity and willingness of Christ "*to save to the uttermost.*"
The reflections into which we have been almost imper-
ceptibly drawn, in this connection, are based on the recollection of conversations we have had with Brother
Thomas, on the subject of indiscriminate efforts, after
the evening sermon on a camp ground. "Brother," he
would say, "you cannot determine who is true, and who
is insincere. One of those outcasts in human estimation,
when raised up out of degradation, by the noble and disinterested sympathy of Christianity, may become one of
the brightest ornaments of society, and a precious jewel
of the Lord."

He had stored in his memory hundreds of remarkable
conversions, and could draw an example or illustration
of every variety of case, from this depository, showing
aptly and conclusively the importance of observing that
command, "Despise not the day of small things."

He would frequently linger at the place of prayer
long after others seemed weary, and alone with some
troubled spirit, would employ all the ingenuity he possessed to simplify saving faith, or ascertain the causes
of doubt and difficulty, where mourners did not speedily
apprehend the plan, and realize the comfort of salvation.

When camp meetings in this region of country are
broken up, discontinued, and only remembered as scenes
of the past, and the causes of their cessation traced
out, it will be discovered that this extraordinary means
of grace has failed from one chief cause; and that is,
not the multiplicity of churches, the altered taste and
inclination of the people, the presence of time-serving
politicians, or the disorders occasioned by the unruly

and lawless; but the *indolence* of professing Christians, who, though they love to tent on the ground, and liberally sustain the hospitality, and other temporal arrangements of the occasion, *do not love the prayer meetings.*

Brother Thomas was severe on those Christians who attend a camp to eat and drink, promenade and talk, and give, as many in modern times do, the altar and its exercises *a wide berth;* leaving the important prayer meetings to their weary preachers, unsupported, except by a few young or inexperienced persons, with an idle, gaping crowd of unbelievers ranged around them, to gratify their callous and morbid craving for what is strange or novel, in the sight of persons weeping for sin, wrestling in prayer, or rejoicing in new found hope.

In the palmy days of Tangiers, there was comparatively little to complain of in this regard. Christians who assembled there, far from their homes, their business, and ordinary associations, gave themselves to the work, and were watered with copious showers, while they came up to "the help of the Lord, to the help of the Lord against the mighty."

There is not a circuit on the lower Peninsula,—hardly a society,—that has not gathered fruit from Tangier Island, in soundly converted souls, who like Mr. Barbon, lived and died in the faith of Christ, and in communion with the church.

We have yet many incidents to recount of the seasons of grace witnessed there, and in a future chapter may attempt something like a verbatim report of one of its characteristic experience meetings, but at a later day than the period of which, as yet, we write.

CHAPTER XV.

Removal to little Deal's Island—Rev. David Wallace—Marriages—Prayer meetings at his house—Jacob Webster—Camp meeting at Todd's chapel —Praying in the rain—"Keep the fire burning"—Death and funeral of David Wallace—Parson Thomas' labors—Success in fishing—Trades to Choptauk—Ebenezer—"It comes to me, I must first shout"—Conversion of an offended hearer—Singularity—Shouting, a means of grace—Shouts while making his child's coffin—Early dead, early saved—Children in heaven—Rev. Wm. Spry.

ABOUT the year 1825, we find Brother Thomas settled in a new locality, surrounded by a large family, and with a much wider sphere of usefulness and duty opening before him. He had been ordained a Deacon in the church, and in this relation became at once the worthy successor of a local minister named David Wallace of Deal's Island, who had for many years been a prominent and useful laborer in the church. No man of his day possessed a stronger attachment to the doctrines, usages, and duties of Methodism than he. As one of the earliest converts enrolled under its banners in Somerset County he aided in building up the wasted places of Zion, and making this moral wilderness to rejoice and blossom as the rose. He was contemporary with the first band of Itinerant preachers who published the message of a free salvation

on the Peninsula, and was highly esteemed by such men
as T. Ware, W. Colbert, Nathan Swain, Thomas Smith,
and Dr. Chandler. As a preacher, he was somewhat
boisterous, and irresistibly earnest, with a voice like a
pealing trumpet, and an unquenchable ardor. In the
great revival which commenced in 1800, he did good
service for God, and was an honored instrument in leading many souls to the " fountain opened for sin," as the
wave of salvation circled wider, in its onward and glorious
progress.

His own awakening and conversion was thorough, and
the fruits he brought forth in all his after years, attested
the genuineness of that work which had translated him
out of bondage to sin, and made him " a bright and
shining light."

We have incidentally introduced his name, in connection with revival scenes on the Islands. When he
became fully aroused in exhortation, we are told, you
could have heard his voice a mile distant, warning sinners,
and dwelling on the hopes and heritage of the children
of God. He was the first local preacher in that country
who was made a Deacon, which office he magnified, in
the multitudes he had the happiness to unite in the bonds
of matrimony. His certificates on file, at the time of
his decease, were, it is stated, over a bushel ! Most of
these marriages were solemnized at his own house on
Deal's Island, which stood on the spot now occupied by
the modern and elegant residence of Captain Wm. Price,
the Custom house officer for that port. The old dwelling was the first place opened for religious worship on
the island. The memory of prayer meetings held there,

will be transmitted from generation to generation among the families of that locality. Persons are yet living who were present on a certain evening when, under the pressure of a " general shout," the sleepers gave way, and the crowd fell through the floor!

This faithful man of God led many a poor wanderer to Jesus. He attended camp meetings far and near, and labored for the salvation of the souls of men with untiring energy, and with great success. He would go round among his unconverted neighbors, and invite them to accompany him to some distant meeting where he hoped they would seek the Lord, and obtain saving grace. He generally provided a way for such to go, and attended to all their wants while in his company, as well as those of their families in their absence.

Brother Jacob Webster, one of the oldest members of the church on Deal's Island at the present time, was converted through the instrumentality of his long and highly esteemed friend Wallace. When a young man he attended the great camp meeting at Pungoteague, where the riot occurred, and at the time the managers, for arresting the wrong person, were indicted and heavily fined. He was on guard in the midst of all the excitement, and heard a Brother Chambers from Baltimore preach on the outskirts of the ground after he had been wounded in the face by a blow from one of the infuriated mob. The text was " Turn ye to the stronghold, ye prisoners of hope."

He returned from this meeting under deep conviction, and Brother Wallace proposed to him to join a company who intended visiting a camp meeting at Todd's Chapel in Dorchester Co. the same fall, (1807.) He excused himself from going, by saying he had a sore foot. "Then," said Wallace, "let me carry you on my back to the vessel." He yielded, and joined the company. When they came to anchor near the camp ground, it was foggy and raining hard. In the discouragement of the moment, "Uncle Davy" ordered all hands on deck for prayer. "Come up," said he, "all you who want to get to heaven, and help me to pray." He bared his head in the pelting rain, and asked God to give them a clear sky and a glorious meeting. His voice rolled out over the waters, upward to heaven, and onward to the encampment, where it reached the quick ear of Dr. Chandler, who was preparing to commence the exercises. The fog dispersed, the rain ceased, and when that long and *strong* prayer ended, the answer had already come. Looking toward the shore, they saw wagons awaiting them, and were hailed by Dr. C. who had hurried down to meet and welcome his Deal's Island brethren to camp. "Come on, Brother Wallace," said he, "I heard you praying, and am glad the fire is burning in your soul; come ashore and let us expect the Lord of hosts to be with us."

Brother Webster, at that meeting, was made happy in a Saviour's love, and says, when he felt the blessed change and arose from the bench, the first man he saw was Brother Wallace. He caught him in his arms, and though he was an immensely large man, he lifted him clear off the ground!

This Boanerges of the Church remained faithful until death, and has gone to receive a many starred crown from the hand of his ascended Lord. He greatly strengthened and encouraged Brother Thomas, in the early periods of his ministry, and enjoyed the confidence of all who knew him, as a sincere, deeply pious, and very useful man and minister.

His funeral was attended by Rev. Wm. Prettyman, then a youth, who preached on the occasion from " Blessed are the dead, who die in the Lord, &c."

His mantle rested on Father Thomas, who now took his place, having become a resident of the adjoining, or little Deal's Island, where he spent the balance of his days.

Brother Thomas now began to extend his labors and visits far into the interior of the country. He navigated the winding rivers, and was present at every quarterly or camp meeting, within a wide circle. He became known as the "shouting preacher;" and, wherever he made a visit, the first families of the neighborhood vied with each other, as to who should have him for their guest. His sprightly conversation, excellent anecdotes, and, above all, the hold he took on the hearts of young and old, while officiating at the family altar, made him a renowned man, and endeared him to all with whom he came in contact.

So heavily did these frequent visits to distant places tax his time, that some of his acquaintances prudently intimated he had better be at home providing for his family, lest they come to want through his devotion to the Church. "No indeed," he would reply, "my Lord will see to that. He will take care of me according to the promise, while I am endeavoring to serve him and do good to the people."

The Lord did mercifully, and sometimes almost miraculously, stand his friend. His granary caught fire, and with it was consumed his little store of provision; but he meets with a floating cargo of flour in the bay, and returns to his empty larder with abundance. His calculating and worldly-minded neighbors had often to return from the fishing-grounds with scanty supplies, but he was invariably successful. People in various places, to whom he ministered in holy things, ministered to him in temporal things, and he could often say, " My cup runneth over."

As acknowledged " Parson of the Islands," he performed nearly all the marriages that took place. The proceeds from this source formed a respectable addition to his means. No man could " do up" a wedding ceremony better than he.

If the call was to a distant " Neck" or " Island," he was prompt and punctual. His simple and affectionate prayer for, and advice to, the newly married pair, was always appropriate; and the festivities of the occasion were generally more pleasant when he remained to mingle with the company.

He had not yet obtained the celebrated canoe "Methodist," but owned a little trading craft in which he made trips to the Choptank, and other places, with the productions of the island and bay, receiving, in exchange, commodities that were needed in his family or in demand among his neighbors.

Whatever bargain he made he always gave a good

prayer "to boot," and faithfully dealt with the souls of persons in whose company he might be placed, or with whom he transacted his business.

His cargo, at a certain place, consisted of clams. The villagers did not seem to appreciate this luxury, and he lay at the wharf all day without a customer.

When school was dismissed towards evening, the boys took a turn in that direction to investigate the new arrival. He determined, if the people would not purchase his clams, to give them away, and calling the school boys on board he filled their caps and pockets.

They reported this fact at their homes, and soon the citizens came hurrying down with baskets and bags, and bought out his load at very remunerative prices.

At another time he had potatoes, fish, &c., to barter for corn, meat, and such articles as were lacking at home. The people were absorbed with other matters, and paid no attention to the stranger. He heard of a prayer-meeting in the neighborhood, and leaving his boy in charge of the vessel, he attended it, and soon made himself known, as a remarkable person, by his exercises. "Who is he?" was the general inquiry. When this question was settled, he had no more difficulty at that place, but was always welcome and successful.

He was in the habit of relating these incidents with some religious end in view, at camp meetings; and could verify the truth in himself, that "the righteous shall not be forsaken," and, "all things work together for good to them that love God."

The place we have named as "Todd's Chapel," was subsequently called "Ebenezer," and has been a famous camp meeting locality for a great many years. It was formerly included in Cambridge Circuit, but, of late years, is one of the appointments of Church Creek. At this place, as shall hereafter appear, Brother Thomas spent many of the happiest hours of his life, in religious labors; and enjoyed an extended acquaintance with the warm-hearted, liberal, and devoted people who attended the meetings there, from Taylor's, Hooper's, and Elliott's Islands,—from up the Nanticoke, the lower Islands,—and various places in Dorchester County; and who always delighted to see him among the preachers at their camp meeting.

He arrived one day while the exercises were in progress, and was called up to "exhort," after a sermon had been concluded. The eyes of the congregation kindled, as they followed him in his movement towards the "stand." Arriving there, he pulled off his low crowned hat and cast it aside, he then took off his overcoat, and laid it away, and, turning to the expectant people, he said, "It comes to me, *I must first shout!*" He thereupon began to jump, and clap his hands, saying, "Glory!" "Glory!" and continued thus until he was in a fine glow of religious fervor.

The people looked at the man, and then at each other, with smiles at the oddity of this movement, but after a little, some ventured an "Amen," and the feeling began to infect those in immediate proximity to the stand, until quite a number were responding, and shouting in concert. He then quieted down, and gave an earnest exhortation, full of good sense, and commanding the eager attention of his congregation.

A gentleman was present on that occasion, and became the subject of deep conviction under this singular proceeding. His statement, afterwards, was in substance .as follows : " At first I thought the man was a fool, and the preachers were to blame for asking him up. I was about leaving my seat in disgust and indignation, and retiring from the ground ; for, though I was not a professor of religion, I respected its order too much, to see it caricatured in that manner. I finally concluded to stand it out, rather than attract attention by my departure. I took a steady look at him, and in that instant one of the strangest sensations I ever had experienced, came over me. I felt that the Spirit of the Lord was there, actuating the man in what he said and did, and for the first time in all my life, I trembled from head to foot, under a new and over-powering conviction that I was a lost sinner.

"I tried to shake it off by going outside among my friends, and made some effort to leave the place altogether, but I could not. The hand of God was on me. I went forward and humbled myself publicly as a penitent seeker of pardon, through the atoning merits of Christ.

" Before leaving that place I obtained an evidence of acceptance with God, and was inwardly assured, ' Thy sins are forgiven thee.'

" I had been all my life a hearer of the gospel. I had paid a decent respect to the observances of the church, and had sometimes thought myself as good as was necessary, or, at least, as good as others around me, until that scene of shouting unsettled my balance, and swept away my false foundation. I can now," he added, "most cordially endorse a good holy shout anywhere, and help a good Christian at any time to praise a pardoning God."

This gentleman became a prominent member of the church, and attributed his conversion to the instrumentality of Brother Thomas, under the gracious influence of the Holy Spirit. "His ways are not our ways, neither are our thoughts his thoughts. He will send by whom he will send," and work out his own designs, according to the counsels of his will and wisdom, by means that human ingenuity is incapable of devising.

Singularity for its own sake is contemptible; but singularity, and, even eccentricity, that may be natural or constitutional in preachers or people, should meet with forbearance; since few or none are moulded by the same model, and "variety is the spice of life."

Sometimes an impulse received in the pulpit, or an impression conceived in a moment, may be from the right source; and to crush or disregard it, would be doing violence to the Spirit, and wrong to one's self, when, if followed, some great and good result might be attained.

Parson Thomas considered himself authorized to shout, as clearly as it appeared to be his duty to sing or pray. Many a private opportunity he has improved in this way, when none but the God he loved and praised was nigh.

Away out on a shoal called "Bird point bar," he had a "good time," one day, while gathering bait at low water. He was "musing" while traversing the mud, until "the fire burned," and "his heart became hot within" him, then spake he with his tongue, and the word was "Glory!" He never stammered on that exclamation. The neighbors discerned him in the distance, shouting, and thought it a strange time and place to indulge his "ruling passion;" but he reported on his return having received a great blessing.

One of the preachers took him to task at a certain camp meeting, for his disregard of propriety in this matter, advising him to restrain himself before large and promiscuous congregations, and not to incur the suspicion which might be created, that he sometimes shouted without any feeling prompting the act.

"Feeling," said he, "I do not wait for feeling. I am prompted by a sense of duty."

"How can you make it appear," said the preacher, "that it is a *duty* to shout, or, rather, leap as you do?"

"Because," replied he, "I regard it to be a *means of grace!*"

He then turned inquisitor, and asked: "Why do *you* pray?"

"To receive good, and to be made happy."

"Why do you preach? Is it not that you may do and get good?"

"Certainly."

"And do you not sing for the same purpose?"

"Yes."

"Well, do you become happy while praying?"

"Often."

"And in preaching?"

"Yes."

"Do you sing yourself happy?"

"Oh, yes, very frequently."

"Good. Now *understand*, I shout myself happy; and if *you* use these means, when you feel dull and uncomfortable, to obtain, through them, light and joy—I shout for the same purpose. Often when I sing, and pray, and preach, I fail to get my own soul blessed; but when I try a good shout, the clouds clear away, and my hope is brightened for immortality and eternal life."

The preacher turned off with a smile, confessing himself to be enlightened in an unexpected manner, and acknowledging himself outdone in the argument.

One touching incident he often alluded to in public : He had a sweet little child that sickened and died. The weary hours of watching spent by the side of the little sufferer, and the chill sense of bereavement which came over him, when death's sad work was finished, made him droop in sorrow and tears. He had to make the little coffin himself, and with his spirit cast down and his soul disquieted, he proceeded with his undesirable task. While planing the boards, his burdened thoughts turned to the eternal world, the home of the pure and the holy, whither his child had gone.

"Is it possible," thought he, "that my little one is now before the face of God, or in the arms of Jesus? Can it be, that the sweet voice we loved on earth, is blending with the angels and saints above, in the 'new song' of heaven, and I am here mourning, and sad of heart? Why should I? Is not this the highest honor I could enjoy? Could my ever kind God have shown me a greater mark of his love, than to take a child of my family home to his own, where 'the Lamb that is in the midst of the throne shall feed them, and shall lead them unto fountains of living waters, and God shall wipe all tears from their eyes?'" This train of reflections set him to shouting at once.

He returned to his plane and saw, but again praised the Lord; and so he continued, alternately shouting and working, until the coffin was made, when he proceeded to bear the little body to its grave, remembering the faith and hope of David, and saying, "I shall go to him, but he shall not return to me."

Happy would it be for all parents whose little olive plants wither and die, if they took a brighter view of the case, and remembered the fact that if early lost to them, their children are *the sooner saved*.

One of the chief deprivations of his later years was the infirmity that prevented his "walking, leaping, and —in this way—praising God." He was, in the days of his activity and strength, unwilling that any person should pray oftener, preach more, sing better, or *shout longer* than himself. At a camp meeting held at Curtis' chapel, he and Rev. Wm. Spry labored at the altar until a late hour one night, and enjoyed a happy time. Brother Thomas retired to the church where the preachers lodged, and went to bed. Brother Spry came in a short time afterwards, and was so filled with joy, that he commenced in a corner of the house to shout. The movement roused his rival, who immediately left his bed, and joined his pious brother in this exercise, unwilling that he should have the slightest advantage over him in this respect.

Meeting with Rev. Joshua Humphriss, when that minister first came on the circuit where Mr. Thomas belonged, and ascertaining his name, he remarked, "Well you are the first preacher I ever knew by the name of 'Joshua.' Now be a brave 'Joshua,' a wise commander of the sacramental host, and lead on your army until every 'Jericho' of unbelief and sin is stormed and captured, and our great 'spiritual Joshua' proclaimed universal Lord.

"You must look sharp, however, for I mean to try and *beat* you in preaching, singing, and prayer, if I possibly can."

The more he knew subsequently of Brother H., the more he had to acknowledge that, in these several departments, his namesake was "hard to beat."

It was at this (Curtis' chapel) meeting, he recommended the Princess Anne ladies to try the kind of piano the Island women practiced on music; said he, "They do not call it by that hard name though—they call it a *spinning wheel!* and make the prettiest music while they make our clothes. Try your hand on our 'spinning-wheel piano!'"

CHAPTER XVI.

Commencement of camp meetings on Deal's Island—Managers—Rev. Henry White—Great sermon on the old hill—Rev. John S. Taylor—The power of a hearty "amen"—The gust camp—Preachers present—Bible meeting —Rev. S. Townsend—Saturday night—The storm cloud—Wild commotion in the harbor—Vessels driven ashore—Tents blown down—Trees prostrated—Distress and fear—Saints and sinners—Rev. E. J. Way— Meetings in tents—A welcome morning—Extent of damage—Wonderful providence—Brother Thomas' celebrated exhortation—The forces rallied —" Our Joshua"—" The devil had a hand in it"—Did not succeed—The meeting goes on—Incidents—Self preservation—An alarmed sailor.

BROTHER THOMAS, soon after his removal to Deal's island, selected a place for camp meeting, and applied to the proper authorities of the circuit for sanction and support, in affording to the people of that locality the spiritual enjoyment and advantages of this, his favorite means of grace.

He had witnessed such displays of the power of God in the preaching of the gospel at Tangiers, and saw so many blessed results in enlarged moral influence on communities, and increasing spirituality in the church at various places, that he hoped for great good to his neighbors through this instrumentality.

Accordingly, we find him at a Quarterly Meeting Conference, held May 24th, 1828, at Curtis' chapel, pleading his cause, and obtaining that which he sought—the appointment of a camp meeting to be held on Deal's Island, commencing on the 17th of July, in that year.

A list of managers for this meeting is found on the old journal, and may be interesting to the reader, if recorded here. The following is the extract from the minutes, as preserved in the handwriting of that devoted servant of the church, and steward of the circuit for a long series of years,—Mr. Richard E. Waters:

"A Board of Managers was constituted for the first Deal's Island camp meeting, consisting of Joshua Thomas, Travers Daniel, Gabriel Webster, John Parks, Charles Parks, Severn Mister, George Rowe, John Webster, Wm. Wallace, Capt. Wm. White, Hamilton Webster, John Waters, Lewis Phœbus, Denard Evans, and Aaron Bradshaw."

The site which had been selected as possessing the most inviting natural advantages, was a bluff, rising abruptly from the water's edge, thickly studded with large pine trees, and accessible to visitors both by land and water. It was situate on the lands of Brother Denard Evans, who cheerfully placed it at the disposal of his intimate friend, Brother Thomas, and the religious community, for the purposes intended.

The "old hill," as it is now termed, was occupied for twenty years successively as a camp ground, and hallowed by many of the most powerful meetings, that perhaps have ever been witnessed since the day of Pentecost. Tangier Island itself, in time, became insignificant in the comparison.

Sermons by some of the most distinguished preachers

DEAL'S ISLAND CAMP MEETING.

in the church, living and dead, have been delivered there, and hundreds untold, scattered over the continent, on both sides of the Alleghenies, in the far west, and in the remote south, as well as in the populous towns and cities adjacent to the Chesapeake Bay, were savingly brought to a knowledge of the truth on that consecrated ground. And hundreds more have "crossed the river of Jordan, happy in the Lord," who were born for glory there.

The converted sailor, passing up or down the Tangier Sound, turns his eye to the well defined spot, and thinks of the hour when, in the language of a fervid poet, he could say :

> " The opening heavens around me shine,
>   With beams of sacred bliss ;
> My Jesus shows his mercy mine,
>   And whispers I am his."

And many a Christian pilgrim who sings, " Heaven's my home," and at the love feast tells the time and place of his start for eternal life, refers to the "old hill" on Deal's Island, and to some memorable camp meeting many years ago, saying, " There God for Christ's sake pardoned my sins."

The first meeting was held, as intimated, in 1828. On the day appointed the old woods were waked to echo with songs of praise, and the God of Israel was earnestly invoked to hear and bless his people, for the first time on that ground.

Rev. Henry White, Presiding Elder, and an able working force of Itinerant and Local preachers were in attendance. People had assembled from Virginia, Dorchester, and the interior of Somerset County. Tents were numerous, order good, and many were converted. The meeting ended satisfactorily to all, and to the extreme gratification of Brother Thomas, who continued it the following years, and the place became renowned for happy and successful reunions of the Methodist people, from various places throughout a large district of country.

Rev. Henry White, whose name occurs here, was in his day a very effective preacher. He literally went forth "*weeping*, bearing precious seed." Those who crowded his congregations, and were unmoved by his arguments, were often melted by his tears.

His most successful efforts, it is said, were made on Deal's Island, and before Sabbath morning congregations at the camp meetings there. The multitude, congregated under the sound of his voice, would sometimes heave like the ocean in time of storm, before the power of Divine truth falling from his lips, while his furrowed cheeks were bathed in flowing tears.

One occasion is remembered, and will never be forgotten by those who were present, when the religious excitement surpassed everything they had previously witnessed or felt. The good old man had produced an intense feeling, while proceeding with his animating sermon, and checked the tendency he discovered in his hearers to express aloud the emotions of their swelling hearts, or exhibit their joy by shouting. "Not yet! Not yet," he commanded. "I will give you the word when to shout." He continued preaching, and the tide of emotion rose still higher. "Not yet!" he urged, and exerted himself some moments longer to reach the climax of his subject. This was grandly done, and he exclaimed, "Now! all here who hope for heaven, rise upon your feet!"

The sudden and spontaneous outburst that then rolled out over the waters, and rang through the woods, we are informed, was indescribable. As by an earthquake shock, sinners fell prostrate; idlers along the shore started and ran towards the camp, and the sensation of that shout was experienced on board the vessels in the crowded harbor. Some unconscious of all surrounding things, mingled with the amazed throng, and joined the general rejoicing, having paddles on their shoulders, which, after leaping on the shore, they forgot to leave with the canoes, in which they had hastened to land, to ascertain the nature of this commotion.

The slain of the Lord were many that morning, and Christian people obtained such a vision of glory and of God, as many of them had never experienced before.

A scene almost similar to this, was brought about some years afterwards in the same place, by a very simple agency. Dearth and dullness seemed to have fallen upon the people, and the exercises of the camp were progressing without much apparent good being done. The preachers labored hard, and those who prayed, tried to reach the throne,—but no move had been made among sinners.

Under these circumstances, Rev. John S. Taylor, a man universally beloved in his day, and one of the most popular and successful ministers remembered by the people of the Islands, arose to exhort, after the evening sermon. The congregation appeared to be unaffected, the unconverted calm and careless. "I want every Christian here, in the stand and out of it," said he, "to join me in one short, simple prayer, and when I utter it, to say 'Amen.'" He then slowly and devoutly prayed, "Lord have mercy on careless sinners!" A few voices responded, "*Amen!*" "Come," said he, "let us try it again: All who have a desire for the salvation of souls, will speak out, and say 'Amen!'" Again he uttered the prayer, and the "Amens" were more emphatic, and more numerous. "Once more," said he, with increasing earnestness, "*Lord have mercy on careless sinners!*" "AMEN!!!" was thundered with startling eagerness by the suddenly aroused people. The next instant a cry arose from all parts of the camp, "Lord have mercy!" "Lord save or I perish!" and sinners came rushing forward in scores to the place of prayer.

The spell was broken, the enemy routed, and victory was gained on the "side of Immanuel."

Such occurrences as these, to the mind of Brother Thomas, were convincing of the truth, "Not by might, nor by power, but by my Spirit, saith the Lord of Hosts."

In his own ministry he disdained no instrumentality that promised effectiveness in rousing the conscience from its delusive slumber, and reaching the heart in its hardness and impenitency. He remembered and practiced the admonition, "Despise not the day of small things."

One of the most numerously attended camp meetings

ever held on Deal's Island was in the summer of 1838. This meeting is remembered as the "great gust camp," and will form the subject of conversation among those who were present, and the "generations following" for years to come.

The meetings of those years immediately preceding this had been crowned with such glorious results, that many strangers had been induced to attend for the first time the great "feast of tabernacles," to share in the "showers of blessing" that fell upon this holy hill.

The Island people had erected permanent tents on the front rows, reaching entirely round the circle. These were tastefully built, and made comfortable by weather-boarding and shingles. The second, third, and sometimes the fourth and fifth rows were occupied by persons from the main and distant islands. On the southern slope of the hill, the Potato Neck people pitched their canvass tabernacles. Along the brow, next to the Sound, large tents from Virginia were erected. On the upper, or northern slope of the ground, immense boarding establishments were allowed; and away towards the eastward, the colored people encamped, and held at intervals their lively exercises. The stand was on the most elevated point of ground, and commanded every part of the enclosure. These particulars the writer learned in a recent visit to that now silent and desolate spot, in company with Brother Denard Evans, who pointed out each place, and gave all the information desired as to the arrangements.

At the time of which we now write, every available site for a tent was occupied, and the exercises of the meeting commenced under the most favorable and promising auspices. Brother Thomas, as manager-in-chief, was active in affording every needed facility to his old friends, or to new comers, as their boats touched the sandy beach.

Rev. S. Townsend and Rev. James Allen were the circuit preachers that year; the former having charge of the meeting. The Presiding Elder, Rev. H. White, who was on the district for the second time, was also present. A number of ministers from various circuits adjacent, were there with their people, and, after arranging the tents and concluding the preparations on Thursday, the religious exercises were commenced with a sermon by Brother Townsend on Friday morning.

An eloquent preacher named McKenny, from Virginia, was also there to represent the interests of the American Bible Society, and did good service in the stand during the meeting. A collection was taken up amounting to $130 for the Bible cause, and Rev. H. White, Rev. J. Allen, Rev. Joshua Thomas, and the preacher in charge were constituted life members of the Virginia State Bible Society.

The Presiding Elder preached on Saturday morning. Service was held in the afternoon; and Rev. J. S. Taylor, who, with his colleague, Rev. E. J. Way, was present from Accomac in Virginia, was appointed to preach at the evening service.

Crowds of people had been gathering in during the day, and when the trumpets sounded, an immense congregation was speedily seated to hear the sermon, and join in the impressive devotions of the hour. The fire-stands threw a halo of light over that sea of upturned faces, and irradiated, with fantastic wreathings, the stately pines which interlaced their branches overhead.

The night was calm and beautiful, as its sable curtain closed around the scene. No sign of danger near threatened the absorbed multitude, except a dark, massive cloud bank, which was discerned slowly rising in the gorgeous west, portending one of those temporary gusts which bring an invigorating shower in times of summer drought.

That man of God, Brother Taylor, introduced the services by holy hymns and a comprehensive prayer, after which he proceeded to announce his text from the Prophecy of Daniel, and every eye and ear became interested in his lucid exposition and winning manner, as the sermon progressed.

Meanwhile that distant storm-cloud has become strangely agitated. From its murky depths lightnings begin to leap, and hoarse mutterings of thunder break upon the ear. Onward comes the war of winds; more vivid and rapid in succession the flashes, and in ceaseless reverberation the thunder. Startled looks are directed to the water, and an uneasy movement begins in the congregation. Brother Taylor held the people until the storm, careering over the bosom of the Sound, burst upon the camp. Then, with a hurried prayer to God for help and protection, the congregation was dismissed to see to their tents, and look after their vessels and boats.

An accurate picture of the awful scene that followed, cannot, at this lapse of time, be drawn. Hundreds remember the scene as if it were but yesterday, but language fails in every attempt at a full description. Wishing to obtain the most circumstantially correct account, the writer applied to Dr. Townsend, now of Philadelphia, who, as preacher in charge of the encampment, was supposed to have retained the most distinct impressions and recollections of this occasion, and received from that gentleman the following account of this thrilling scene :

"The storm commenced on Saturday night about the close of evening service. The clouds had been gathering portentously, and seemed to settle down on the earth enveloping all in blackness and terror.

"The lightning flashed through the air, the thunder uttered its mighty voice in the heavens, the rain descended in drenching torrents, the winds blew a perfect hurricane, the trees were uprooted, the tents were razed to the ground, the fire flew in whirling sparks, and threatened a conflagration among the tents ; the people, filled with sudden dread, commenced screaming wildly in their apprehension of destruction and death. The appearance of the air was unusual, sometimes red, then changing to blue in the gleaming light of burning torches, and the general aspect of things seemed to presage the appalling magnificence of the day of judgment. Indeed many supposed "the great day of his wrath" had burst upon them.

"The spacious harbor was crowded with vessels, far as the eye could reach. The fury of the gale first burst upon them, and pressed by its force, with severed cables, dragging anchors, and crashing spars, they were thrown into a confused mass, and swept in towards the shore.

Many of the people in attendance at the meeting had
made no other provision for their lodging than their vessels, and were constantly plying to and from the camp
ground. Some were asleep in their cabins, when the
wind and waves began to roar around them; and, being
awakened, rushed on deck, and rent the air with cries,
which were borne across the angry waters to the ear of
their friends on shore, 'We are lost! we are lost! Save
me! help me!' They expected every moment to be
crushed to pieces, or drowned in the boiling surf.

"The danger seemed to be not less imminent on shore.
The stately trees yielded before the blast until their
boughs almost touched the ground, and it was feared
every instant they would snap like pipe stems, and,
falling, crush the tents. When the rain came opportunely down, and quenched the spreading flames, the
situation of the people was rendered more wretched still.
But in a short time the force of the hurricane was spent,
and silence and gloom fell upon the scene. The beach
was strewed with boats; the people who, on the shore,
vainly tried to shout encouragement and hope in the face
of the tempest to those in the vessels, still called the
names of their friends, and searched for missing members of their families; but darkness was upon the face
of the waters, and confusion on the land, like that which
prevailed before the Spirit of God moved upon the great
deep, and brought order out of chaos, and light and
beauty over the dreary scene of old.

"In the morning, which was anxiously longed for,
and which, when it rose, was one of the calmest and
most lovely that ever broke on this world, the effects of

the storm became fearfully apparent. Many of the
tents were prostrate, the people were uncomfortable,
and in complaining humor with themselves for having
come to the meeting, or with those at whose instance
they left their homes.

"Two or three, only, of the larger class vessels were
high and dry on the shore, and only a few injured. One
old craft was an entire loss, but the amount was made
up, in a short time, by the generous people to her owner.
Not a life was lost, or even a limb broken. No person,
it was ascertained, was even seriously injured. God
took care of the lives and property of his people, and
preserved the multitude gathered there to hear his holy
word.

"The ground, tents, and clothing of the people were
too wet to have much religious service on the following
day. The people sauntered from place to place, making
arrangements to leave the camp early on Monday morning, and with the fixed determination never to return to
that spot again.

"Brother Thomas, who had been on the alert all night,
became painfully aware of the discontent prevailing.
His soul was stirred, and his spirit grieved within him,
at the prospect of disappointment and dismay in the
event of breaking up the meeting. Great trouble and
expense had been incurred in the preparation, and great
good was expected to be realized, as in former years,
from the exercises; but here was an event that threatened
to record 'Ichabod' on Deal's Island camp-ground, and
leave this holy hill deserted and desolate.

"The people had assembled as upon the day of Pen-

tecost, from almost every part of the land. The rich
and the poor, learned and ignorant, male and female,
parents and children, bond and free, saints and sinners,
were there with one accord.

"The preachers were ready to preach, exhorters to
work, the people to pray and sing praises: God was nigh
at hand to bless, Christ to save, and the Holy Spirit to
quicken and renovate the heart. Faith was in exercise,
hope beating high with expectation of victory and triumph
in the success of the meeting.

"And now, to be baffled and disappointed of all this
prospect of good before his eyes, and in his heart, was
too much for the noble soul of Brother Thomas to bear.
He applied to me, as the preacher in charge, to summon
a meeting of the managers, that he might obtain permission to have the people assembled at the stand, and address them before any further steps were taken to leave
the ground. The meeting was called, permission given,
and the trumpets sent out their call to the multitude to
come into the congregation. The people obeyed with
seeming reluctance, and an evident purpose not to be
persuaded to remain. They seemed determined to
leave the ground at all hazards. The old gentleman approached, looking solemn as the grave, and slowly
ascended the stand, where he knelt down in silent prayer,
to cast his burdened soul on God, and plead for direction
and help.

" As he arose from his knees it might be discovered
that his countenance shone with a placid lustre, and confidence appeared to take the place of anxiety. Brushing
the hair that lay in straggling locks over his noble fore-

head away, he swept the congregation with an eagle eye, penetrating the thoughts, it would seem, of the discontented and murmuring masses before him. A pause ensued. The people seemed spell-bound, looking first at this old hero of a hundred battles, in the army of 'Immanuel,' then in each other's eyes until shame for their lack of firmness and faith began to operate, and a mighty reaction from that moment set in on their feelings.

"With commanding look, and tones as confident as those which stayed the storm on the lake of Galilee, he said, 'In the name of the adorable Trinity—Father, Son, and Holy Ghost, I want this congregation to remain quiet, and give me your attention; and not a man, woman, or child to move till I deliver to you a message from the Lord!'

"No man living will ever write the address which he delivered that day. I believe he was as much inspired of God to deliver it, as was St. Paul to preach, or write his Epistles. Memory retains but a meagre outline, and can only recall the substance of his memorable exhortation.

"He said, 'Brothers and Sisters! we came here to hold our annual feast of tabernacles. This is God's house. This ground has long since been dedicated to his service. Here he has recorded his great saving name, blessed his people, and converted sinners. Here believers have been sanctified, and his church built up on the foundation of its most holy faith. New born souls have gone forth east and west, north and south, connecting themselves with the redeemed of the Lord,

swelling the number of his elect, and marshaled under
the great Captain of their salvation, to be conducted
on to glory and to God. This ground has gained a
widely extended fame, for the large and successful camp
meetings held on it. The eligibility of this island for
such purposes; its accessibility to every part of the
country, both by land and water; the ample accommodations, health-giving salt breezes, right from the Atlantic
Ocean, fine shade; and more, and better than all—the
return of numerous converts, the fruits of our toil and
tears, every year to the consecrated place of their conversion, who are ready to fall down and kiss the very
earth, where, from above, in years gone by, they first
received the pledge of Jesus' pardoning love—these considerations should weigh strongly against an abandon-
ment of the meeting.

"'We assembled a few days ago,—as the Parthians,
Medes, and Elamites, and the dwellers in Mesopotamia,
Pontus, and Asia, of old,—from Delaware, Virginia,
Maryland, the Eastern and Western Shores, the towns
and villages around, the great cities of Baltimore, Philadelphia, and New York, from Norfolk and other places
in that direction,—all with one accord in this grove,
awaiting the fulfillment of the ancient promise, the de-
scent of the Holy Ghost, like a rushing, mighty wind.

"'*It has come.* The mighty trees have been uprooted,
the tents strewed on the ground, the hearts of the people
have quaked with fear, their tongues have cried aloud,
the sea has been agitated, and its mighty billows have
moved from beneath, and lashed the time-worn shores;
but God has spoken to the proud waves, "Hitherto shalt

thou come, and no farther," here they have been stayed and stilled by his voice.

" ' The clouds have passed away, the rain is over and gone, the flowers appear in their beauty, the time of the singing of birds is come again, and the voice of the turtle is heard in the land. The fig tree putteth forth her green figs, and the vines with the tender grapes give a good smell. "Arise my love, my fair ones, and come away ;" but not to break up the camp meeting, and leave our goodly heritage in confusion and dismay, where God has so often come to us and blessed us, " but from the clefts of the rock, the secret places of the stairs, let me see thy countenance, let me hear thy voice, for thy countenance is comely." These poetic effusions are full of comfort, and indicate the day of gladness and joy, that shall succeed the season of gloom and heaviness now hanging over your souls, shutting out every prospect, and destroying every purpose of good to yourselves and your friends at this meeting.

" ' Come, then, give up this determination to forsake the place, and abandon the God-honored enterprise that brought you together, and has cost us such an expenditure of time, money, and prayer. Is it possible that you can so suddenly cast away your confidence, and give place to the enemy ?'

" (Here he gave a paraphrase of Job and his calamities, arising from the malignant power of Satan, the prince of darkness, and applied it to the storm of the preceding night, saying, ' *The devil had a hand in it*, and wanted to prove whether we had true faith in God.')

" ' Shall he gain the victory, and "scatter, tear, and

slay" our hopes in this manner? Is it so? Shall we
receive good at the Lord's hand, and not evil? Can it
be that your Christian integrity, your faith in a benign
providence, is so easily shaken and destroyed? Do you
not believe "all things shall work together for good to
them that love God?"

" ' Has he blessed us with *so much* good weather, good
health, prosperous seasons, happy meetings? has victory
so often perched upon our banner, and glory, through
our instrumentality, redounded to Christ? have we sent
abroad in former times an odor of sweetness, that has
attracted around us the thousands now present, who are
looking to us for instruction in the good and right way?
And shall we now, instead of breaking to their hungry
souls the manna of the gospel, break up our meeting,
and send them away without supplies, to faint and die
by the way? Shall believers fear, and like cowards fly?
No! desponding Peter, wherefore didst thou doubt?
Come and have thy faith made strong by earnest prayer!
Come, Andrew; bring the lad with the small basket of
loaves and fishes. "All things are ready." Let us look
for a great blessing, that we may be enabled to praise
our God with a loud noise, and feed the hungry multitude
with the bread of life!

" ' Jesus is here to perform a spiritual miracle, conquer
and renew the old rebellious heart, and bless the poor
with bread! Nearer and nearer we find him coming
now to our weak and wavering hearts! Glory be to
Jesus! glory! glory!'

" Here a hearty response, like the sound of many waters
broke in from the excited multitude. The tone of feel-

ing had undergone a total change, faith sprung up, hope revived, and voices were heard in every direction shouting, 'Go on, Brother Thomas! we are listening to what you say, and are ready to follow. Give the word of command, our Joshua, and we will press forward, though it be through the wilderness or sea, in fire and fagot, in rain and storm, through peril and fear!'

"Pausing while these responses rolled in upon him, he felt that his message was delivered, and its burden gone. His soul was full of holy fire, and again rising, he soared upon the wings of his faith, and carried his hearers into the state of intensified emotion which swelled his own heart. As they responded, he replied, 'That's you, my brethren! brave soldiers in the army of our Lord Jesus Christ; like our veteran fathers, fight and conquer! fight and you shall win the prize, and wear the palm of never fading bliss—the unsullied crown of victory and glory which our King shall give unto all them that love his appearing, and are "faithful unto death."'

"He made allusion in the course of his exhortation to the dark days of the revolution, and the energy, perseverance, and bravery of our ancestors, who fought for liberty and independence, in some such words as the following:

"'Oh! think of the struggle, through poverty and peril, in winter's biting cold, and summer's torrid heat, in danger, discouragement, and distress, for nine long years, to gain our nation's freedom from the yoke of despotism, that we might be permitted to repose in the shade and safety of that glorious tree our fathers planted in a soil enriched by their blood! Did one shower of cannon balls, one defeat, the loss of one battle—the taking of one town or city by the enemy, intimidate those brave men ?   [The people shouted " No !"]   Did not our noble American soldiers stand to their guns, maintain their position, and without shoes to their feet, track their path over snow and ice, still hoping against hope, and trusting in the wisdom, and skill of their General, the great and good Washington ? ["Yes."] Yes, brethren, as one fell, another took his place ; as one platoon gave way, another came to the rescue ; as company after company melted away, from hardship and danger, others took their place, filled the ranks, and urged on the fight for victory ! Sometimes they advanced—often had to retreat—now a battle is gained, then two lost, but still they were invincible.   They collected the shattered fragments of their forces, and braced up their wasted energies for another onset.   They were unconquerable, by their powerful foes, and in the face of their darkest trials shouted, " Give us liberty or give us death !"

" ' Were they at last successful ?' [" Yes ! yes !"]

" ' What made them so ?   Not their might, their numbers, equipments ; these were far inferior to the well trained foe they had to encounter—but they overcame with the blessing of God, by perseverance !' [" Yes !"]

" ' Is our cause less righteous ; less urgent, than theirs, and shall we give up the strife ?' [" No !"]

" ' Look at Martin Luther and his contemporaries struggling for long years to free their country and the world, from the withering blight of popery ! The Apostles preach, the martyrs suffer, a Wesley toils his life away to fan into a living fire the flickering spark of an expiring spirituality, and we, oh! for shame! we seem to become weary in a day. Shall we let go our hope?'

"'*No !* no !'"

"'There is a crown reserved for us if faithful!'"

"'We'll have it! we'll wear it!'"

"'How shall we have it? What is the condition? Is it to succumb to the prince of darkness, as some of you were about doing?'"

"A loud and long response of 'no!'"

"'The patriot of old believed in the justness of his cause, and the skill of his general. Who is our Captain?'"

"'*Jesus !* jesus ! !'"

"'Yes, King Jesus is our Captain, Hallelujah! Let this be our sentiment :

"Here I'll raise my Ebenezer;
Hither by thy help I've come;
And I hope by thy good pleasure,
Safely to arrive at home."

"This was sung amid great excitement, and Brother Thomas was shouting happy. He waved his hand to the people saying, 'Go on! my brethren in Christ, go on, I'll meet you there. "Allelujah! the Lord God omnipotent reigneth!" "The kingdoms of this world are becoming the kingdoms of our Lord Jehovah, and of his Son Jesus Christ!"'

"The old veteran left the stand in glorious triumph, borne away on the affections of the people, and filled to overflowing with the love and power of God.

"There was nothing more intimated about striking tents, or leaving the camp until its close. The meeting received a new impetus, which carried it forward to a glorious issue. Hundreds were converted, and no doubt some in glory were that morning moved to give themselves to God;—others are still on the way, and will be owned in that day when the Lord shall come to make up his jewels."

A few incidents of this gust camp meeting, as it is termed, remain to be noticed.

Brother Poulson and his company from Accomac had a large tent on the brow of the hill. It was exposed to the fury of the wind, but it stood the storm; being held fast by several strong hands. Rev. E. J. Way was stationed at the outer, or windward post, and while holding on for life, received a stunning blow, by the falling of a large shelf, loaded with crockery ware and provisions, on his head. His situation was so critical, however, that he dared not let go, long enough to rub the sore place!

As soon as the gale subsided, this tent was cleared for action, a prayer meeting was started, and mourners fell on their knees in penitence before the Lord. A young woman came in, clapping her hands, and saying, "Hallelujah! the storm did not drive me to Jesus; it has no terrors for me; my feet are on the Rock of Ages."

A brother, now a leader and exhorter in the church, informs us that he was at the meeting that terrible night, and was at that time a wild, thoughtless young man. Passing near where a tent had been dismantled, he saw the occupants huddled together praying, and the head of the family engaged in calling on God for protection and help. He was very hungry, and seized upon a tempting looking pair of fowls, that lay amid the wreck, thinking that the theft was justified under the circumstances, by the "first law of nature." With his appropriated supper he took the way to the shore, to be beyond reach of danger, should the trees fall, as was expected every moment; and there, alone, spent the night.

Some persons seemed to lose completely their wits and self-possession, and said and did a great many singular things. A sailor sought religion in the great meeting following the storm, on Sabbath, and was converted. He stated that he was in his berth on board a vessel when the hurricane came on. The cries of distress and the dashing of the waves aroused him; he sprang on deck, where the first object he saw, was a large steamboat, with vapor hissing, lever working, wheels revolving, (to keep her to her anchor,) and the lights from her furnaces, cabin, and decks, flashing through the darkness, on his bewildered gaze. He thought he had, sure enough, reached the bad place at last, and became filled with terror and despair. He promised, if spared to reach the shore, the very first thing he did, would be to repent and turn to God. He kept his purpose, and rejoiced aloud in the mercy that found him a lost and ruined sinner, and removed the burden of his guilt that day.

CHAPTER XVII.

Rock Creek Church—Preaching of Brother Thomas—Conversion of George Washington Rowe—His zeal and success—Rev. Z. Webster—Great revival—Rev. Shepherd Drain—The Rowe family—Captain Rowe converted—Parents and Children happy in God—Mortality—Gathered home —Funeral of Rev. G. W. Rowe—Effects of a hymn—The sick restored— A Baptism of the Spirit—Faith of Parson Thomas—" Lord cure the boy" —Signal answer to prayer—Rev. Z. Webster a traveling preacher—His dying mother—" We shall meet in heaven."

ROCK CREEK Church was the first, and for many years the only place for public worship, in the vicinity of Deal's Island. The large congregation at Dames Quarter above, and that on the island below this central locality, formerly united here, having no church at either place. Incidental allusion has been repeatedly made to the meetings held at this mother church in the preceding chapters. Its history, if written, would be a stirring record of revivals; for hundreds, now among the glorified, found peace, and learned the way to heaven within its consecrated walls.

Brother Thomas attended and conducted service at this appointment, for a long series of years. Some of his happiest efforts in the pulpit were made here, and the effects of his ministry, in explaining and illustrating the truths of the gospel, like "bread cast upon the waters," may still be discovered in the conversation and experience of the more aged Christians in that community.

To reach the Rock Creek church, he had about four miles to walk on Sabbath mornings, besides the trouble of crossing the upper and lower Thoroughfare, in doing which he was exposed to wet and cold; but nothing impeded him in regular attendance. It is thought that his health received irreparable injury from his fastings, (for he never took breakfast before leaving home to preach,) his long walks, and his excessive labors there. After preaching, and meeting the large class, he generally returned to the island, and assembled his neighbors for prayer-meeting, which sometimes continued until a late hour of the night. It mattered not with him how weary he might be in body after his Sabbath labors, if he only could feel assured that some one had been benefited at his meetings, or induced by his influence to accept the mercy he offered to all whose " repentance toward God, and faith in our Lord Jesus Christ" gave evidence of sincerity in seeking religion.

At one of the prayer meetings he conducted, an interesting young man, who had grown up without the advantages of parental example, or encouragement to piety, became a subject of converting grace. He "followed on to know the Lord," by reading the Scriptures, secret prayer, and a studied avoidance of all surrounding dissipation. The eye of the church soon marked him out for usefulness. He was appointed class leader, and made such proficiency in grace that he soon became an

earnest and faithful exhorter.   His intense soul longed
for a mighty, and extensive, revival of the work of God.
For this he prayed and labored, persuading his young
companions to think on their ways, and turn their feet
to the testimonies of the Lord.   He was in very many
instances successful, and in due time, feeling moved by
the Holy Ghost to believe that a " dispensation of the
gospel had been committed to him," accepted license to
preach, and the good old Parson, Brother Thomas, had a
warm coadjutor in the person of George Washington
Rowe.

Rev. Z. Webster, also, about this time became an active laborer, and took his part in the exercises of the
meetings.   At a protracted effort commenced in the
month of September, 1840, which continued four weeks,
one hundred and ten persons professed religion, and
joined the society at Rock Creek.   Such a revival had
never been known in that vicinity.   Nearly every adult
person within a wide circle, who had not previously become a member of the Church, was included in this overwhelming work of grace.

The circuit preachers at that time were Sheppard
Drain of precious memory; and Isaac. R. Merrill.   These
faithful ministers were constant in attendance, and aided
in the arduous labors, which this revival meeting imposed,
by Rev. M. Willing, now a minister in the P. E. Church
in New York, and others from a distance ; but the chief
instrumentality, in leading trembling sinners to Christ,
and carrying forward the prayer-meetings, was Brother
Thomas and his two young Island preachers, Rowe and

Webster; they were "fervent in spirit, serving the Lord."

During this remarkable outpouring of the Spirit, salvation came to Captain George Rowe, and all his house! He was father to Rev. G. W. Rowe; and, up to that time, had treated religion with almost total indifference. He was a man of large influence among his neighbors, a captain of militia, and regarded as one of the most unlikely subjects to be affected by the exercises of an excited meeting. A sight that will never be forgotten by those who witnessed it, was presented when this proud, impetuous man bowed down in penitence, with his wife and children on either side of him engaged in prayer. They were all made happy in a sense of pardon, near the same time; and parents and children, around the altar, rejoiced with exceeding joy. They also joined the Church, seven of that family, standing side by side together, and taking her vows upon them, began to "journey toward Zion, with their faces thitherward."

The change in that family was wonderful. Boisterous passion and unguarded profanity were hushed, prayer and praise sweetly blended around the newly erected altar of devotion, and gentleness and peace made their abode in that happy home. All but two of the members of that once united circle are gone. Mortality has reaped a fearful harvest, and tombstones only tell the once cherished names of both the united head, and amiable children of the Rowe family. Sons that were the promising stay of their beloved parents have fallen, one by one; and accomplished daughters, whose intelligence and kindness made them endeared to all their associates, have followed their parents to the silent grave; but they still live in the affections of many who shared their hospitality, and enjoyed their society on earth, and who bade them farewell in the dying hour, with hope to meet where parents and children part no more; but where all we love shall live forever.

In the lamented death of Brother G. W. Rowe, a void was occasioned in the church, which, it seemed, would be impossible to fill. At his funeral, Rev. Wm. Campbell appealed to the young people who had followed with sadness and tears his remains, saying, "For your salvation this departed brother spent his strength, and gave his life, in incessant labors and prayers. Will you promise, in your hearts, to-day, to try and meet him in heaven?"

The wife of Captain Rowe, and mother of this large and interesting family, professed to have been changed in heart long before the Rock Creek meeting, but finding no sympathy in her companion for this state of life, she did not connect herself with the people of God, or take a public stand in religion, until he led the way; then she gladly reconsecrated herself, and was enrolled with him in the militant army.

She was a lady of sterling worth, and greatly beloved by all her friends. A remarkable instance of the efficacy of prayer in her behalf, occurred during a severe spell of sickness. She was given up to die by her physician and family, having become so weak by prostration and illness that she could not turn herself on her weary bed. The preacher, Brother Townsend, called a company of devout persons together at her house, and held a prayer meeting there for her benefit.

Brother Thomas was present, and at a certain stage in the exercises proposed to sing a favorite hymn, during which, he said, he expected God to bless Sister Rowe, and give them all an evidence that she would recover. He then gave out, and sung with great pathos and fervor, the beautiful words :

> " How happy every child of grace,
>   Who knows his sins forgiven!
>   This earth, he cries, is not my place,
>   I seek my place in heaven.
>   A country far from mortal sight,
>   Yet oh ! by faith I see—
>   The land of rest, the saint's delight,
>   The heaven prepared for me."

This hymn he sung entire, adding to it a couple of disconnected stanzas, as follows :

> " To Father, Son, and Holy Ghost,
>   Who sweetly all agree,
>   To save a world of sinners lost,
>   Eternal glory be.
>
>   Oh ! what are all my sufferings here,
>   If, Lord, thou count me meet,
>   With that enraptured host t' appear,
>   And worship at thy feet!"

As the last lines were repeated, the expected blessing came, and filled the soul of the sick lady with "joy unspeakable, and full of glory." She clapped her hands in holy exultation, and all who were present participated in the happy experience she obtained. Next day she was greatly improved in strength, and in a very short time after that baptism, was out of bed, and able to attend her ordinary domestic duties.

The circumstance made such an impression on one of her sons, (Mr. Gabriel H. Rowe, then a small lad,) that he committed to memory the entire hymn, as sung by Father Thomas, and to this day remembers both it and the tune, and can vividly recall the whole scene of that remarkable night.

Another instance may be given, showing the power of prayer, and the ready, implicit faith of Brother Thomas.

When Rev. Z. Webster was a small lad, he had a very severe attack of illness, and was supposed to be at the point of death. His father, Brother Jacob Webster, already introduced to the reader as an intimate friend of David Wallace, in his day, and one of the oldest members of the Island church at present, was grievously troubled about the condition of his favorite child, and greatly longed for his recovery, if consistent with the Divine will. He had the utmost confidence in Brother Thomas, for whom he entertained an ardent affection; and in this emergency called upon him, as one who had power with God, to intercede for the boy, that he might be spared to his parents, and raised to usefulness in the church.

The Parson came with alacrity, and knelt down by the cot of the little sufferer, imploring God to interpose and save him. "It may be, Lord," he said, "that this child will choose thy ways, and walk in them. Oh spare him to be a blessing, and to do good." No immediate effect appeared, and a meeting was called, to be held in the little school house, where united supplication should be offered for the sick youth. The people assembled, the exercises progressed, and all who were called upon to pray referred to one special object—the sick child—in their petitions. At length Brother Thomas gave an exhortation, quoting certain promises, and showing the power that Jesus employed in the days of his sojourn on earth, to cure the sick, and even raise the dead. " Come, brethren," said he, " let us all have faith in this same Jesus, who is still ' strong to deliver, and mighty to save,' let us pray." He led in prayer, and made " Brother Webster's child," the great burden of his pleadings. He moved about the floor on his knees, wrestling with God, and settled down in one exclamation, "Lord cure the boy! Lord cure the boy!" Obtaining what he regarded as an answer, he leaped to his feet rejoicing, and expressed his confidence that prayer had been heard, and would be answered.

" Go home, Brother Jacob," said he, " your boy will recover." He came home, and found Zach. much better. The crisis had passed, and his health rapidly returned.

That little boy was, as has been intimated, converted in his youth, became a leader and exhorter, was in due time licensed to preach, and recommended by his brethren to the Philadelphia Annual Conference, to be received into the traveling connection.

He was received, and gave several years of earnest labor to the church, when he took a location and engaged in mercantile pursuits, preaching whenever and wherever called upon, and is at this day, all that was comprehended in the hopes and prayers of Brother Thomas, "a good useful man in the church," and a very zealous, and effective minister.

When the good old "father in Israel," Brother Thomas, died, Brother Webster by request preached his funeral sermon, an abstract of which will be found in this volume. His services are greatly in demand, and are always cheerfully given, in this department. He has attended as many funerals within the last ten or fifteen years, as any man that could be named, as he lives in the heart of a teeming population, remote from the residence of the circuit preachers, and enjoys withal the universal esteem and confidence of the community. This duty devolves upon him to such an extent, that we heard him declare a short time since in the pulpit,—when about to preach a funeral sermon,—he hardly knew where to turn in the Bible for an appropriate text which he had not already used on some similar occasion.

Through his almost unaided efforts, the time-honored church at Rock Creek is sustained in its financial and Sunday-school departments. The society there has dwindled considerably, since the erection of large and elegant churches on Deal's Island, and in Dames Quarter, which have drawn off the congregations that in former years crowded its walls, and enjoyed their chief Sabbath-day privileges, in its holy services.

Its present membership is not as zealous as they should be in attendance, and prayerful waiting on the Lord to secure spiritual prosperity and religious enlargements.

" Wilt thou not revive us again, that thy people may

rejoice in thee? Show us thy mercy and grant us thy salvation!" " *O Lord, revive thy work!*"

Before closing these memorials of Rock Creek and Brother Webster, a touching incident relating to his departed mother may be introduced. While he was off on his circuit when an itinerant preacher, she was called away to a better home. Before she died, they asked her, "Shall we send for Zachariah?" "No," she replied, "though I should love to see him before I go; it is not necessary, we shall meet in heaven; tell him to be faithful to God and the church, and I shall wait on the blest shore to hail him there among the saved."

The present wife of Brother Jacob Webster, who worthily fills the place of his former, and departed companion, is a daughter of the late Father Thomas, and was by him "picked out," as the most suitable for his friend.

She is a lady of great energy of character and devotion to God. On her memory, as sufficient authority, the writer relies for many incidents of, her honored parent's earlier life. He is also indebted to her for the gift of her father's old hymn book, from which numerous quotations are made as they were found, marked, and emphasised there.

To Mrs. Hester Webster, therefore, in the name of our readers, we tender respectful acknowledgments for her invaluable aid in the compilation of these memoir.

CHAPTER XVIII.

Brother Thomas ordained an Elder—Preaches in Baltimore—Rev. G. G. Cookman—William St. Church—Great sensation—Meeting at the house of Mr. Crouch—People happy—Rev. I. P. Cook at Deal's Island—Local Preachers—The Parson in Baltimore—The guest of Mr. Cook—A leaping blessing—Exhortation to the colored people—Jacob's sons—Corn in the land—" Godliness with contentment"—Poor prospect—God's blessing and a good harvest—" What he says is first rate"—Popularity in the city—A new overcoat—The prayer and its effects.

BROTHER THOMAS was recommended for Elder's orders, and ordained in 1835. His presence at the session of the Philadelphia Annual Conference that year, enabled many of the preachers who previously had heard of him, to form his acquaintance, and show him the respect to which his name, and valuable services in the church, entitled him. When his recommendation was read, and the vote was about being taken on his election, his good Presiding Elder had only to represent him as the man who preached on Tangier Island before the British army, and who was ever the devoted friend and helper of the preachers laboring in his vicinity, to secure for him a unanimous and hearty reception by the Conference. When called in to answer the usual questions propounded by the Presiding Bishop, as to his faith and obedience, with reference to doctrine and discipline, he appeared for the moment to be under considerable embarrassment, but put the brethren in great good humor by his simple and emphatic answer: "I don't understand as much about these matters as my beloved brother ministers here, but *as far as I know*, to the best of my ability I will conform to all the rules of the Methodist Church; *you may depend on it!*"

On his way to Philadelphia, he, in company with Rev. Thomas Summers, who was ordained a deacon the same year, had to pass through the City of Baltimore. To this place, his fame had preceded him, but he did not make himself known to any of the preachers or people, until circumstances brought him into prominence. The Baltimore Conference had just closed its session, and the ministers had not yet become settled in their stations.

The Rev. George G. Cookman had been announced to preach on the Sabbath Brother Thomas was in the city, at William St. Church. A great crowd had been attracted to hear this celebrated minister, Brothers Thomas and Summers, among others, repaired to the place, but Mr. Cookman did not reach the city, and the people were disappointed.

One of the official men of the church arose, and, after making explanations, and regretting the fact that they had no preacher, proceeded to announce a hymn and offer prayer. While he was offering his apology, Brother T. turned to his fellow traveler, and inquired, "Ought we let this good brother know that *we* are preachers?" Brother Summers modestly advised against this, as it might involve them in responsibility which they were not prepared to assume.

During the prayer, however, the soul of the "Parson" was fired up, and his responses became notable. To every petition he would say with earnestness "amen!" and at times would utter the word "glory!" and "hallelujah" in a very animated and emphatic way.

"Who is this old chap?" whispered one of the brethren in the ear of Brother Summers. "That is Joshua Thomas," replied he. "What!" said the other, "*Parson Thomas, from the Islands?*" "Yes," was the answer.

As soon as the prayer was ended, there was a hasty consultation, and the leading brother turned to the congregation, saying, "We are favored to-night with the presence of Brother Joshua Thomas, and another Local preacher; these brethren will please go into the pulpit and take charge of the meeting."

There was quite a flutter of excitement through the crowded house when it became known that Thomas was there. He regarded this unexpected turn of affairs as an opening of providence, and immediately ascended the pulpit, calling on his brother preacher to follow. This, the other was reluctant to do, but took a seat in the altar. After singing another hymn, Brother Thomas announced the text, "Ye must be born again," and, after telling the people, that he only rated himself as an exhorter, proceeded to give an able, and very interesting exposition of the doctrine of regeneration, and illustrated his points in his characteristic manner, ending with a shout; to the great delight and profit of his congregation. Brother

Summers then took part in the services, which were continued until a late hour.

A gentleman named Crouch—father of the Rev. C. J. Crouch of the Philadelphia Conference, took the strangers to his house on Light Street, and insisted on their making it their home. The door was besieged early next day by a large number of people who came to pay their respects to our Parson.

He proposed to "hold meeting" there, and did so the greater part of the day. The parlors were crowded, and the people wept under his artless eloquence, or joined him in shouting the praise of God. Some, it is said, were brought under conviction, and became the subjects of united prayer, until they were converted and made happy in a Saviour's love that day.

Before leaving the city he met with several of the preachers, and others whom he had previously known, and gave them all a pressing invitation to the Deal's Island camp meeting.

At that place, during the following years, he had the pleasure to meet many of them, and renew the fellowship and friendship which he had formed for these whole-souled brethren.

Among the visiting ministers at Deal's Island, on the occasion of a camp meeting in August, 1842, was the Rev. Isaac P. Cook, who became a great friend and favorite, of the Island preacher. His labors at this meeting were extensive and very successful, and the intercourse between him and Brother Thomas and others who occupied tents on the ground, was very intimate and pleasant.

As a local preacher, Brother T. was especially interested in him, since he was himself of that class ; and
shared the honor which he considered due to such
brethren, when they exceeded in pulpit power, or maintained equality, even, with the regular, or "traveling"
fraternity. His Baltimore preacher, he considered,
as do all who know the man, a credit to that noble
band, who form the "right arm" of the Itinerancy itself.

By invitation of Rev. I. P. Cook, Brother Thomas
visited Baltimore in 1842, and again, accompanied by
Mrs. Thomas, in the month of September 1844. During
these visits, he was the welcome guest of Mr. Cook and
his family, and received marked attention from both the
Methodist people, and the community generally.

The periods of his sojourn in that hospitable city, were
among the most pleasant recollections of his after life.
A number of incidents occurred in connection with his
social and public career, that will not only bear repeti-
tion, but will be found both interesting and instructive.

A number of ministers were invited to dine at the
house of the late Mr. Joseph T. Ford. In the course
of conversation, Brother Thomas inquired of a worthy
minister, since deceased, "Brother, did you ever 'leap'
while praising God ?"

The minister replied, "No, I never did."

Brother Thomas continued, "It is as much a gift of
God to 'leap,' as to weep, or shout in his service.. I
remember the first time the power of the Lord came on
me, in that manner. I was in my canoe, and earnestly
engaged with God in prayer, I asked that I might be

enabled to 'leap' and praise the Lord ; the power came in answer to prayer ; I sprang from the canoe, and in the water and mud near the shore, I leaped and glorified God." He then added, "Brother, you have never received a leaping blessing, because you have never exercised faith that God would give it to you."

Whatever doubt may be expressed of the propriety of his views concerning what he termed a "leaping blessing," no one who knew the man could doubt his sincerity in what he stated.

He accompanied his good friend Mr. Cook one Sabbath to the colored peoples' church, where he had an appointment. After sermon, Brother Thomas had the privilege to speak a few words, and delivered, as we are told, one of his most unique, and remarkably successful exhortations. He stated, in substance :

"There was a good old patriarch named Jacob ; he had twelve sons, but they did not all love each other. Ten of them took one, named Joseph, and sold him as a slave into Egypt. After a long time, a great famine arose, and his father and brothers were in want of food. A visit was made to Egypt by his brethren, to buy corn, and they obtained some, which lasted them awhile, but soon gave out. They had to go down there a second time, as the famine continued, and there was plenty of corn in Egypt ; and during this trip, Joseph made himself known to them. The old father and his family were sustained through the provision that had been made by Joseph, under the direction of God himself.

"Now," said Brother Thomas, "your fathers inhabited the same country ; they did not love each other, but engaged in wars, took prisoners, and then sold them as slaves.   Many were *thus* brought to this country, where they have found that there is *corn in the land*—the blessed religion of Jesus Christ.   But spiritual famine reigns in Africa your father land!   Your brethren are calling for bread!   The church of God is sending it out, but the famine is not abated.   You should aid not only in sending, but in *taking* the gospel of Christ to your benighted brethren ; for there is an abundance of corn in the land !

" Would you not rather labor, and dig, and toil, and enjoy the religion of Jesus Christ, than be where there is no corn ?"

The appeal was answered by a universal response and a scene of rejoicing, in which Brother Thomas participated, until he became weary.   He would then request them " to rest a while," when the same scenes were renewed, and much enjoyment seemed to prevail.

All who know the sensitivenesss of the colored population, on their relation to Africa, may clearly discover the delicacy of the position assumed by Brother T. ; but his evident piety, simplicity, and earnestness, bore down all opposition, and disarmed their resentment, while he won their respectful admiration.

He was with the same minister, (Brother Cook,) on another occasion, in one of the largest churches in the city.   Mr. C. preached a sermon founded on the text, " Godliness with contentment is great gain, for we brought nothing into this world, and it is certain we can carry nothing out."   1 Timothy, vi. 6, 7.

Brother Thomas followed in an exhortation, remarking, " It would be strange if the people of Baltimore were not contented, with such fine houses, furniture, and clothing, as you possess. If you lived where I do, and saw how the Islanders have to labor and toil, and suffer, to make their daily bread, you would be contented with your condition."

He then said, when God converted him he was very poor, without comfortable clothing, or even shoes to his feet! He worked a small patch of ground, in which he raised corn and vegetables. After his conversion he felt it to be his duty to visit his neighbors, and tell them what the Lord had done for him. This occupied much of his time, day after day, but he devoted the hours of night to labor, that he might not be a loser by his religious efforts, for the welfare of his neighbors. After one of his excursions, in visiting and praying with the people, he returned to his home, went out into his little field and engaged in working his corn. "It looked very unpromising, indeed," said he; "my adjoining neighbor was a man of the world, who gave little or no attention to religious things, and his corn was taller, greener, and gave promise of a far better yield than mine. Satan suggested this to my thoughts, 'If God loved you, as you suppose he does, he would take better care of your crop, while you are away exhorting your neighbors; look at that other field! see the great difference between your worldly neighbor and yourself; you had better stay at home and mind your own business.'

"My feet," said he, "had well nigh slipped, but I thought I would pray over it, and I knelt down beside one of my little corn hills, and called upon God. I told him in sincerity, that I was anxious about the souls of

the unconverted, and wanted them to seek Christ—that
I wished to devote myself to his blessed cause, and if I
was right, to bless me there.

"Well, the Lord poured down on my soul the most
abundant blessing I had ever received. I rejoiced in
the God of my salvation.

"In the midst of my rejoicing, I thought I heard a
voice saying to me, 'Joshua Thomas, do you want any
more corn?' I replied, 'Not another hill, Lord!!' and
before the time for gathering corn had come, my stalks
were just as high, and my crop was fully equal to, my
neighbors; and, you see, I exhorted the people nearly
every day besides." "Godliness with contentment is
great gain."

During these visits to Baltimore, he preached at
several churches, in, and adjacent to, the city. He also
delivered various exhortations, attended several official
meetings, and gave, on these occasions, interesting state-
ments concerning his awakening and conversion to God;
which produced a great desire on the part of the people
to see the venerable man, and receive his blessing.

A friend states that he was in the city about the time
Brother Thomas was there, and heard him talked of
everywhere. Two gentlemen met in the street and engaged in conversation. One inquired of the other:—
"Have you been to hear Mr. Thomas?"

"No," was the reply, "who is he?"

"An old gentleman from the Islands who is visiting
the churches and making people cry and laugh every
time he talks!"

"Ah! a preacher, is he?"

" Well, I am not sure that he is a preacher."

" One of their ' exhorters,' then, I reckon."

" Don't know about that; but, preacher, exhorter, or whatever he may be, I never listened to a more interesting man in my life."

" I must try and hear him too."

" Do, for what he says is *first rate !*"

It is said that even Mr. Maffit, then in the zenith of his popularity, could not attract a greater crowd in Baltimore than the "Parson of the Islands," who, in homespun dress and in simple language, told inquirers the " way of salvation," as he had learned it, when the Holy Spirit became his light, and guide, to the cross of Calvary.

The house of Rev. I. P. Cook, where he was being entertained, was frequently crowded, as that of Brother Crouch on his former interview with the people. Visitors poured in and kept him constantly employed in telling the wonderful works of the Lord to himself and his neighbors; repeating instances of conversion, and describing the early camp meetings and revivals, in the exercises of which he had participated.

Until his dying day he remembered, and conversed about that loving people who made so much of him, and conferred upon him, by their kindness, a weight of obligation which he tried to discharge in his usual way—by praying for them.

He retained a number of little presents, made to him on those occasions, and beguiled the solitude and weariness of his last days, by recalling the circumstances, and mentioning the names of his warm-hearted friends.

One of the most interesting, and affecting incidents of his sojourn, occurred just prior to his departure to his Island home. The circumstances are furnished by an eye witness of the whole proceeding, and are as follows:

"It was noticed by his host and a few others that the old gentleman needed an overcoat, and Mr. Cook took him to a clothing establishment, where he selected a suitable article, to keep him warm and comfortable during the approaching winter. Brother Thomas was asked if the coat would be of service to him, while conveying the ministers of Christ in his canoe to their preaching appointments.

He replied, he had not the means to pay for it.

The overcoat was ordered and sent to the store of Mr. Cook without his knowledge. The parson was then informed the coat was his property.

He answered, "No, I did not buy it." He was told that it was a gift of several friends who had contributed to purchase it for his comfort.

"What shall I do for those kind friends?" said he.

"Pray for them," was the answer.

"Well," said he, "let us pray now."

He was then in the public store, and was about kneeling; for it was immaterial to him where he prayed, so that he could pour out his full soul before the Lord; but Brother Cook stopped him, saying, "Not here; not in this public place; let us retire where the family are, and have them to join us."

All then repaired to a private room, where a scene took place, that never can be forgotten. They bowed in prayer, and Brother Thomas proceeded in something like the following language and order to say : "O Lord, thou hast been good to thy unworthy servant all his days. When he was a poor, miserable sinner, thou didst awaken and convert him for Christ's sake. O Lord, thou knowest how poor I was, when I was converted. I had but little clothing, no shoes to my feet, and scarcely bread to eat; but thou hast fed and clothed me, and given me many friends. All I have the religion of Christ has given me.

"Lord, thou knowest how greatly I needed warm clothing for the coming winter, that I might aid thy ministering servants in preaching the gospel, and doing good : and this morning thou knowest I counted my little money, to see if I could buy an overcoat for the winter, and thou knowest I could not do so.

"And now, Lord, these kind friends have supplied me with what I needed so much. Thou didst put it into their hearts to help thy poor old servant. O Lord, let these good brethren be clothed with salvation as with a garment; and may they never lack any good thing. They have asked thy servant to pray for them. It is all he can do. Lord! Lord! bless and save them for Christ's sake. Amen."

Tears and sobs were seen and heard throughout that company, and a share in the cost of that overcoat could not have been easily purchased, after the melting prayer was ended. It seemed to have been uttered in the very presence of God, and was answered as soon as offered.

"Years have passed away since that occasion, but the memory of that precious saint of God will not soon be forgotten. He was indeed a living example of the power

of Christ to save from sin, and to consecrate to holy purposes, even 'one talent,' in the vineyard of the Lord
of the whole church.

"Many far more elevated in society, educated, and talented; have done less, much less, for the cause of God
and humanity, than the simple hearted, honest, and
faithful Island exhorter, Joshua Thomas."

"Give my love to all my Baltimore friends," said
Father Thomas, a short time before his departure, to a
person from, and about to return to, that city.

"All!" was the rejoinder; "that would be next to an
impossibility; unless I put your kind message in the
papers, and have it announced in every Methodist
pulpit!"

"Well, do so," said he, "for I love everybody there!"

When, on the occasion of the Deal's Island camp
meeting, large numbers of what was called the "rowdy"
class, made excursions on the steamers chartered for that
purpose; and, by their restiveness on the Sabbath day,
gave trouble to the managers and order-loving citizens;
Father Thomas would plead: "Treat them well; bid them
all welcome; show a loving temper, and they will behave
right; and perhaps some of them may be converted
through our instrumentality."

CHAPTER XIX.

NANTICOKE POINT was another celebrated camp ground,
and Brother Thomas was always welcome, when permitted by his numerous engagements, to attend the services of the meeting there.

In the days of Lawrenson, these two notable men gave
celebrity to any occasion of worship where they were
present to participate, in preaching, exhortation, or social
intercourse.

At one of the camp meetings remembered in this locality, a number of preachers—traveling and local—had
assembled, and both these brethren were among them,
to take their share of responsibility and labor. A gentleman who resided in the neighborhood, and who took a
lively interest in all the meetings, but was not himself
religious, took great delight in the forcible and masterly

discourses of Mr. Lawrenson, and also in the quaint
exhortations of Brother Thomas. The latter was an
especial favorite with Captain ———, but for one or
two things in which he indulged, to the disparagement
of his character in the estimation of his friend; those
were, to repeat so often the story of his childhood's
poverty, and shout so much at camp meetings. "Why
don't you preach to us like the other ministers, Brother
Thomas? We would rather hear that, than have you
going over your anecdotes, or jumping about in the
pulpit," the Captain would say.

"Well," rejoined Brother T., "I do not know how to
preach like anybody but Joshua; but, to please you, I
will not do what you dislike, if I can possibly avoid it."

He entered the stand soon after, and commenced the
exercises of the morning prayer meeting, during the
progress of which, he delivered a very impressive exhortation, confining himself to one particular theme, at
the suggestion of his critical friend, who sat before him;
he alluded to the astonishing contrasts between time and
eternity, in relation to human character and the condition
of men.

"Could we penetrate that vail," said he, "which
hides the glory world from mortal sight, who, think you,
would we behold nearest the throne?" He looked, and
pointed upward for a moment, and then continued, as
if he saw a particular object—"Who is that yonder in
a shining robe, among the company of the 'blood be-
sprinkled bands,' with a form more lovely, a face more
joyful, and a song higher and holier in its strain, than
all the others there? See! Jesus smiles upon that spirit,

while it casts a jeweled crown before him! Who can it be?"

After a short pause, he turned his gaze from the blue arch of the heavens, slowly round toward the rear of the stand and—pointing his finger to one of the pious old colored persons, who, with flowing tears were listening to his talk about "glory," he said, "It may be some one who was a poor, neglected, suffering saint of God here on earth, like one of these! In this world of woe she had afflictions and persecutions, but she loved her Lord, and though often, it may be, was hungry and weary, she held fast to the hope set before her, believed the promises, and died well!

"Her sufferings in this present life were more than many others, and—understand—her joy is now greater, her song sweeter, and her mansion more glorious than some who did not live so faithful. The hymn tells us:

"Through great tribulation, my people I bring,
And the deeper their troubles, the sweeter they sing."

(This couplet was doubtless one of his own getting up, as he spent much of his own unoccupied time, when on the water, in re-arranging stanzas, to suit his own views.)

"What," he continued, "is the worth of a world, in comparison with yonder crown! What signifies it, colored people, if you are laughed at, and scorned, if you but learn the way to Jesus, and *He*, at the last 'great day,' shall say to you, 'Well done!' Be faithful; live holy; sing on:

" Give me Jesus, give me Jesus,
You may have all this world,
Give me Jesus."

This encouragement was appreciated by the poor
neglected ones, to whom it was addressed, and who are
too often slighted, or forgotten by the minister.   They
responded rapturously; " Yes, glory *be* to his name!"

"And now," he went on, with more stern emphasis
and an overcast brow—"Now, let me show you a picture
of the other place; for we are all traveling to heaven or
hell; to eternal salvation, or to 'everlasting fire!'   Look
at the lost!—there they are weeping and wailing, and—
Who is that?"   Here he made a rapid gesture with his
hand, while terror gleamed in his eye.   With finger
pointed he repeated, "Who is that?   I see one there
who in this world lived high, had plenty, owned horses,
and carriages, and farms—who attended camp meetings,
respected the preachers, was good to his neighbors, but
after all lost his soul!   There he is among ugly fiends,
himself as ugly as a *big black ram!*"

At this point, the people who were in a strain of eager,
and very serious thought, felt themselves irresistibly
impelled to laugh, and many eyes following the index
of the speaker's hand rested on one particular man, to
whom it pointed.   The man was Captain ——, the
friend of Brother Thomas, who in a moment began to
wince under the ludicrous comparison, and the startling
suspicion which flashed upon him—" *He means me!*"

No, he did not mean him.   It was a mere accident
that his finger pointed in that direction, but, without
thinking, or designing it, he drew an accurate portrait.

Nor was he responsible for the comparison that seemed so incongruous; he could not help it. He made people laugh and cry within one minute's time. His discourses were full of homely but striking comparisons, causing a smile to flash like a ray of light, over a thousand up-turned faces at once; but without losing his pathos, and that power over their sensibilities, which touched on keys he understood, and vibrated to weeping at his will.

He continued his description of the lost man, and so vividly pictured his misery and hopeless despair, in con-trast with a "fast" life and abundance of worldly com-forts; that, weeping himself over such a fall, he made others tremble, hold in abeyance their very breath, and let the tears spring unbidden from their "eyes unused to weep."

But, without his knowing it, that friend of his felt himself aggrieved, and in hot resentment left his seat and started for the "outskirts" of the camp.

Here he was rallied and joked by his boon compan-ions, until he threatened severe measures on the head of the unoffending man, whom in his petulance he char-acterized as "an ignorant old islander."

When Brother Thomas finished his exhortation, and the people were allowed a short interval before the 11 o'clock service, he ascertained the difficulty of which he had been the cause. To hear that his warm friend the captain was "out" with him, filled his meek soul with distress. He could not bear the thought of enmity against a living person, or rest, if others had ought against him. He was on the way to find the offended

hearer, and humbly apologize for what had given offence,
when he met Brother Lawrenson. "Never mind," said
the latter, "it will blow over. Don't go near him."
"Oh," said T., "I must go and make up. I would give
or do anything to regain his good will, and save his
soul."

"Well," said the other, "leave the matter to me. I
am going to preach this morning, and will make a suitable apology for you." To this he agreed, as Brother L.
insisted on the arrangement.

Before the congregation gathered, which was in a few
minutes, the subject was whispered round, and reached
the captain's ear. He was mollified considerably by
what he understood to be the consideration of Mr. Lawrenson for his wounded feelings, and invited all his
friends to come and hear the concession to his wounded
vanity, which he supposed the Elder was about to make
in a public and ostentatious manner.

The preacher commenced his exercises, and in due
time announced his text. It had been evidently suggested by the circumstances, and related to ministerial
fidelity and responsibility. It was one of his mightiest
efforts, and carried away the people in rapt admiration for his lofty genius and commanding eloquence.

There sat the "worldlings," whose pride had been
touched, and whose vanity craved a humiliating acknowledgment from the pulpit, that the good brother of the
morning was indiscreet, or presumptuous, in allusions
made, which, however remotely, referred to their vices
and sins, and told the truth as to the end of their careless career.

Lawrenson at length, in an indirect, but scathing rebuke, made the promised apology. He had referred to the adjustments of the "last day," when God's administration and man's accountability should appear in the light of the "great white Throne." "There," said he, "I must stand, and these my fellow laborers, to answer as to motive, word, and deed. No dissimulation there! No excuses for a time-serving, man-fearing, world-pleasing policy, can stand the scrutiny of the august Judge. We must speak the truth,—'declaring unto you the whole counsel of God;' and wo unto us, if we fail to 'warn the wicked,' neglect our duty, or lack in our own behalf personal holiness.

"And you, oh! ye godless men, how will you stand in the presence of that God you heedlessly forget, or madly spurn, in this your day of mercy?

"Here you carp and cavil about your honor, name, and character! Here you show a silly head as well as a depraved heart, when you imagine an insult, because we rush in your hellward path with messages of terror and gentle grace, to save you, if we may, from the curse and consequences of your sinful ways.

"You must have an apology to soften unwelcome truth, and degrade God's ministers into miserable time-servers! You would have us beg your pardon for preaching in your refined ears, the living word, which as a keen edged sword, I am glad to believe, has this day aroused the conscience within your breast, to feeling and to fear.

"No! no! we stand on an eminence too high, to come down to this! Whether you hear or forbear, bless or curse, believe or, doubting, go down to hell, we are not ashamed of the gospel!

"This controversy we throw on the Master 'whom we preach,' and who will settle it with you soon.   To that day we bind you over.   There we would appear—may Almighty God grant us to appear free from the blood of all men; free from blame in that we set 'life and death' before you this day; free, when the issues of this meeting are made known, from tampering with your souls, and by a craven spirit, unworthy those who stand on the watch towers of Zion, exhibit to the derision of devils a fear of man!

"No! no! our apology is, 'Repent or you shall perish;' believe or you will surely be damned."

Like the bursting of a bombshell, these red hot truths fell, and scattered dismay in the midst of our friends referred to, who, at the close of the sermon, beat a hasty retreat beyond the circle, admitting, and even admiring the worth of men who would not quail from duty to gratify their greatest friend.

Brother Thomas, during the sermon, and at its close, confessed his faith, and adherence to the principle of a firm and distinct utterance of truth, and discharge of duty, regardless of consequences; although he never could bring his mind into a patient indifference to the opinions and regard of his friends.

The sermon, a sketch of which has been attempted, made a deep impression.   It was so far, in severity, beyond the morning's subject, that Brother Thomas regained the respect and friendship of the enraged captain, who was now in a milder mood, and remarked, as he met the Presiding Elder, " Lawrenson, *you've swept me !*"

A neighbor of Brother Thomas', whom he highly esteemed, took umbrage once at something he said or did; and being of an unfortunately high and hasty temper, would admit of no overture for reconciliation. This grieved the good man exceedingly. He could neither eat nor sleep, so deeply was he troubled by day and by night, about this misunderstanding.

Hearing that his offended brother (old Captain Mister) was preparing to start for Baltimore in his vessel, he paddled up to where the schooner lay at anchor, and went on board. Captain M. rudely ordered him from the deck. He happened to be unusually cross at the moment. Brother Thomas meekly retired to his canoe which was alongside, and, with sadness and pain expressed on his face, remained there for some time in silence. At length the captain in a rough way asked him why he did not clear out, and told him he did not want to see him about there. Brother Thomas replied, " I cannot leave you in this way, brother ; you are bound on a voyage, and something may occur to prevent your return. This is an uncertain world, and yours is an uncertain life ! What if you should go to the bottom, and to the bar of your God in the spirit you now show, and with the feelings you bear against me. Would he justify you ? Or suppose I am removed by death, before your return, and leave you with this malice in your heart, to carry on with you to your grave ! Is this right for neighbors, and Christians ? Think a moment, dear brother."

It took the other but a moment, rough and petulant though he was, to see, and feel the force of this appeal. His breast heaved, his eyes became dim with gushing tears, and walking aft, he gave his hand in pledge of love, as a conquered man, to his Christian neighbor.

He stepped on board again, and ratified the act of reconciliation by kneeling down, and offering prayer and thanks to God while the other sobbed, and said "amen." They never had a misunderstanding afterwards, but were knit together in bonds of strong and mutual affection.

Brother Thomas was equally successful when called in to mediate between parties estranged by temporary difficulties, or when, as was generally the case, he volunteered to arbitrate cases and reconcile brethren who were divided in opinion or interest, until their respective families were not on terms of friendship. He had one protracted siege of this kind. Concessions were suggested, and carried between the parties, until one of them absolutely refused to negotiate any farther, and ordered the man of peace to desist from troubling him.

This was a sad turn of affairs, but did not discourage the soul of Brother Thomas. He prayed, and fasted before the Lord, over this perplexing case; and had a dream one night bearing upon it.

Early next morning he hastened to the obstinate party, and reached the house before the breakfast hour. He was asked to join the family at the morning meal, but said he could not partake until he had told his dream, and prayed with them ; to this arrangement consent was given, and during the narration of his singular dream and while engaged in prayer, the heart of his neighbor was touched. At first he felt ashamed of his uncompromising and selfish conduct, then began to mourn his sin before the Lord, then fell to weeping, and promising any and every concession, towards a speedy settlement of existing difficulties.

In this mood Brother Thomas left him, and forgetful of the waiting repast, ran at once across the fields for the other party, and returned bringing him along. They met, rushed into each other's arms, and became fast friends, while he went off in a great shout, during which they all became "high," and gave God the glory.

Instances of this kind illustrate the man's sincerity of heart, and show his value in such a community as that, which from its peculiar complexion afforded him ample scope for his benevolent interference, as the representative of a peaceful gospel, and a peace-promoting Saviour; among men, who, from the circumstances surrounding them, and the nature of their business, were often brought into competition and collision, unchecked by calm and sober reflection.

"What will become of us now?" said an old citizen of Deal's Island, and a remarkably wicked man, when the not unlooked for tidings of the old Parson's death ran like an electric thrill through the community. "What will become of us?"

"Why?" asked the person addressed. "In what respect?"

"Why!" said the other. "I fear we shall go to ruin!"

"Hope not," replied he. "What makes you think so?"

" I think so, because we are so bad and wicked, and
there is now nobody to pray for us as *he* did, and watch
over us with the anxiety of a father."

This man became deeply concerned, and, it was observed, for some time attended the house of God more
punctually than he had ever done before.

The religious history of the Island, since he first made
it his place of abode, until the present, would be a curious and correct illustration of the idea he occasionally
advanced with reference to the Devil's untiring contest,
to keep possession of that place originally called by his
name.

It was the first care of Brother Thomas to " pray
him off " the little Deal's Island, the place of his own
family residence.   He had a place in the tall sedge
grass, and a well-worn path leading to it, which he called
his " closet in the field."   There he spent many an hour,
pouring out his soul, and seeking help and success in his
humble endeavors to extend among his neighbors and
their children the fear of the Lord and a knowledge of
his name.

Whenever an impression would strike him to go and
pray, if at work in his field, or building a canoe at his
landing, he would drop his hoe, or leave his plough or
plane, and be off to the silent sanctuary, and there hidden from view wait upon God until he should renew his
strength.

He stated on one occasion, that he thought he had a call,
but could not determine with clearness whether it was the
Spirit's voice.   If it was, it came only in a " small, still"
accent, and he resolved to go anyhow.   He had not been

at this "Bethel" but a few moments until his soul was overflowed with Divine influence, and he concluded if God gave him such a great blessing, from a slight call, it was an encouraging token that obedience to louder and more distinct drawings that way would bring correspondingly increased enlargement of soul, and greater manifestations of saving and sanctifying power.

In this exercise, he believed Satan received notice to quit, and entrenched himself the more firmly on the larger island. But his fortifications were often assailed, and his citadel taken. Revival after revival has but barely sufficed to keep the Church in a state of grace. Of late years the annual camp meeting is comparatively barren of results in strengthening the Church or adding largely to its numbers. The excellent preaching is appreciated, but the necessary prayer-meetings, altar work, and individual zeal, are not attended or exhibited, to that extent, that will warrant success.

The immense influx of population, also, and the readiness with which money can be earned, has had a tendency of late, to sustain the usurper's sway, and encourage immorality among the young.

What the issue may be, as to the proprietorship of this place, whether it will be filled with righteousness or become an utter moral waste, will depend on God's Spirit poured out in answer to united, earnest, unwearied prayer, and a waking up to diligence in duty, by those on whom rests the responsibility; or, failing to secure a perpetuation of the Divine presence, and "given over" to backsliding, money getting, and selfishness; it will inevitably be the "Devil's" Island, at last, as it was nominally, at first.

It might be a paradise on earth, and will be, if the Church is faithful; but, if not, a forgotten God, a forsaken Saviour, will say, "Let him alone." Which, may God, in infinite mercy, forbid.

The writer would never have assumed such an undertaking as this, but that the devoted Thomas through such means might revisit every house, and speak to every heart, in this favored locality, words whereby sinners may be saved, and believers quickened in the race for eternal life, and be led nearer to God in holy living.

CHAPTER XX.

Severn Mister—An invalid Captain—Prayer on the road side—The day of miracles—Signal answer—Wonderful faith—Strange dream—Premonition —Three young men drowned—Grief for the lost—Bodies found—Funeral sermon—Rev. V. Smith—A delicate subject—Sympathy—Words of warning—Casualties among the watermen—" Be ye also ready."

SEVERN MISTER was a prominent and wealthy citizen of Deal's Island for many years, and was on very intimate terms with Father Thomas. Their friendship continued after Captain M. removed to the western shore of Virginia, where he settled in Northumberland County.

He was at one time involved in a protracted law suit, to recover property which he claimed from another, and the parson being acquainted with the case, was called upon to leave his home, cross the bay, and attend a session of the county court, as an important witness for his old friend.

In connection with this transaction, some of the most remarkable events in his history are found.

He was expecting a vessel to be sent over, to convey him to the court which was about to convene. It was in the month of March, 1843. The appointed day approached and no vessel came.

He had given his promise to be there, and as he never violated a promise, if within the range of possibility to fulfill it, he became very restive under these circumstances.

When he could wait no longer for the expected conveyance, he set about providing a passage on his own account; and one afternoon, started up the island to make inquries. He ascertained that there was a schooner in the harbor belonging to Captain P., which was at the time unemployed, and might be secured. Her captain, however, was at the time an invalid at home, and had been unable to attend to any business for some time. His complaint was something like a severe rheumatic affection, and confined him, in a crippled condition, to his fireside.

Weary of his confinement, he, with great effort, hobbled out on this particular day, as far as the public road, leading up the island, and sat down to rest a moment after his painful, though short journey. While there, Brother Thomas appeared in sight, hurrying towards him. As soon as he came up, he stated his business, which was, that Captain P. should have his vessel ready at an early hour next morning, and take him across to Northumberland.

"Can't do it," said Mr. P.

"I *must go*," said he, "I have engaged to be at my old Brother Mister's to-morrow. I know of no other way to get there. Now get ready, and let us start early."

"Why," said the other, "I am hardly able to return to my house, let alone—going across the bay."

"What is the matter with you, brother?" asked Brother T.

"Matter? I have severe pains in my back, and am almost helpless with rheumatism."

"Would you go to-morrow, if you felt clear of your pains, and in your usual good health?"

"That I would," said he.

"Very well," said the persevering man. "I will pray to God to cure you, and he will do it; for he knows I must keep my promise, and this is my only chance."

By this time, two or three of the neighbors had joined the party, and were interestedly listening to the dialogue.

The afflicted captain smiled at the proposal, and seemed incredulous as to the result of prayer. The others laughed at what they considered one of the old man's vagaries; but he sternly reproved their rising levity, telling them, he believed in the power of God to accomplish all things, and that *He* could in a moment cure his friend, the impotent captain.

They admitted this, but intimated that the day of miracles had ceased, and the "Son of man" was not now on earth, to work such a wonder.

"Let us try the power of prayer, right here," said Brother Thomas. "Come let us now call on the Lord in faith."

He immediately dropped on his knees, and the others could not well avoid following his example. There they were, on the public road side, feeling very much surprised as they, too, bowed in the attitude of supplication.

Their disposition to laugh at the position so unexpectedly assumed, was soon dissipated by the solemn tones of the man of prayer.

He began by rehearsing the nature of his business, the importance of the case, in which he was to appear as a witness, and the fact, that his God had never yet deserted him in extremity, or disappointed him in prayer. " Now, Lord," said he, here is poor Brother P—— with a severe backache, and he has suffered considerably from his pains. I have no other prospect of fulfilling my promise, as thou knowest, but in his immediate recovery. I believe in thy great power. I trust in thy good providence. Thou wilt not suffer me to violate my word, or fail to help in this time of need. Now grant to cure this thy crippled servant, that he may take me across the bay. Lord! thou art able; do the work, and I will go home and make ready to leave in the morning. Amen!"

Up he rose, and said to Captain P.: " Now go home and you will be all right in the morning. I will expect you at the landing, or meet you at the vessel. Be sure you are there."

The Captain was still incredulous, but promised, if he was well, to be on hand. Brother Thomas hurried back home, full of faith in his power with God. The other also returned, and weary with his walk, soon retired, and fell asleep.

At a very early hour next morning he awoke to consciousness, and the first distinct thoughts that entered his mind, were of the road side prayer, the faith of Brother Thomas, and his own promised recovery. With this, he turned himself over, and found to his astonishment the pain all gone!

After various stretchings and experiments, he could not doubt his complete and effectual cure; and remembered, in this connection, the promise he had given to be at his vessel at an early hour.

He called his good wife, and told her all the circumstances, proposing to her, as he had to cross the bay, to get ready, and take a trip with them. She arose and prepared to go, wondering not a little at this whole proceeding.

On reaching his vessel in the harbor, Captain P. found Parson Thomas *already on board!* There he stood, with a twinkle in his eye, indicating his entire satisfaction with the course of events so far, and certain ropes and sails all adjusted, and ready for a speedy departure. "I knew you would be well," said he, "and now you see what God can do."

They quickly made sail, and were under way down the Sound, with a stiff breeze, and a somewhat rough sea, from the effects of a severe blow, which occurred the day before. "Now be very careful," said Brother Thomas, "for something is surely going to happen, or has happened, in which we are deeply interested."

This admonition alarmed the captain, who inquired as to the reasons for what his passenger had just told him.

"I had a strange dream last night, brother," he said, "and it makes me fear some trouble ahead. I dreamed that I was upset in the water, and was trying to scramble up on a vessel's bottom, and that others were in distress around me. So, be careful."

This statement and warning made the captain waver in his purpose to proceed; until the other assured him, "It won't be us; you need not fear that. We shall be taken care of; but it is always wise and right to exercise caution."

In due time they arrived at their destination, and were warmly welcomed by Brother Mister and his family. The business on which they came over, was to be attended to next day; meantime inquiries were made about a vessel despatched the previous day, with Capt. Mister's three sons on board, to convey Brother Thomas from Deal's Island to Virginia. No such vessel had arrived there, or had been discerned on the bay, or in any of its harbors, that they had been able to identify. This intelligence awakened much concern in the minds of the family, and deep anxiety in that of Brother Thomas. He thought of his dream, and felt more alarm than he considered it prudent to express.

The case was viewed in every possible aspect. It was remarked that the boys went out in a gale, and were overtaken by a snow storm, which swept the bay the day before. It was remembered that they were hardy, adventurous, and thorough seamen, as far as disregard of danger, and a manly defiance of hardship was concerned. Some one added, that they crowded on all sail, and as they disappeared in the blinding snow storm, were seen to be making fearful headway over the surging waters.

These considerations gathered force, and gave strength

to the agonizing suspicion that they were lost! This dreadful thought made all the family intensely anxious. Old Brother Mister wrung his hands, and walked the floor all night, crying, "My sons! my sons! my noble boys are lost!—they are gone! gone!!"

It was a distressing night, but relieved somewhat by the prayers offered, as Brother Thomas assembled the family around its domestic altar; or uttered every word of probability and hope he could command, to relieve their dark uncertainty, and terrible forebodings.

The proceedings of the Court, however, admitted of no delay, and called off the attention of Brothers Thomas and Mister for a while from the subject that gave them so much agony. The trial came on, the case was decided in favor of Mister; but, though he had spent his energies and means for years to secure this desirable result, his victory was embittered by this greatest calamity of his life. He returned to his stricken home, only to find that all search had been fruitless, and no intelligence of the safety or fate of his sons had been gained.

One hope only remained. They might have been driven outside the Capes, and have boldly steered for the open sea. If so, they would run in again at the first favorable opportunity. Days and weeks passed away and they did not come. Every harbor was searched, and every source of information applied to, but still these young men were missing. Soon the last ray of hope expired in the tidings that the vessel had been seen bottom upwards in the bay.

In that raging storm, these three adventurous, promising, but, alas! irreligious young men, went down; and it might have been, and probably was; about the moment when, in the "visions of the night," Brother Thomas had a startling view of the mode by which they perished.

The event spread a sickening sense of bereavement over the hearts of that large circle of friends connected with the family, and shocked the entire community where those fine young men were known, up and down the waters of the Chesapeake.

The most intolerable thought connected with their sudden call into eternity was the fact that they had not been known as "on the Lord's side." This, in the brimming cup of their stricken father's grief, was the most bitter drop of all. Not merely lost to him and to society, but, as he would exclaim, "lost forever !"

He brooded over this until reason almost became unsettled on its throne, and existence itself, to him, was a burden. In his racked anxieties he would recall their childhood, review their youth, and linger over the traits of character which distinguished those sons.

He had taught them of God and heaven. He had led them to the house of prayer, and to the camp meeting, where they heard the invitations of redeeming love. A thousand times had he borne them to a throne of grace in prayer ; but, like those of Eli's house, they were restless under holy restraints, and willfully chose their own way. Now came the question, as they were suddenly cut off, was it "without remedy ?" When going down, they called on their father's God ; was it a fruitless cry, finding no response in that Being, whom *they* had not served in their youth? Had he "cast them off forever?" Or, did they find a long suffering Saviour, in the hour of their peril, and, like Peter, sinking, cast themselves on His power, which, "to the uttermost," can save ?

"May be so," whispered hope, as it tinged the dreary cloud with a gleam, and came to keep the hearts of those mourning parents from breaking under the pressure of their anguish.

In a short time one of the bodies was recovered, then another; and, almost simultaneously, the third was found by Brother Thomas and the circuit preacher on their way across from Holland's Island, after holding service there.

Side by side the remains of those three young men, Richard, Lowder, and David Mister, were buried, and over each, a stone erected, to tell the name, and record the date of that dark day in which they lost, with all its opening hopes and joys, their place among the living.

The occasion was suitably improved by a funeral sermon preached by the Rev. Vaughan Smith, from the text: " *Son of man, behold, I take away from thee the desire of thine eyes with a stroke !*" &c., Ezekiel xxiv. 16.

There was an immense crowd in attendance. The preacher felt all the delicacy and responsibility of his position; and avoiding, almost entirely, any allusion to the dead, except their sudden summons into the eternal state, where their spirits had met, and were in the hands of a just and merciful God; he pressed home upon the living the obvious lessons of such a startling event; and vindicated the Divine character, under whose omniscient control, all pervading power, and inscrutable will, rest the issues of life and death; leaving man to learn submission and wisdom; and, avoiding that presumption which would say unto God, " What doest thou ?" meekly bow and bless his name, in the faith which, unquestioning, exclaims, " It is the Lord, let him do what seemeth *him* right," and, " Good is the will of the Lord."

After the discourse was ended, the desolate and afflicted father made some remarks which indicated the depth of sorrow in his lacerated heart.

He unthinkingly reflected in some bitter words on the preacher, (who did not and could not, at that time, argue out the probabilities of his children's safety.) His poor, yearning spirit longed for light on this impenetrable problem; and, compassionating his affliction, the multitude dispersed in tears and sympathy, strongly impressed by the sermon they had listened to, and which, at this day, many can still distinctly recall, as a most judicious and timely effort under peculiar circumstances.

The impressible nature of Brother Thomas drank in the wormwood of his old friend's sorrow. He wept with him, and, to relieve the dark doubt that, like a poisoned arrow, embittered his life, he unwisely attempted to know, by an impression from the Lord, the fate and condition of those departed spirits.

This, we must say, was one of the mistakes of his charitable and impulsive nature. He fasted and waited in prayer for days,—musing, at intervals, on the ways of God, and setting in array the promises of his word, as a foundation for hope.

That salvation is possible at any moment this side the dread boundary of time—that some in the eleventh, or last hour, have been reached and redeemed; and that the God who keeps "mercy for thousands," and "will not that *any* should perish," *might have* interposed to save in the case under consideration, was all plain to his mind. Here he founded a hope, and clinging to it, was enabled by easy transition to believe and rejoice.

He therefore encouraged Brother Mister, who gratefully accepted the consolation offered him. But Brother Thomas ventured, in this case, on a realm which mortals are forbid to invade, and mooted a subject, vailed from human vision by the all-wise Deity.

Of this he was convinced subsequently by Mr. Smith, for whose ability he entertained the highest respect. His exposition of the question of human accountability and duty, with its appropriate scope and settled limitations, Brother Thomas accepted and ever afterwards remembered.

This whole matter would have been designedly overlooked by the writer, but for the reason that a revival of the harrowing memories of that event, may, and doubtless will, in this connection, prove a standing beacon to the many—oh! how many! who are pursuing the perilous life of a sailor, in jeopardy every hour, and yet, "having no hope, and without God in the world."

Sons of pious mothers and praying fathers! will you risk not only your own souls, but the terrible adventure in case of your untimely death—of filling their cup with blank, hopeless grief, to bring them down in sorrow to the grave?

A "chapter of accidents" might be compiled from the events of every year, in the vicinity for which, and of which these are written, revealing many a heart-saddening, and hopeless termination of life, by exposure to casualties, and too great a recklessness in danger.

The most gloomy feature of the record would be, not merely the homes left desolate and friends bereaved, or the anticipations which naturally wreath in bloom the future of enterprising youth, with prospective joy; but wicked lives, without a moment's warning, dashed out into a dread eternity; and souls, priceless beyond all comparison, sinking down forever without accepting the hope which a divine Saviour offers, in the day of gracious visitation.

Let the unconverted reader pause, and ponder the momentous subject of sudden death! "Let the wicked forsake his way, and the unrighteous man his thoughts; and let him return unto the Lord, and he will have mercy upon him; and to our God, for he will abundantly pardon."

> " Now God invites ; how blest the day !
> How sweet the gospel's charming sound !
> Come, sinner, haste—oh haste away !
> While yet a pardoning God is found."

CHAPTER XXI.

Range of travel—Camp Meeting visits—Impulse—"I am saved"—Sermon
on fashion—Rev. E. J. Way—The Devil's things—Love conquers—Fishing lines—Getting tangled—Satan's ways—Socrates—Rev. W. Quinn—
The School-house meeting—An enraged young man—His sudden death—
Presumption fatal—Danger of displeasing God—Stingy people—An ox
lost—The law of giving—Pay and pray—Good measure—Rockawalking
—Following the best light—Christian fellowship—No sects in heaven—
Opposition to revivals—Help one another—Attends church service—Makes
a " joyful noise"—Transcends prayer book proprieties.

THE range of Parson Thomas' travels and labors, during the years immediately preceding that affliction which
confined him to the limited sphere of the Island, was
quite extensive; embracing all the camp meetings
from Dorchester County, Md., to the eastern shore of
Virginia, and several places across the Chesapeake
Bay.

He so arranged his time in summer, that he could
visit six to eight, and sometimes ten, in the course of one
season, always allowing himself a full week at his own
Island meeting, where he was every year a tent-holder,
and an efficient manager.

His family tent stood next to that occupied by the
preachers, and his table never was without some of them

at the daily meals. The amount of labor and care he assumed, was extraordinary.

At the commencement of the meeting he settled disputes between the people about choice places for tents; while the meeting progressed, he included in his oversight the outsiders, among whom his mild manner was an effectual check to boisterous levity, or exciting debate; and the altar work, to which he always paid particular attention.

To visit neighboring meetings, after his own closed, was a great means of recruiting his wasted energies of body and mind, and enlarging his stock of experience, with regard to men and things. Traces of his journeyings are still distinct in nearly every neighborhood, within the extremes mentioned. We have only to refer to his name, to open the fountains of grateful memory, and gather the facts of his life, as they are reported by those who hung upon his strangely interesting ministry, at Witipquin, Nanticoke, and Rockawalking; Curtis' Chapel, Colbourn's Creek, and Accomac; and numerous other places more remote.

His movements were sometimes as rapid, and his manner as impressive as that of the eccentric Lorenzo Dow; though two men, in most respects, could not well be conceived more dissimilar in character.

When he arrived at a camp meeting, and was invited to preach, he would not positively consent, until he felt an impression, and received a text from the Lord. At Ebenezer, on a certain occasion, the preacher in charge assigned him an appointment; but he was undecided, until a few moments before entering the stand, as to whether it was his duty to preach at that time, and would not have attempted it, had he not obtained what he believed to be the concurrence of the Spirit, and a special subject of discourse.

So in exhortation. He obeyed the impulse, when *it came to him*, and at such times his word was with power. He had an impression one day while a minister was preaching, that his old friend, Rev. Henry White, must follow in exhortation. He told him to be ready; but Brother W. shook his head. Thomas insisted, and urged the matter so earnestly, that, rather than hurt his feelings, the good Elder yielded, and was most powerfully aided and blest while exhorting the people. It was one of the best and most effective efforts of this man of God. At its close Brother T. was happy, and remarked, " I thought he would come out right!"

When feebleness and pain unfitted him for active service, he still claimed the privilege to speak, when he felt moved to do so. "At a camp meeting on Deal's Island," says Rev. E. J. Way, "the old man was carried into the stand one morning, and heard a powerful discourse by Brother V. Smith from Jer. viii. 20. " The harvest is past, the summer is ended, and we are not saved." He remained quiet and thoughtful, during and after the discourse. Again, at afternoon service he was present; and while one of the brethren was preaching, he intimated that at the close, if he was to be allowed, or expected to say anything at that meeting, he felt this to be the time. When the preacher finished, he was assisted to stand up, and leaning over the Bible-board, he surveyed the congregation for a moment; then, without any allusion to the subject just presented, he seemed to recall the text and sermon of Brother Smith that preceded it, and in a tremulous voice began to say :

"Friends and brethren, you see here a poor, feeble, broken down man. My harvest is very nearly past ; my summer is almost gone ! The brighter days of my youth and strength have fled ; the evening of weakness and weariness has come ; my opportunities have been many, but they are getting few ; my sun will soon go down ; I am hastening to the grave—but, hallelujah ! *I am* SAVED !"

That was enough. The word took hold, and a thrill ran over the people, that affected some to weeping, others to unbounded joy, and all with a sense of the "unction of the Holy One." God was in it.

Brother Way relates, among other incidents, an interview he had with Brother T. when he was but young in the itinerancy. He had preached a sermon on the evil tendencies of fashion, and was very pointed and severe on the inconsistencies of professors generally. He showed the absurdity of that taste which seeks gratification in tinsel baubles, and fantastic apparel. When he met Brother Thomas in the preachers' tent, a short time afterwards, the good man took him aside, and said, " Brother, if you want to get sinners converted, let the devil's things alone. Don't make his people mad by ridiculing their follies, or they will not love you, nor can you persuade them to come to the altar. The way I do, is to get these poor creatures converted, and made happy in religion, before I raise a quarrel with them and their cunning old master. The best way to loose his hold, and ous him from their vain hearts, is to show them what is so much better than all *his* pleasures—the love of Jesus."

He also told a little "circumstance," which proved conclusively his point : " I was talking to a mourner," said he, " and there came near the bench one of these young butterflies, to watch the weeping penitent. She had ear-bobs, finger rings, flowers, and finery, without stint. Now if I had begun to tell her to take off her rings, and throw away her jewelry, she would have said, '*I wont !*' I knew this and said not a word against the devil's things; but reached out and took hold of her hand. I said, 'Daughter, do you love Jesus?' her countenance fell. I then said ; 'If you do not, oh ! what a pity it is, for he loves you, and died on the cross to redeem you from sin and hell.' At this she burst out crying. 'Come,' said I, 'give your poor heart to God to-day ! Seek him while he may be found ;' and, brother, down she fell by the side of the other mourner, and was soon converted; then she loved these things no longer. Her heart was set on Jesus."

When Rev. L. (now Bishop Scott) was Presiding Elder on the Peninsula, Brother Thomas was frequently at the places where he preached, and occasionally exhorted after him. Once at a camp meeting the Bishop delivered one of his very clear, convincing, and effective discourses. It evidently made the Island preacher feel his own little-ness in comparison. "But," said he, rising to speak, " there must needs be great preachers, and small fry, like our fishing lines down yonder on the islands. Some are great long ones, and some are little short ones. I once went out with a neighbor to fish; he had one of those big lines, and would swing it and throw it (suiting the action) away off yonder. I had a short line, and dropped it out near the canoe, and I caught as many fish as he did! His line would sometimes become *tangled* and his fish escape, but I had no trouble in pulling them in. So with preachers and exhorters; the great point is to catch the fish; and, brethren, if some of us cannot throw out as long a line as others, let us not be discouraged; for, if we are faithful and holy, our Master will bless our labors, and give us souls for our hire."

"That he will," said the good Bishop, who enjoyed the illustration greatly.

At another time the same preacher officiated, and at the close Brother Thomas remarked, "Friends, our good Brother Scott has told you much about the ways of the Lord: let me finish by telling you something of the ways of the devil! It seems to me we ought not to be 'ignorant of his devices,' but well posted, and completely fortified against our common enemy." He gave the people several illustrations of the power, malignity, and ceaseless influence of this "deceiver," and closed by quoting the stanza:

> " Leave no unguarded place;
>   No weakness of the soul;
> Take every virtue, every grace.
>   And fortify the whole."

Still another anecdote of his intimacy with our excellent Bishop, is current in Annamessex.

The sermon embraced the subject of Saul's journey to

Damascus, and when the preacher referred to the wonderful light which appeared, he said he was not sure whether it was outside and around him, or within him,—"Both, brother!" said Mr. Thomas. "Yes," said he, "very likely, brother, you are right!"

A remark he once made while listening to a sermon from Rev. W. Quinn, is remembered, and often repeated. Brother Quinn was preaching on the hope and assurance of believers, and quoted the words of Socrates, when his friends were leaving him to die: "You are going to your friends, and I am going to die: which is best, the gods only know: no man does." "Bless God, brother," said he, "I know more than he did! I can say, 'For me to die is gain.'"

He and Brother Quinn were intimate for many years, and were often brought by circumstances together. They were returning one night in company from a camp meeting, which was held at Wesleyville, beyond Snow Hill, and found themselves somewhat bewildered in the matter of a stopping place, as it had become quite dark. They drove on, however, until they came upon a light, and ascertained that they were at a school house, where a prayer meeting was about being held. They determined to remain for the meeting, Brother Thomas remarking that "perhaps God had something for them to do there."

The people, having ascertained who they were, invited them to conduct the meeting. Brother Quinn preached an awakening sermon. Thomas followed with an invitation to persons present, who might be under concern about their salvation, to come forward for prayer.

A bench was provided, and several bowed there as

penitent inquirers; among them a young lady who was much engaged, until interrupted by her brother, who came up rudely to take her away. Brother Thomas talked very kindly to him, and tried to persuade him to desist from the course he was pursuing. No, he considered it to be humiliating and disgraceful for his sister to be at a mourners' bench, and with vile words he ordered her to leave. "Young man," said Brother Thomas, "you are acting wrong in this matter. Take care how you displease Almighty God; for he could kill you and send you into eternity in less than three weeks." The young man appeared to be reckless of consequences, and paid no attention to the admonition.

In less than one week after this time, that young man was cut off from among the living. He had gone to his home in a rage, boasted of his prowess in withstanding the preacher, and moved on in his prayerless condition; until, in a few days, he was out in the woods cutting timber, and a tree fell on him and killed him.

This startling event, when viewed in connection with his conduct at the meeting, and the warning of the good man, who tried to persuade him to "cease to do evil," created a great sensation in the neighborhood. It was conjectured by many that Brother Thomas was in some indirect way accessory to this visitation, from the fact that he merely stated a possibility, remembering the predicted fate of all who harden their neck—that they shall "suddenly be destroyed, and that without remedy."

A number of instances might be given, where, in the workings of Divine providence, those who crossed his way, or spurned his message, were made to remember it with deep regret. Before his death, he stated to a preacher that he had become afraid, almost, to ask a favor for himself or his God—in the form of contributions to the cause of religion or obedience of heart and life to the Divine will—and be refused; for in many cases he had seen the interposition of that hand that shapes the ends of men; vindicating the claims of God to all that human beings held, and called their own.

He could point to cases, where persons, made aware of a brother's need, or solicited for aid to some religious enterprise, had closed their ears and their pockets to the call; had met with calamity or loss—sweeping away from their selfish grasp a hundred fold more than the amount solicited. He knew from observation and experience that the Bible rule was safe and right. "There is that which scattereth and yet increaseth, and that which withholdeth and it tendeth to poverty," and also, "He that soweth sparingly, shall reap also sparingly."

"You had better pay what you owe the Lord," he would say, "or he will have it out of you in some way."

A man on one occasion had been solicited by him for a contribution to the missionary cause, and refused to give. He was urged by every consideration, but believed what he had was his own, and laughed at the foolishness, as he termed it, of those who "threw away" their money for such purposes. On returning from the meeting he found a valuable ox drowned in a ditch! "There now," —he was forced to admit. "Old Thomas was right. Had I given a dollar, I might have saved my ox, and not lost *twenty* by his death!"

He pictured various ways in which stingy Christians,

by placing themselves in array against the mandate
" Give," should find out their mistake and meet with unlooked for loss.   He said *he* never lost by his labors, and
time, given to the service of his heavenly Master, and
believed it to be as much the duty of men to *pay*, as it
was to *pray;* for praying is dull work and very often
fruitless, unless we have a heart to "praise" as well, for
the rich blessings of God's mercy and love.   " Give and
it shall be given you, good measure pressed down, shaken
together, running over !''

An exhortation he delivered at Rockawalking, many
years ago, is often referred to by those who were present
on the occasion.   He was discoursing about the different
denominations, and their relation to the general Church
of Christ.   "Not one branch of the true Vine," said he,
"but brings forth *some* good fruit.   I love all the people
who love my God in sincerity ; but I love the Methodists
a little more than any other.

" The reason of this I will show you.   I always tried
to follow the *best light*, wherever it could be found.

"When I grew up, the best light I had was the good
old prayer book, and I followed it, trying to conform to
its devotional requirements.   Then the Baptists came
along, and I heard them preach with more earnestness
and spirituality, and pray with more directness, than the
church preachers; I tried to obtain some of their light,
and it helped me on.   But when I became acquainted
with the Methodist people, I was convinced they had the
best and most, both of light and power; for under their
influence, the Holy Spirit reached me, the scales fell
from my eyes.   I first saw men as trees walking, but

soon the glorious Sun of Righteousness shone upon my heart, and that light was 'marvelous' and glorious!

" Now if I knew any better light, I would forsake all, and follow it; for we are advised to ' prove all things, hold fast that which is good.'

" But I think I cannot hear more sound saving doctrine, than you preach, brethren; nor do I wish any higher privileges than you afford me—I wish our people lived up to them better. No brighter, happier day, do I expect to share, than a good day at a Methodist camp meeting where the people are alive, and God is worshiped in the ' beauty of holiness'—until I reach the City above, and walk the golden streets.

" In that place, however, we shall drop these names, and all be one glorified company of sinners redeemed through the precious blood of Jesus.

> " Names, and sects, and parties fall;
> Only Christ is all in all!"

" Now, understand, I hope to meet people there out of every profession and place in all this world; and while here, I want my good Presbyterian and Episcopal brethren to help me, and to let me help them, and we will both get along the better by doing so. I am sorry that some of these nice people who come to our meetings stand off, and do not approve of the altar work, or shouting ' Glory' when we are happy. Why, it is this very sort of work that is keeping them, as well as ourselves, alive in religion. Were it not for these camp meetings, and good old-fashioned revivals, both your churches and ours would soon go down, or go back to the dry and barren days, which, we are told, prevailed in this country before the Methodists were known.

" Come then, friends, when you warm yourselves, and light your lamps at our fire, do not be so unmerciful on us, as to go away and call it ' wildfire !' You know better than that, for most of you, that have any religion, can remember where you first found it. Yes, right at our 'mourners' benches,' and at such meetings as this, you sought and found mercy. Let us then be friendly on earth, if we hope for heaven ; for our Lord won't allow any bigotry there."

He surprised the people at this same place once by abruptly appearing on the ground, after he had bid them farewell, and was supposed to be on his way home.

A lady, hearing that he was at the meeting, and wishing to see him, left home early one morning, and on the way to camp, met him near the ferry,—on his way to where he had left his canoe. He generally timed his departures to suit the tides.

This lady reached the meeting, and in due time took her seat in the congregation, regretting that she had missed seeing Brother Thomas. To her surprise he was the first person she saw entering the stand. He told the people, when he reached his canoe, it came to him, to return, and wait another tide, as he had some things to say which had been forgotten in his previous exhortations.

He happened into the " good old church," in the ways of which he had been brought up, on a certain occasion, some time after his conversion, and took his seat in the gallery. During the reading of the service, he startled the parson and congregation by his loud "Amens," and a frequent utterance of "Glory!" at places where the book did not say so. The worshipers looked hard towards the corner where he was, but he seemed oblivious to the proprieties which they thought desirable, and could not restrain a full heart from expression, as the beautiful and impressive prayers and psalms were said and sung. He obeyed to the letter that part of the prayer book which invited him to "make a joyful noise unto God," and "bless his name"—making "the voice of his praise to be *heard*" among the people!

CHAPTER XXII.

Letter from Rev. R. E. Kemp—First acquaintance with Joshua Thomas—
Bishop Emory—Rev. Wm. Evans—Ross' Woods Camp Meeting—Ebenezer—Rev. Wm. Spry—Serving God at home—Reminiscenes — Afflictions of the righteous—House burned—A "God send"—Truthfulness—
He prays for wind—Shouts on the shore—Politics—Habits of prayer—
Wm. Rea, Esq.—Stolen money restored—Last visit to the Island—Sacramental occasion—Lines to his memory.

REV. ROBERT E. KEMP writes the following sketch:—
The name and fame of Joshua Thomas had reached
my ears long before I was permitted to see the man and
enjoy his acquaintance. I counted it as one of the anticipated pleasures of my itinerant life to be permitted in
the course of providence to witness the zeal, piety, and
great devotedness to God, which, from what I had heard
of him, I was persuaded he eminently exhibited in his
life and labors, in the cause of the Redeemer.

The first time we met was during the Session of the
Philadelphia Conference, at Philadelphia, in the spring
of 1835. He came up that year for Elders' Orders, on
a recommendation from Princess Anne Circuit, within
the bounds of which he lived. The same year I was
thought by my brethren eligible to that order in the
church, and side by side with this good man of God, I

stood before Bishop Emory, and was duly ordained by the imposition of hands, after a sermon by the Rev. Dr. Holdich. I have always regarded it as a privilege to have been set apart for this office in company with the apostolic Joshua Thomas, and by that prince of Bishops, John Emory.

Our intercourse at the conference was limited, and I was not much in his company until several years afterwards.

In the summer of 1842, we met again at a camp meeting at Ross' Woods, near Seaford, Del., where we became more intimately acquainted. He came to the meeting in company with Brother Wm. Evans of Smith's Island, a man greatly beloved for his work's sake, who accompanied him on many a tour to distant places to advance the cause of the Master whom they served, and exhort sinners to embrace the free salvation of the gospel. The souls of these men were as the souls of David and Jonathan.

At the meeting referred to, their united labors were much blessed of the Lord, and many are yet living in that vicinity who have not ceased to remember their "holy conversation and godliness."

When the time came for their departure, Brother Taylor, who had charge of the meeting, requested them to give the congregation a parting address at the morning prayer-meeting. The Divine word informs us that " as iron sharpeneth iron, so does the countenance of a man his friend," and this was abundantly verified on this occasion. The people were edified and greatly quickened while these simple-hearted men exhorted them to a holy life, and took the parting hand in pledge to meet again, where parting should be no more. As they ministered in spiritual things to us, the generous people showered upon them temporal things, to bless their basket and their store, and showed by their tears and prayers for them, that they had a warm place in their hearts.

Being appointed the next year to Cambridge Circuit with that truly devoted servant of God, Rev. Wm. Spry, we had again the pleasure of meeting Brother Thomas, who came to camp meeting, bringing his brethren, Wm. Evans and J. Parks, with him to aid in the work. It was truly a time of refreshing from the presence of the Lord, as these faithful laborers toiled in the stand, at the altar, and in the tents; preaching, exhorting, praying, and talking about the religion of Christ, which in rich measure they themselves enjoyed.

On leaving the ground they were accompanied to the shore by a great number of the people, and before they set sail we all joined in prayer, committing and commending them to the watchful providence of that God who had directed their course to the meeting and made them a blessing to many.

It was on this occasion I first saw Brother Thomas' far-famed canoe, "The Methodist," in which he had made so many voyages to carry the glad tidings of salvation to distant places on the shores and islands of the Chesapeake, and to many points in Virginia, Maryland, and Delaware, where his visits and ministrations were always held in the highest esteem by both preachers and people.

In this canoe, also, did he carry or send the ministers laboring on Princess Anne Circuit to their appointments on Smith's and Holland's Islands, and none who have had the happiness to be in his company on these trips could forget his conversation, or feel the time irksome while he was in their company. Many of those who were delighted passengers in the "Methodist" have now with him gained the port of peace, and are rejoicing in the light of the Lamb which is in the midst of the throne.

A singular incident occurred at the Ebenezer camp meeting of the previous year, which shows the simplicity and earnestness of Brother Thomas' religious character. He had heard much of Brother Spry, and greatly longed to meet with him. Here they became acquainted, and their spirits blended in sweet sympathy while they labored in prayer for the conversion of souls.

He watched Brother Spry very closely, and, although he thought no man living had greater cause to love God than himself, or tried to love him better, yet it was impressed on his mind that good Brother Spry really did excel him in this grace. He had been invited to dine with Brother C——, who, when the dinner-hour arrived, went in search of his guest, to bring him to his tent. After a long search he found him alone on his knees weeping. "Come," said Brother C., "dinner is waiting, and I have been looking for you to come and dine according to engagement." "No, brother," was Mr. T.'s reply. "I cannot dine with you to-day. I do not wish to eat. I am in affliction, and you must excuse me. I have thought there was none on earth that loved my Lord more than I did; but this I find is not the case. I have been watching Brother Spry, and I am convinced he has greater love for my blessed Jesus than I have—and I cannot eat until I obtain more of the love of God shed abroad in my heart."

How few do we find thus exercised in a holy rivalry to love and good works! How many are content with that measure of religious enjoyment that barely prevents the apprehension of being lost, and may avail them to enter at last into the kingdom; or are trying to see how *little* religion will save them from sin here, and wrath hereafter!

This was not the case with Brother Thomas, he ardently desired to love the Lord his God with all his heart, mind, soul, and strength; and in the fullest sense his neighbor as himself. He did not wish any to excel him in this character. There were but few indeed that did. If the general church of Christ was composed of such fervent and faithful Christians, how soon would she " come up out of the wilderness, clear as the sun; fair as the moon; and terrible as an army with banners," spreading life and light around, until the world would be speedily converted to God.

Both the sainted Spry and the devoted Thomas have finished their work—fought their last battle, and have gone up to see the King in his beauty. Oh that their mantle may fall on those left behind!

During the summer of 1844, I again met with Brother Thomas, who, with J. Parks, paid his last visit to old Ebenezer. Infirmity had begun its work on his active limbs and robust frame. His exposure to cold and rain had brought on rheumatism, and greatly impaired his activity. But he could say with the man after God's own heart—"My heart and my flesh faileth, but thou art the strength of my heart and my portion for ever."

He took a final leave of the brethren of Cambridge Circuit at this camp meeting, and many were deeply affected, as he left the ground.   I took him in my carriage to the shore where his canoe was in waiting, and after receiving his blessing saw him depart to his own home.

Many from the old Ebenezer camp meetings, will rise up and call him blessed in the great day of eternity.

At the Conference of 1849, I was appointed to Princess Anne Circuit, with Rev. Wm. Rink as my colleague, and on reaching this field of labor, made my arrangements to pay Deal's Island an early visit, that I might see Father Thomas at his own home, and renew the pleasant intercourse of former years with him there. After preaching on Sabbath morning at Rock Creek, and Deal's Island in the afternoon, I crossed the " thoroughfare," which separates the little from the larger Island, early next morning, and had the pleasure of spending the entire day with him, before starting across the Sound to fill my appointments on Smith's Island.   I found him seated in his large arm chair, to which he had been confined for some time : the Holy Book his companion, and his excellent wife, and affectionate sons ready to minister to him in every thing that tended to his comfort.

My visit that day—and whenever subsequently I could spend a while under his roof—was a time of great spiritual refreshing and encouragement.

It is said, to know a man perfectly, you must live with him at the fireside, and be acquainted with his most private life. None could form a less favorable opinion of Father Thomas, by residing under his roof, and witnessing his daily and hourly devotion. I could not but be reminded of one of his own shrewd remarks, " If you can serve God at home, you can serve him anywhere;" during my two years as his pastor, he emphatically *served God at home.*

His conversation was chiefly of a religious kind, and often turned on his youthful days, which he said were spent in great ignorance on the subject of true religion. He and his neighbors, though attentive to the teachings of the church, thought it not wrong to participate in the vain and sinful amusements of that day, such as dancing and frolicking.

He remembered no real conviction for sin in his own mind, or among his neighbors, until brought in contact with Methodism. He referred to a meeting which he attended as a careless spectator, or prejudiced opposer of the work of the Lord, and dates his first serious impressions from what he then and there observed. The Holy Spirit came upon the people in mighty effusion; many ran away, leaping out at the windows in their alarm. He was also inclined to run, but looking around to see who had fled, and who remained, he noticed that the best of the people staid under the influence, and the worst had run away. This moved him to remain among the praying ones.

He related the impressions made on his mind at the first camp meetings he attended, and the novel and won-

derful scenes witnessed then. His own conversion was
an untiring theme with him; also the rise and spread of
religion on the islands among his neighbors and friends.

The attempt you are making, my respected and much
beloved brother Wallace, to portray those scenes of revival in which he bore so prominent a part, is a worthy
one, and will be owned of God, in stirring up many who
may have grown lukewarm, to greater zeal and diligence.

All his own children, and many of his grand-children
have been converted and gathered into that church he
loved, and which honored him, as far as was possible, in
its confidence and affection. May the generations of
his posterity be useful and faithful, and walk in his foot-
steps, as he "walked with God."

The remarkable incidents of his life that I have heard
from his own lips, would make a thrilling volume—how
God provided for him in his poverty, defended him in
danger, blessed him in prayer, and hundreds of times,
as he verily believed, made even the elements and the
laws of the natural world subservient to the safety and
success of his humble servant.

It is beyond all doubt, that the Divine hand was in a
very signal manner with him. Such results, as no calculating, worldly mind could expect, were gained by his
pleadings at the throne of heavenly grace.

He delighted to speak of the ministers whom he had
known, from Dr. Chandler down to modern times, and
had his mind stored with many an anecdote about them,
and the texts and sermons he heard from their lips.

Chief among all the worthy names he cherished, was
that of Brother Lawrenson, who was instrumental in

bringing him into the public work of the ministry, and instructing him in the doctrines of the Bible, and the ways of religion. He could talk for hours of his travels and labors with this extensively useful minister.

Brother Thomas valued camp meetings as being the chief means of grace. To his instrumentality belongs the credit of originating them on Tangier, and also on Deal's Island. At the former place he persisted in holding them, sometimes even against the wishes of the officiary of the circuit, and by the Divine blessing, his views were sustained and owned of God in doing great good.

I heard him deliver the last sermon he ever preached at Deal's Island camp meeting, in August, 1850. He was seated in a small carriage, and very feeble in body, but roused the people as of old, by his pathetic appeals.

To his instrumentality in a great measure, also, may be attributed the erection of the church on Deal's Island. He so loved the house of God and the tented grove, that he desired to be interred near the new church and camp ground. This desire was fulfilled, and there sleeps his dust "till God shall bid it rise."

To him and his friends it would have been a dark and inexplicable mystery why he was so greatly afflicted in body, had it not been placed on record. "Whom the Lord loveth he chasteneth, and scourgeth every son whom he receiveth."

In various ways was his cup mingled with disappointment and bitterness. Soon after he moved to his new home on Deal's Island, and had comfortably settled him-

self and family, one of his out-buildings caught fire, and
with it was consumed all the provision he had on hand.
If he did not take joyfully this spoiling of his goods, he
at least took it patiently, and could say, "Shall I receive good at the hand of the Lord, and not evil? The
Lord gave, and the Lord hath taken away, blessed be
the name of the Lord."

Through the kindness and liberality of his friends, his
loss was mostly made up to him, and another house
erected in the place of the one consumed.

Soon after this event, having an errand to the western
shore of Virginia, he started in his canoe, and called up
at Smith's Island for his fellow-laborer, Rev. Wm. Evans.
While at dinner, the wind hauled round so as to be ahead
when they made sail. The course they had to steer
brought them in contact with a number of barrels of
flour afloat in the bay, which had been washed off the
deck of some vessel in a recent gale.

They viewed this as a God-send, and secured about a
dozen barrels which were found to be but slightly dam-
aged when brought home.

They could have secured a number more, only for the
fact that he was already loaded with sweet potatoes,
which he was carrying to a friend to whom he had promised them; and would not break his word, or throw
them overboard for the more valuable freight which fell
in his way.

He that sweareth to his own hurt, and changeth not,
hath the promise of abiding in God's tabernacle, and
dwelling in his holy hill; and Brother Thomas lived with
an eye single to this thing.

His love of truth, and character for integrity, was one of his distinguishing traits. Unable to write, so as to sign a note or bond, he made his word always binding, and in no known instance failed to make the promise, " I'll do it, my brother," good to the letter.

On one occasion he had been out on a fishing excursion, for this was one of the chief means of his family's support. He had promised to call at a certain place for a person who wished to come back to the island with him. He had been very successful in his fishing, and in his canoe lay a fine lot of large fish. The day promised to be very hot, and any delay in getting home would be likely to spoil his cargo; but having given his word, even casually, he would not for all the fish in the ocean break it, or disappoint a person who had expected at his hands a favor. The result was, that while he tacked in, to take the person on board, the breeze freshened up, and enabled him to make a rapid run home. " Godliness is profitable to all things."

Being on another fishing excursion, and with every prospect of a dead calm—he found himself unequal to the task of rowing—or pulling his large craft, so great was the distance—and, if he delayed, his fine supply of fish would become tainted and spoiled. He had recourse to prayer, remembering that He who sent rain to the prophet was the same, and could send wind across the glassy waters to his relief. After prayer he unfurled his sails, and no sooner had he spread his canvas to the breeze than it came—first as a " cat's paw" across the surface of the deep, and then a delightful breeze before which his canoe soon sped to the distant shore. Why

should we be sceptical on such a subject as this? Has
the Lord not said, "Ask *what ye will* in my name, and
it shall be given?" And does not the "wind and the
seas" still "obey his voice?" Is it too much for His
almighty power, who holds the winds in his fist and
makes the clouds his chariot, to send a breeze in answer
to prayer? "Not too much," some would say, "but
too little a thing to suppose God would concern himself
about."

A mistake, my friend—nothing is too little to be beneath his notice, or too great to baffle his infinite skill.
" Are not the very hairs of your head all numbered?"

Another of his fishing incidents may be given here.
Returning home with a fine mess one day, for it was
rarely his misfortune to toil and catch nothing—he
reached his landing and fastened his canoe to its accustomed stake, and on surveying the silvery heap of
fine trout, mullet, and crocus, the Lord had given him,
his heart was filled with gratitude for these blessings,
and he gave vent to his feelings in a great shout, which,
with him, was to leap and praise God—regardless of the
mud and water which flew over him, his fish, canoe, and
all around, bespattering everything; he continued his
shouting for some time.

It was rarely he meddled with the exciting subject
of politics, particularly after one unfortunate adventure
which he always regretted.

When General Jackson was a candidate for the Presi-
dency, one of the charges brought against him by his
opponents was, his having six militia men shot. Brother
Thomas heard of this, and in one of his sermons, ex-

pressed himself rather strongly on the impropriety of this act, and pronounced it out of all character—inhuman! A Mr. M., who had been a great admirer and friend of Brother T., became much offended, and left the congregation in a pet, remarking, that if he lived until his head was as gray as an eagle's, he should never listen to him again.

This, coming to the ears of Brother Thomas, caused great distress and grief;—he could not bear the ill will of any, and especially his friend, Mr. M. After consulting the circuit preachers, he went to the offended party and made humble acknowledgments—promising never to touch politics again; this settled the difficulty.

His habits of prayer were remarkable. He stated to me that he had never spent a half hour in any family he visited, without having prayer, and never was refused a request by any person to pray in his house.

It mattered not where he was, in the company of Churchmen, Presbyterians, worldly persons, or even Atheists, he was always prompt to pray, and welcome to commend them to God at a throne of grace.

The instance of his paying a certain debt on one occasion by prayer, has been often repeated, and perhaps heretofore published, but I will relate it again, and here:

Having business in the Register's office at Cambridge, the gentlemanly clerk at that time, Mr. Wm. Rea, promptly waited on him, and attended to all his wants.

After he had finished his business, and put away carefully the papers he had obtained, he asked for the bill. "Nothing, Mr. Thomas," said Mr. Rea. "Nothing at all to you, but your prayers." "Then," said Brother T., "I never like to be in debt. Let us pray." Down he knelt on the floor, and offered up an earnest petition to God, for his good kind friends there present, and their families, with all that appertained to them. This made a deep impression on the mind of Mr. R., who, at that time, was an irreligious man; but shortly afterwards was converted, and has remained ever since a prominent, useful, and intelligent member of the Methodist Church. He will, perhaps, never forget that unexpected prayer.

It is written, "He that converteth a sinner from the error of his way, shall save a soul from death, and hide a multitude of sins." How Brother Thomas succeeded in a very delicate and difficult case, we learned as follows:

A youth, whose moral training had been greatly neglected, came to reside on the Island. A sum of money was purloined, soon after, from one of the neighbors, where this young man had access. He was strongly suspected, but no direct or positive evidence could be adduced against him. Brother Thomas was deeply grieved for the character of the Island, and troubled about this young man. He sought an interview with him, and by affectionate entreaty melted him down, to confess his guilt and restore the money, and at once resolve to avoid in the future such a course of conduct as would most certainly bring him to shame and ruin.

My last visit to him and to the Islands will never be obliterated from my memory. Nowhere in all my intercourse, have I become so strongly attached to any people as those on Deal's, Smith's, and Holland's Islands. On the occasion of my farewell trip, I was accompanied from the house of Father Thomas by his son Seymour, in the "Methodist." I crossed the Sound to preach to the dear people once more. On reaching the Island after a very pleasant run, I was soon at the ever happy home of Brother William Evans, where I remained until the hour for worship ; then in company with the family we went to the house of God. As I tried to preach, their tears would flow, and responses rise, until my soul was carried away in love for them. Our separation will never be forgotten, as we stood on the shore and embraced one after another of the old soldiers of the cross, in hope of a happy meeting in the realms of eternal love. I had received from them not only grateful blessings, but substantial marks of their favor, in numerous presents.

Leaving this dear, loving people, we steered for Holland's Island, and there put up with my old friend, Richard Bradshaw, around whose family altar I had often knelt,—and now bowed for the last time. We repaired to the little sanctuary, and in singleness of heart, worshiped together ; mutually pledging each other to be faithful until death, and to meet again, if no more on earth, in the city of the New Jerusalem.

Some who were in those congregations have gone on before, and others are on the verge of Jordan, with a hope full of immortality.

Returning to little Deal's Island, I had a last interview with Brother Thomas. We met at the bedside of a dying saint, Brother Aaron Bradshaw, one of the purest and best men I have known.

Brother Thomas had been carried over to administer the sacrament of the Lord's Supper to his neighbor and friend, before he should bid farewell to earth.

As the elements were handed round by the old Apostle of the Islands, God was present to bless us by a revelation of Himself to our hearts.

These two men, long united in holiest bonds below, are now safe at home, in the land where the inhabitants never say, " I am sick."

Suffer me to conclude this sketch with a few

LINES TO THE MEMORY OF JOSHUA THOMAS.

Christian friend, must we resign thee—
    Dear to many as thou art?
Sacred ties are they which bind thee
    To the wounded, bleeding heart.

Rest thy form beneath the willow ;
    There thy dust shall sweetly sleep ;
While the friends who smoothed thy pillow,
    Shall in sadness often weep.

Now thy spirit, far from danger,
    Safely rests in Jesus' love ;
And, to grief and pain a stranger,
    Ever lives in heaven above.

All thy conflicts here are ended ;
    Over is the weary strife ;
Up to God thou hast ascended—
    To the joys of endless life.

There amid unfading pleasure,
　Where the mourner weeps no more;
Count with joy thy garnered treasure!
　Sing on the eternal shore!

We expect ere long to meet thee,
　With the holy to be blest;
Happy dawn, when we shall greet thee,
　Where "the weary are at rest!"

R. E. K.

At the Ross' woods camp meeting—referred to by
Brother Kemp—Brother Thomas made some remarks
about worshiping God under such circumstances as then
surrounded them, "without distraction." Said he, "You
ought to leave all your worldly cares at home, and trust
in the Lord. The devil sometimes troubles Christians
very much, by suggesting that things are not going on
right at home. This very morning he has been telling
me that the hogs are in my potato patch; but I told
him, if they were, and eat up my potatoes, I would *eat them*
next winter, and that will make it all square!"

He also related that when out in his "blind," waiting
to shoot ducks one day, he began to pray; while at
prayer the ducks came within range, but he became
happy, and began to shout, and scared away the entire
flock. "Let the poor things go," said he, "with their
'quack! quack!' for they seem to be happy too!"

CHAPTER XXIII.

The Canoe "Methodist"—The original tree—Hance Crosswell—Dimensions —Little Deal's Island—Voyage to the Island Churches—Reminiscences by Rev. Dr. Townsend—The fence-log story—Rev. J. Hargis—Preaching on Smith's Island—Rev. R. E. Kemp—Lively hearers of the word— "You're right, brother!"—Class meetings—Thomas Tyler—Theological controversies—"Just as I said!"—Deference to the preachers—Effect of the gospel on the Islanders.

THE celebrated canoe, "Methodist," of which an accurate and beautiful engraving is here presented, demands for itself a particular history.

It is said to be the largest canoe afloat in these waters, which has been constructed out of one tree, and is one of the most trim and tastefully modeled crafts of its class. It has been admired wherever it has gone, bearing Brother Thomas in his itinerant labors; and has gained its chief notoriety from the fact that in it, the traveling preachers performed their voyages to the Island appointments for a great many years.

Next, in interest, to a portrait of the Parson himself, will be that of this far-famed canoe, as a memento to his memory. The sketch we have secured, will not fail of a ready recognition by all who in past days have been acquainted with the original.

The tree, out of which it was built, grew in the neighborhood of Curtis' Chapel, on the lands of a Mr. Broughton, and was so large that it was regarded a curiosity in the neighborhood. A well beaten path led through the tangled swamp to where it stood, so many had traveled there to look at it, and measure its dimensions. It had long been offered for sale, but no person was found with sufficient courage to purchase and remove it, until it arrested the eye of a man named Hance Crosswell from Annamessex.

He bought it for ten dollars, and, singlehanded, in the space of two or three hours felled it to the ground.

Its fall was like the roar and reverberation of heavy ordnance, and shook the ground for many miles around.

Two canoes were rough hewed from its mammoth trunk: the largest, afterwards called the " Methodist," and another, which is now owned by Mr. D. Evans, of Deal's Island. These were hauled to King's Creek, a distance of five miles, and towed by way of the Manoken River, round Jericho, to the place in Annamessex where they were subsequently finished, and launched.

The length of the "Methodist" is between 20 and 30 feet, and its width from side to side about five feet. It is capable of bearing a heavy freight, and can live in very rough weather under skillful management.

It came into possession of Brother Thomas about 30 years ago, and was left at his death as an heir loom in the family. William Seymour, one of his sons, is its present guardian and proprietor, and places such an estimate on it, that, except for the service of the Church, and the dissemination of the gospel, as in former years,

money could not purchase it.   It is newly painted every
year, and in as good condition now as when it was built.

The scene and surroundings of our picture are strik-
ingly appropriate.   Standing on the lower point of Deal's
Island, or on the front porch of that well remembered
home for the preachers, the house of Brother T. Daniel,
and looking across the lower thoroughfare to the little
Island, we see in the foreground, getting under way,
the gallant Methodist : named in honor of that wonderful system, which, under God, has brought light and life
to thousands "afar off;" and still bears the message of
salvation, through its energetic agencies, in ever widening
circles, to the ends of the earth."

Her prow points toward the south, where Smith's
Island, at a distance of ten miles, dimly shows itself on
the horizon.   This is the destination of the voyagers,
who may be recognized as Brother Thomas and one of the
preachers.   The former sits in the stern sheets with
tiller in hand, and a keen, critical eye for wind and
weather, scanning the condition of his sails and the
bearings of his course.

To the left may be seen that Eden spot, the little
Deal's Island, where he resided.   The large house
nearest, is that erected and occupied by Aaron Bradshaw
until his decease ; now the residence of S. Evans.

In the distance may be seen his own house, and to the
right of it, and nearer the water's edge, that of Wm.
Seymour Thomas.

Leaving this scene to stand as " a thing of beauty,"
let us accompany the good pilot, and in his entertaining

THE CANOE "METHODIST," WITH A VIEW OF LITTLE DEAL'S ISLAND.

society, make the round trip contemplated before returning to the point from which we have just now embarked.

The passenger, if the reader will take one more look
at the engraving, is represented in the act of pointing
out some object in the distance, and beginning to ask a
series of questions, which the Parson takes great pleasure in answering.   Traditions of early times in these
latitudes ; the names of head-lands, shoals, and marshes;
adventures in storm and calm—the latter dreaded nearly
as much as the former, when distances have to be traversed—and a thousand personal recollections of men
and things, are related in a manner that enlists the most
absorbed interest of the hearer, and often excites his
laughter, so inimitably humorous are some particulars in
the detail.

Soon we cross the Sound channel, and stretch down
towards Kedge's Straits, taking care, if the tide is not
full, to clear the Musclehole Bar, and make a landing
at the Light House on Fogg's Point.

Captain White, who for a great many years kept this
establishment, took the greatest pleasure in accommodat-
ing his old friend Thomas and the Circuit Preachers.
Rev. J. L. Tyler, a subsequent incumbent, also made
them welcome to his home and hospitalities.   The present officer, Captain Tyler, is clever, and kind as any
of his predecessors.   He is a member of the church,
and a generous host to all who seek the shelter of his
house.

The arrival of the preachers, and the hour for public
worship, is made known on Smith's as on Tangier
Island, by hoisting a flag at the little church.   The

signal flag was procured by the Sons of Temperance, who have a flourishing division there. It bears their motto—" Union Band," and when unfurled to the breeze, may be seen from every part of the Island.

The people mostly come to meeting in canoes, and a more picturesque sight cannot well be imagined, than that witnessed about the time of service. From every point they come, some careering before the breeze, boomed out, and almost smothered in the spray; others close hauled on the wind, holding their course for the landing, and some expertly tacking against the wind, to reach their destination.

Warm hands and hearts give us welcome, and at the conclusion of worship bid us adieu. Brother Thomas has his exact time specified for starting, and wo to the laggard wight who is not ready when tide makes, or wind is fair, to continue the voyage to Holland's Island. This is at a distance of eight miles from Fogg's Point, and is reached by a rapid run up the Bay.

The " Methodist" is seen in the distance, and old Brother Price is at the landing to welcome us to his house. Then, after a pleasant night's rest and preaching next morning, we are homeward bound, through Holland's Straits or the " Gun Barrel" channel, to Deal's Island again.

A number of communications have been sent us, embracing recollections by ministers, of these voyages, and incidents connected with them. This may be an appropriate place to introduce a few of such reminiscences.

Rev. S. Townsend enjoyed very intimate acquaintance with Brother Thomas, and was, when in this part of the work, a highly esteemed minister by all the people. He writes as follows:—

"Rev. Joshua Thomas was truly a most extraordinary man. His like, in many respects, will never be seen in this world again; and every thing that can, ought to be done to preserve the memory, and perpetuate the true piety of so great and good a person. His life, in the form of a biography, will prove a blessing to the world and the church, affording a medium through which, like the blood of Abel, he may speak to the present, as well as unborn generations from the ground.

"Thousands of times, in imagination, he has come up before my mind, and with feelings of inexpressible delight, I have fancied myself, as in former days, traveling with him through the dense forests of Delaware and Maryland, penetrating the populous "necks," or crossing the marshes along the Chesapeake Bay, the Manoken, Wicomico, Pocomoke, Nanticoke, or Choptauk Rivers, by day and night; or in his noble old canoe, "Methodist," gliding over the Tangier Sound, through Kedge's or Hooper's Straits, to Smith's, Holland's, or Deal's Island;—interested, cheered, captivated, lost to every thing else, by his delineations of Bible doctrine, Christian experience, and historical incidents, relating to his own life or to the lives of others,—especially the preachers whom he had known personally in former years.

"Of the first class of preachers, such as Dr. Chandler, Rev. Lawrence McCombs, Solomon Sharp, and Lawrenson, he had an unfailing fund of anecdote, and delighted to talk of the times when they traveled in his

vicinity. He would often refer, also, to the circumstances with which he had been surrounded, during the
war, the rise and spread of Methodism, where previously
' the people sat in darkness,' and were ' dead in trespasses and sins ;' until hours have passed by unobserved,
and voyages amid scenes of danger and peril have been
made in his captivating company, as we went from place
to place, or enjoyed the warm and generous hospitality
of such families as the Waters', Maddux', Miles', Coul-
burn's, Fontaine's, Phoebus', Smith's, and Williams', on
the Main ; or Daniel's, Mister's, Parks', Evans', Bradshaw's, and his own home, on the Islands.

" I have often been astonished to think over the time
elapsed, the dangers escaped, and the sufferings endured;
all of which has been brushed from our feelings, as the
dust from our garments, by the smiling countenances,
cordial welcome, and unparalleled kindness of our never-
to-be-forgotten friends and benefactors, through all that
region of country.

" Many of these have since gone to their graves, and
to the home they hoped and lived for, beyond them in
heaven. Oh ! how often has imagination followed their
triumphant spirits through the trackless air, witnessed
their reception into the celestial city, and almost envied
the angels their blest society. Nothing but a reunion
with them can satisfy the restlessness of our feelings, or
fill the void made by their removal from earth.

> " O for the death of those
> Who slumber in the Lord !
> O be like theirs my last repose,
> Like theirs my last reward !"

"Three of my first four years in the Itinerant ministry were spent on Princess Anne Circuit—the place of my nativity, and where rests the dust of my honored parents. It then comprised twenty-three regular appointments, including three on the Islands. The circuit, as it then stood, has since been divided into two general, and two or three subdivisions.

"The preponderance of religious sentiment and feeling in the community, was greatly in favor of the M. E. Church. Many of the most intelligent, wealthy, and influential of the land were in her communion. The simplicity, piety, and devotion of her members, equalled that of the primitive Christians, of whom we read: 'They that gladly received the word were baptized, and continued steadfastly in the Apostle's doctrine, and in fellowship, and in breaking of bread, and of prayers; * * * with singleness of heart praising God, and having favor with all the people. And the Lord added to the church daily, such as should be saved.'

"Brother Thomas contributed greatly, in his simple-hearted devotion, exemplary spirit, and untiring zeal, to this condition of things, wherever he moved. He loved God and his fellow man with all his mind and soul; and exerted an influence that was general and powerful in the spirituality of the church. He often remarked, humorously, that he could not allow any person to love God and the church more than himself; or any preacher to preach better or oftener than he did; and though he was keenly sensible of his deficiencies in mental culture, yet with a manly ambition, under the restraints of reason and religion, he sought rank with the purest and mightiest

of God's servants. He was largely gifted by nature,
sanctified by grace; and, availing himself of every
means within reach for improvement, he became a perfect man of God, furnished for and ready to every good
word and work."

An incident often referred to as "the fence log" story
is also related by Dr. Townsend, as having occurred in
connection with himself:

"Brother Thomas and I met at the house of old Brother
Wm. Miles, in the neighborhood of St. Peter's Church,
in Annamessex, one Saturday evening. On Sabbath
morning at the breakfast table, he appeared to be unusually concerned about something that rested on his mind.
In a solemn tone he remarked, 'Brother Townsend, I am
afraid you will not preach well to-day, I had a bad dream
about you last night.' I replied, 'It is no strange thing
for me to fail in preaching; ut you must pray for me.'
'I will,' said he, 'and,'—stammering very badly—'you
must pray for yourself.' 'What did you dream, Brother
Thomas?' said I. 'Why,' said he, 'I dreamed you and
myself were making fence together, and I thought you
made the roughest fence I ever saw. I thought you had
great crooked logs, and left large holes in it as you went
on. I was ashamed of it, and felt very bad when I
awoke. I still feel unpleasant about it, and think you
will not get along well to-day.' Brother and Sister
Miles, the only persons at the table, listened with serious
attention, and began to look somewhat distressed at the
idea of a 'bad out' in preaching, and acquiesced in the
propriety of prayer, to make it efficient. When we left
the table, he went down to the creek to see that his canoe

was all right, and I went up stairs to read and study. When I came down he had just returned to the house. Brother and Sister Miles had gone to the church, and we hastened on after them. While walking along, forgetful of the dream, as if I had never heard of it, I said, ' Brother Thomas, you have never preached for me at this place; preach for me to-day. I know the people love to hear you, and I shall be pleased to hear you myself.' He stammered long in trying to reply; at length, said he, ' Do you think I had better preach?' I knew that his preaching depended altogether on impulse and feeling, and replied, ' If you feel any impression of duty in that way, I wish you would.' He became silent, as if absorbed in thought, and when we reached the church, consented to preach. The introductory services were performed, and after announcing his text, he proceeded for about ten minutes, in a very interesting manner, to explain and enforce it.

" He then seemed to become confused and embarrassed, not knowing what he was talking about. The congregation noticed his incoherency and evident distress; but instead of sitting down, he talked away at random, worked himself into a great excitement, and every moment became more tangled in his train of ideas.

" At length he turned abruptly round to me, and, as if his dream had suddenly flashed across his memory, said, ' Brother Townsend, bring on the chunks!' meaning that it was himself who really made the bad fence, and that it devolved on me to roll in large ' chunks,' to stop up the holes. The congregation looked amazed, not knowing anything about the dream, and Brother Miles could not refrain from laughing, neither could I, at this turn of affairs. I closed the services as best I could, while Brother Thomas was overwhelmed with grief at the result of his effort."

The above was a rare case of failure, and however unpleasant to him at the time, afforded him a lesson which he always remembered; often telling the circumstance to his own disparagement, and with this moral: " Dreams are not an exact criterion, or delineation of coming events."

Rev. J. Hargis, another of his friends of former years, writes :

" The first time I ever saw Father Thomas, was at a camp meeting near Guilford, in Accomac County, Va. While I was trying to preach, he came up and took a seat behind me in the stand, and commenced to respond to what I was saying. As soon as I concluded the sermon, he sprang to his feet, saying, 'Bless God ! now I will have a shout !' This was the man I had so much desired to see, and now heard his voice for the first time. After he had rejoiced for some time, he delivered an exhortation which was sensible and very animating.

" In 1843-4, I was on the circuit where he resided, and spent many an hour in his company. He told me most of the remarkable events in his life ; such as his early sufferings—attachment to the Episcopal church—his adventures with the Baptists—his love for Methodism— the story of his conversion—his great meetings on the Island—preaching to the British—second marriage— removal to Deal's Island, and various camp meeting anecdotes, which interested me very much. He was a good, holy man of God ; very simple, full of faith, and successful as a preacher of the gospel, which he knew to be ' the power of God, to his own salvation.'

"The Island people, when I knew them were, and I hope are yet, as a general thing, devoted to God, love the church, and keep the discipline. Brother Thomas, when he carried the preachers over the Sound to break the bread of life to them, would take his share of all the exercises, and never seemed happier than when at work in the pulpit or class meeting. He was an example in this respect to many of our Local and Itinerant preachers, who content themselves with doing ordinary service, and never care to go out of the beaten track to save souls.

"He was a very industrious man when about home, and was considered an excellent canoe builder, as well as one of the best fishermen on the island.

"He devoted much time to prayer and communion with God, and was of that happy, hopeful kind of temperament, that looks on the bright side of life, and magnifies the mercies enjoyed from day to day. In his room over the fire place, he had a sign painted, ' Take up thy cross and follow me.'

"This was his rule of life. To obey it, he had to spend much of his time away from his comfortable home and beloved family, to be occupied like his Master in doing good. I have been with him, as have been many ministers of the Philadelphia Conference, who have labored on the Peninsula, in his canoe, in calm and storm, cold and heat, up and down, and across the waters of the Sound and Bay, and ever found him the same meek, humble, teachable, and fervent-spirited follower of Jesus. I hope for a renewal of our happy intercourse, in the home of the blessed :

> "There all the ship's company meet,
>   Who sailed with their Saviour beneath ;
> With shouting each other they greet,
>   And triumph o'er sorrow and death.
> The voyage of life's at an end ;
>   The mortal affliction is past ;
> The age that in heaven we spend,
>   Forever and ever shall last."

Preaching on Smith's Island, as on all the islands named in this vicinity, is referred to by the brethren who have enjoyed that privilege, as among the most interesting occasions of their ministry.

The sketch presented will recall, to many, the joyous moments they have spent in the pulpit and among the people there. The congregation consists of " old men and fathers" of over four-score years ; mothers in Israel, and young people of all ages, down to the little infant of days carried out to be consecrated to God and the church, in holy baptism.

The little sanctuary is capable of seating between one and two hundred persons, and is kept in very neat condition, with " whitewashed wall and cleanly sanded floor," and is the scene of very lively exercises when the people assemble to join in praise and prayer.

The minister represented in the pulpit, we will suppose, is Rev. R. E. Kemp, than whom, but few of modern days was more popular or better adapted to this people, from his use of similitudes, and his style of illustration, when preaching to them.

REV. R. E. KEMP PREACHING ON SMITH'S ISLAND.

Whenever the preacher utters a sentence that may be striking or forcible, his hearers will express audibly their appreciation, as " good !" " true !" or, " first rate !" and this is continued all through the sermon. The brother alluded to had learned most of their nautical terms, studied their habits, and, in the pulpit, would " box the compass," " bear away," or, " hold your luff," while he pictured the voyage of life, and the duties of godliness; or refer to weaving, spinning, hoeing corn, and raising potatoes, with the design of simplifying truth, and making the commonest objects convey instruction, admonition, and wisdom.

Here is an example of one of those colloquial services, that may give the reader an idea of the mode in which the gospel is preached and listened to; making each sermon a feast of fat things; and every visit, to both preachers and people, a time of refreshing:

" The text, my brethren and sisters, tells us, ' This is a faithful saying, and worthy of all acceptation,' (Yes, that it is !) Now, many sayings among men, and many things in books are not of this character. (No !) Some things said by neighbors about each other are *un-worthy* of any acceptation or belief. (Ah !) They are not true ; (That's a fact !) and those who speak evil of their neighbors—are they faithful ? (No, brother !) Take care, then, of evil speaking ; for this vice will ruin the Church and community as badly as that brother's cabbage garden, which is all eaten by worms ! (True, brother !) A tattler is worse than a grub worm, (You're right !)

" In this false and faithless world there is not much

to rely upon; but, bless God! one thing is faithful. We can all accept it—the truth that Jesus Christ came into the world to save sinners! (Bless God! Glory to his name!)

" The needle never points more truly to the pole—the north star is not more stable—the sunshine is not more clear than this ' saying.' Do you receive it, and believe it, to-day, my friends? (I do, brother!—So do I—Yes, hallelujah!)

" The compass may deceive you, the lights may go out, and your reckonings all fail, on some dark night, when bound up or down the Bay; and the first thing you know you are hard ashore, or out of the channel; (Yes, that's all true!) but Jesus Christ will not fail his people in the time of doubt or danger. (No, glory be to Jesus!) He can save sinners. (I *know* it!) Even Paul, who tells us he was 'chief.' Some of you may have thought, if you did not say, the same thing; that you were the worst, the most wicked, and unworthy of all sinners.

" Have you felt that way? (Yes, often!) Well, he is able, he is willing, doubt no more." (Lord, help!)

Complaints are never made of a long discourse; for time is not noted in the animated and happy spirit in which it is delivered, and received, into good, honest hearts.

The preacher, in view of the fact that he is so rarely permitted to visit this flock, does his best; the people, from the same consideration, " hear, as for eternity," and, " in the love of the truth," receive it, as food to the hungry, and, to the weary, rest."

Brother Thomas, when in company with the preacher,

was given to expressing his mind during the delivery of the sermon. Sometimes, if feeling ran high, he would say, "Hold on, brother, and let us shout a while!"

The class meetings, held after preaching, are always interesting. As one after another is called, and relates his or her experience, a bashful minister will often be startled to hear so many allusions to his sermon; as, "Brother, you did me a heap of good to-day;" "Your sermon was food to my soul;" or, "While you were preaching so powerful, the Lord shone into my soul, and I am happy!"

The old gentleman seen in our engraving with his head protected by a handkerchief, will be recognized as Brother Thomas Tyler, an exhorter, and cotemporary with the first Methodists on the Island. He has been a reading man, and is the standing reference, in the absence of the preachers, on all questions of theology, as he owns the writings of Wesley and Dr. Clarke, beyond which authority, there is no disposition to appeal.

The face of Brother Laban Evans, another of the exhorters, will also be seen in the congregation.

An anecdote is told of two brethren who disagreed on a certain question of doctrine or morals.

They were both obstinate in opinion, and so the controversy remained until next preaching day, when, without knowing anything of the matter, the Circuit Preacher touched on the mooted point, and gave his view of the case. One of the brethren, finding his side of the question sustained by the pulpit, exclaimed, to the surprise of preacher and people, "Do you hear that, Brother John? *I thought so!*"

The deference paid to their preachers is profound, by the Island people. They could hardly be persuaded, but that the Itinerant knows every thing between the extremes of correcting the erratic tendencies of a super-annuated clock, and explaining the system of the universe;—the science of raising beans, and that of reading stars !

In the social circle, as in the pulpit, his opinions are sought, and his advice followed in every particular thing, that lies within the scope of his relations, as their pastor, guide, and friend.

Our canoe voyage has been protracted, and yet a tenth part of its stirring associations have not been told. Few incidents, in either the light or shade of a Methodist preacher's life, is calculated to leave a more durable and agreeable impression on his mind, than this trip to the islands, in the companionship of Brother Thomas. If the water is calm, and wind light, and the preacher feels weary after his morning labors, he may take a nap on some clean sea grass which has been provided for such a contingency, while the Parson will sing a hymn or preach a sermon, as he sits at the helm, with sheet ropes at hand, and thinking over the promises of his heavenly Father's love.

CHAPTER XXIV.

Letter from Rev. L. W. Nottingham—Brother Thomas and Rev. W. Spry—An affecting scene—An angry sinner converted—Personal violence prevented —Rev. J. A. Brindle—Anecdotes—"Better late than never"—Aaron Thomas reclaimed—Becomes an Exhorter—His father's joy—Farewell meeting at Tangier—His regard for Local Preachers—Rev. John Laws— An Experience meeting—Rev. H. Dalby—Jacob's Ladder—Rev. L. Moore —Rev. B. T. Ames—A Sailor's experience—The drops before a shower —Rev. W. Evans—Evans and Thomas at Ebenezer—Remarkable scene.

BEFORE closing our record, there remain a few incidents connected with Tangier Camp Meeting, which claim a place in these pages.

"I shall never forget," writes the Rev. Luther W. Nottingham, "a parting interview I witnessed on Tangier, at a camp meeting, between Brother Thomas and Rev. William Spry. The dear old man had become feeble, and could not move about, except when carried in a large chair.

"He was about to leave the ground, and at his request a meeting of the brethren and sisters was called in the tent where he was staying.

"Brother Spry was at the meeting, and came in to bid farewell to his beloved friend. A prayer meeting was held, and when the time came to part, Brother

Thomas requested Brother Spry to come and kneel before him, and let him place his hands on his head, that he might invoke the blessing of God upon him. The good minister of Jesus Christ, who for years had been proclaiming the glad tidings of salvation, did not consider this act a condescension, but an honor,—an exalted privilege to kneel before the patriarch, 'Parson of the Islands,' that he might receive his benediction. We stood around, and felt the power of the Highest to rest upon us during this solemn act. The place seemed to be filled with the Holy Ghost, and was awful by reason of the heavenly influence that came down upon us.

"After he had laid his trembling hands on Brother Spry, he requested him to place *his* hands on his head, and invoke for him a special blessing. He did so. It was a glorious privilege to be there. It seemed nothing less than God's house, and the very gate of heaven. I doubt whether there was one in the tent, whose cheeks were not bathed with tears. We felt in our souls a joyful anticipation of meeting, after these earthly scenes were ended, in the glorious kingdom of God, to shout redeeming love around the throne. That these two men of God are now in heaven, and compose a part of 'the church of the firstborn,' I have not the shadow of a doubt. They have gone to reap the reward of their labors, and by the aid of Divine grace, we expect to meet them there, and with them walk the golden streets of the new Jerusalem.

"I have been much edified and interested by some of Brother Thomas' exhortations. He said many excellent things, and in such an original way, that none could help feeling their force, and seeing their appropriateness.

"At one time he was speaking of temptations from the adversary, and,—as was his invariable custom, he brought forth instances and illustrations from his own experience. He said there was a large sinner at a place where he was holding a meeting, and the man became angry with him for something he said, which the other regarded as personal. The devil tempted him sorely to believe that this man would beat him the next time they met. He was greatly perplexed in mind about it, but went on with his prayer meeting, and soon God sent the power down, and his big sinner, among others, was convicted, and led to cry for mercy.

"He told of meeting a man on Tangiers, who threatened to whip him, if ever he caught him on the Main. One day having gone to the Main, he was traveling along a certain road, and saw in the distance this identical man, coming towards him. He lifted his heart in prayer to God, but expected the promised beating; but lo! and behold! when the enemy approached, he fell upon his neck, wept bitterly, and asked his forgiveness for what he had said and done. 'So, brethren,' he would say, 'do your duty at all times, and leave results to God. He will take care of you, for he is more than all that can be against you. Men and devils combined cannot harm a hair of your head, without his permission.'

"In conclusion," adds Brother Nottingham, "with all the eccentricities about him, I believe he was one of the best and holiest of men; and if the church had

more like him, she would have more power, and greater
success."

Rev. J. A. Brindle, of the Philadelphia Conference,
in a letter full of encouragement-to the writer, and hope
that this memoir, which has so long been desired, will
accomplish good, says:

"My first interview with Father Thomas, was many
years ago, at a camp meeting, and my attention was attracted toward him by a singular, and somewhat trivial
circumstance.

"He came up into the stand, and took his seat. After
some time had elapsed, there came a preacher up, and
knelt down to offer prayer, preparatory to the devotions
of the occasion.

"The old Parson dropped down alongside of him,
and also engaged in silent prayer. When they arose,
the preacher said to him, 'Why, Brother Thomas, had
you not said your prayers?' 'No,' said he, 'I forgot it
until I saw you, and then I thought it was better late
than never.'

"Thus he showed the simplicity and sincerity of his
heart.

"Our next interview was on Tangier Island, in 1846.
Brother Hargis held a camp meeting there. I traveled
Northampton Circuit that year. It was the last time
Brother Thomas was permitted to visit that place, where
in former years he had enjoyed so much of the presence
of God. He was greatly afflicted with the rheumatism,
and could neither stand nor walk. I took his youngest
son to the altar, or a mourners' bench, in a prayer meeting tent, where he was reclaimed from a backslidden

state. He afterwards became an exhorter, and a very useful laborer in the church. I well recollect hearing the old man shout for joy when it was told him, 'Your son Aaron is reclaimed, and made happy in God.'

"One evening the old brother had retired to bed, feeling very much indisposed. The trumpets sounded for preaching, and rising up in bed he inquired of me, who was going to preach. I told him it was Brother John Laws, a Local preacher. 'Well,' said he, 'I must go to the stand and help him. I feel a great interest in Local brethren, and am proud of them when I think they outpreach the traveling ministers.' He did not design by this remark to convey any disparagement or envy to the traveling preachers. He loved them all; but he had a special regard or sympathy for Local brethren. He went out to the stand, feeble as he was, and prayed for his brother; and while the other was preaching, he responded from a full heart, in the words, 'Amen,' 'Glory,' &c. He was in this way of much service to Brother Laws, as he told me next day.

"One more event,—the most interesting and affecting I can remember in connection with this truly remarkable man. At the camp meeting referred to, he took a final leave of his Island brethren, and the preachers present. He had arranged a kind of programme for his valedictory services, which he communicated to the preacher in charge, (Brother Hargis,) and which was in something like the following order:

"'Now,' said he, 'I want Brother Brindle to give out a certain hymn, and sing, after which I want Brother Laws to pray. I will then give an exhortation to the people, and you will have me carried by two of the largest men you have on the ground to my canoe—(the Methodist,) when I will pronounce the benediction.' His wish was carried out in every respect.   One of the men who carried him, was his oldest son, John, who lives on Tangier.   There were many tears shed that morning, at parting with this dear old Father in Israel, and hopes exchanged that we might all meet to part no more at last."

The interest of the Tangier camp meeting began to wane, with the beginning of that unfortunate state of agitation, and disturbance connected with the separation of the Southern section of the M. E. Church, in 1844, from the Northern.   Much unnecessary bitterness of feeling was engendered, by the continuance of the ministry connected with the Philada. Conference, to exercise their office in that time honored territory; and the progress, as well as the peace of the church, has been retarded by sectional prejudices.

Every trace of the old camp ground is now obliterated, in the building and appurtenances of the "Chesapeake House," on the spot so long hallowed as a place of prayer.

The writer remembers his first visit to the celebrated beach, on the occasion of a camp meeting in 1849. From lower Annamessex, he found a passage down the Sound, and, to his intense gratification, stood amid the clustering associations of that far famed spot.

The preachers in attendance that year were Brothers Mullen, Maddux, England, Lacey, and others of the traveling ranks; and Dalby, Ames, Leatherberry, Evans, and several other Local preachers.

On our arrival, an experience meeting was in progress —one of the most deeply interesting we had ever attended. Brother Dalby from Northampton was speaking. This beloved man has since gone to heaven. He was very happy that morning. Alluding to a sermon preached by Dr. Lacey on "Jacob's ladder," he said, "Nearly forty years ago, at a camp meeting on Hog Island, away out yonder on the Atlantic coast, I found my feet taken out of the horrible pit and miry clay, and placed on the first round of this glorious ladder! I have been climbing upward ever since, with the help of my God. I can now see the city!

> "My hope is full, oh, glorious hope!
> Of immortality."

This excellent brother preached at that meeting from the text: "Whose fan is in his hand, and he will thoroughly purge his floor, and gather his wheat into the garner; but he will burn up the chaff with unquenchable fire."

Another text, on which we remember having heard him deliver a good sermon, was: "Wherefore, holy brethren, partakers of the heavenly calling, consider the Apostle and High Priest of our profession: Christ Jesus."

One of his sons is an able minister in the Virginia Conference. Two others, who preached and labored there, are also in the traveling connection; Rev. Benjamin T. Ames and Rev. Lloyd Moore. When the latter was beginning his ministry, and had preached a sermon at the camp one day, which produced a marked effect, Brother Dalby, whose sympathies had been with the young brother, caught him in his arms at the close of the discourse, exclaiming, "Well done, good and faithful servant."

Brother Ames, in relating his experience, said, "I can face ten thousand without dismay or embarrassment, and preach to them the gospel of the Son of God, or tell the love of Christ which I feel within my heart."

A sailor looking man arose and deliberately said, " I am not ashamed of Jesus. I feel it to be my duty, as well as a privilege, to own him wherever I go: among his friends who love him as you do, and among those who hate him; for my lot is often cast among the ungodly."

One of the brethren remarked, that religion is suited to a man in every condition of life. "I know this to be true. I have been in every condition—in sickness and health, in poverty and abundance, in sorrow and surrounded with happy scenes; and I have found my Saviour precious at all times, in all places, and under all circumstances. At the mast head, and in the cabin, with a smooth sea, and in the midst of the storm, everywhere, religion is the same; only that it gets better and brighter as I near the port of eternal life."

> " Sweet peace it brings wherever it arrives:
> It builds our quiet, as it forms our lives—
> Lays the rough paths of peevish nature even,
> And kindles in the breast a little heaven."

One of the island sisters gave an experience which we still distinctly remember. By this time the tide of religious emotion had swelled high. Brother Dalby was shouting, and the singing was thrillingly grand. This pious woman arose, and pointing towards the stand with her fan said, "A preacher up there, by the name of John Allen, was telling us how the Lord sends his showers of grace, like the rain upon the earth. He said, first there comes a cloud, then a single drop, then two or three large drops, then faster and faster until it pours! Well, friends, I feel it pouring now. A while since I felt a big drop, then I began to see the drops falling on the brothers over there; and I prayed for a powerful baptism. My soul is full of joy; my hope is clear, and I expect to meet you."

Thus the hour moved sweetly on, and the exercises closed with the experience of Rev. Wm. Evans. As near as we can recall this remarkable statement it was in substance: that the Christian who lives with heaven in his view, and redeeming grace in his soul, never fears to die. "Twice," said he, "have I been overboard in the Bay; several times capsized out of my depth in the Sound, and could not swim; but I cast myself on a present God, and was enabled to feel calm and happy. At one time I expected to be ushered into the presence of my Judge in a moment. It was one dark stormy night, when I was struck by the boom, in going about, and fell overboard. I went down amid crashing ice, and as I went, I called to my son on board, 'Farewell, tell your mother I have gone to dwell with Jesus!' In the providence of God, I had grasped a rope when falling over, and by this means, after long delay, I succeeded in regaining the deck; and here I stand to-day, a witness still to the power of Christ to save a sinner, and the power of his grace to make the soul happy in danger, and triumphant in prospect of death."

Here an invitation was given, and was accepted by many, who felt their need of religion. At this meeting, Brother Lacey preached a sermon to the fishermen, in which he displayed a very intimate acquaintance with the different kinds of fish, their habits, and the modes of taking them—also the varieties of hook, bait, and management to ensure success; using all this to illustrate the text, "Behold I make you fishers of men."

Brother Evans followed, and gave an exhortation of telling power. We never knew him to fail in awakening the undivided attention and enlisting the hearts of a congregation, by his pathos and earnestness.

He and Brother Thomas were said to be a "whole team" at any meeting they attended, and left their impress wherever they had access to promiscuous crowds.

The last visit they ever paid in company to the Ebenezer camp meeting, was, we are informed, a time of extraordinary interest and success. They spent the Sabbath, and part of Monday laboring in the meeting, without much apparent good being done. Other engagements demanded that they should leave the ground that day, and at an hour when there was no opportunity afforded them for a parting word, or a farewell hymn. Rev. J. T. Hazzard was about to preach, and had commenced the opening services, when our Island brethren quietly withdrew, and took the way to the landing where the "Methodist" was moored.   Their departure was observed, however, by a few persons, who whispered the fact around, until about eighty persons arose and followed them.   They formed into a procession two and two, and commenced to sing as they walked on.   The singing was led by a whole-souled brother, named Holmes, from Baltimore.   Thus they marched on until they came to the shore.   "Now," said Brother Thomas, who was somewhat concerned lest this movement should disturb the congregation they had left, and yet felt deeply grateful for such a mark of respect and kindness, "let the sisters step on board my canoe, and Brother Evans will stand on the seat and give us a word of exhortation." This was done, and while Brother E. became fervent, eloquent, and overpowering in his farewell words, the fire caught from heart to heart; six persons fell on the shore, under deep conviction, and every Christian man and woman in the company began to praise the Lord. Several prayers were offered, some of the mourners blessed; and such a meeting, it was declared, they had never seen before.

Brother Thomas went round to each and bid them farewell, asking them, as he took their hands, to meet him in heaven.   He then requested them to return to the camp singing as they came; and when they entered within the circle, to march round three times before they stopped.

This they promised, and while the "Methodist" spread her sails to the breeze, the brethren on board could hear the sound of the hymns sung by the returning escort. When the company reached the ground, the sermon had just been concluded, and as they encompassed the camp, they were joined by many others, until the whole place was a scene of the greatest excitement. After they had marched round, according to order, three times, they turned in around the altar, which quickly became crowded with penitents. This gave an impulse to the meeting that greatly contributed to its success, and made it one of the most glorious seasons of revival remembered on that camp ground. Some in eternity, and others on the way to join their friends above, were happily converted through this God-honored instrumentality.

CHAPTER XXV.

In his journeys to and from Princess Anne, the centre of the circuit, and the County town of Somerset, Father Thomas invariably took the river route, and used his Methodist canoe.

He had a number of stopping places along the winding Manoken, where, should night overtake him or the tide turn, he was always sure of a cordial welcome.

His name is as precious ointment, in many families, where he was in the habit of spending an hour, or a night, as the case might be. It mattered not with him, what their denominational proclivities might be; he sung his hymns, called them to prayer, (white and colored people,) and was treated with the highest respect by all.

He was passing the beautiful residence of Mrs. W.

one day, and as it was about the hour for dinner, he
turned his canoe to the shore, made fast, and walked in.
His reception was, as usual, kind and affectionate.
Several visitors were present, who became greatly interested in his conversation; among others a young gentleman, who, he supposed was there paying particular respects to the amiable daughter of his hostess. At the
conclusion of dinner, as the company were rising from
the table, he said, " Let us. pray." This was a rule he
never deviated from, when casually sojourning with a
family. In prayer he named each person present, adverted to their age, circumstances, and, what he supposed
to be their moral condition. This peculiarity of his,
when officiating at the family altar, made his prayers
memorable, and gave him immediate access to all hearts.
On this occasion he had incidentally learned that three
of the ladies present were widows; he prayed devoutly
for them all. When he came to the young gentleman
visitor, divining his intentions, he asked the Lord to
bless the dear man, give him grace and favor in the eyes
of that lovely lady, and so dispose her heart, that his
suit might be successful! However diffident he might
have been, and confused by such an unexpected interest
in his affairs, it may be seen at once, that this occasion
gave him an excellent opportunity to propose.

Many happy nights did our Parson spend with the
family of Brother John Fontaine, when bound for
Quarterly Meetings, or passing on business.

His custom, we are informed, was to assemble the entire household in the large kitchen, and preach or exhort
until they were all made happy. Good sister F. and

her servants have had many a shout with the old gentleman on these occasions.

When visiting Princess Anne, he was sometimes the
guest of General P., who, with his lady, treated the
Island Parson with the utmost consideration, and greatly
enjoyed his devotional exercises, although the General
had no particular inclination to any of the existing
churches, or forms of faith, respected in the community.

The hotel keepers also regarded it as a special favor
to obtain his company, when in the town. Their parlor
or porch was generally crowded with the neighbors, when
" Brother Thomas" was stopping there.

He is the most popular man to-day, at these same
places, who can repeat the best and most anecdotes of
the simple-hearted Parson. The only difficulty in this
case is the temptation to exaggerate, for the purposes of
adornment; or to tickle the risibilities of the irreligious,
by perverting the well meaning satires in which he indulged, against the popular vices and follies of his times.

He was as plain and simple in his dress, as was the
heart and its intentions underneath it. His portrait
represents the old fashioned style of coat, to which, as a
Methodist institution, he was indissolubly wedded. A
number of his friends at one of the Dorchester camp
meetings, once presented him with an excellent coat.
It was made of the best material, but, on close examina-
tion after it arrived at his house, and was in the act of
being tried on, he discovered that its cut was carnal, and
style conformed to the fashion of this world. He pulled
it off in a moment, and sadly laid it aside. His family
and friends used every persuasion they could devise, to

weaken the force of what they termed his silly prejudices, but in vain. He prayed over it. He asked light from above as to this perplexing question, but not receiving what he considered a sufficient authority to justify his change, he never wore the coat. Had he done so, the portrait of good Bishop Asbury, and that of McKendree, which hung on his wall, would have reproved him daily, for thus departing from the wholesome example these pure men set before the church, in the article of clothing.

The reader will find it difficult to form a just estimate of his preaching abilities, from the seemingly contradictory intimations scattered over these pages. When, as was often the case, he would pleasantly remind a preacher that he would try to "outpreach" him, it was never understood that this remark savored of vanity. His own opinion of whatever preaching abilities he possessed, was poor. He once stated in an exhortation he was called upon to give, after a rather feeble effort by one of the preachers, that men had various callings. Some were called to plough, some to hew, and some to make shoes; every man to his trade. In the church, some are called to preach, and expound the great lessons of divinity; and in this department, one is adapted to proclaim "the terrors of the law, another the glad tidings of the gospel. But," said he, "I am inclined to think that Brother— (naming the one who had preceded him) and I are called only to exhort! If we put on the airs of these big preachers, we spoil the work, and reveal our ignorance!"

At another time he remarked of himself, that in comparison with most preachers, he was but a *corn field nag!*

"In fact," said he, "I am about just such a preacher as Brother Gardiner—sitting over there—is a doctor!"

Brother, or Dr. Gardiner, to whom this personal reference was directed, was a respectable practitioner of the "Thomsonian" school; and very useful in his day, and mode of treatment, but was underrated by the "regular" profession; and, as a simply self-taught votary of the healing art, discarded from fellowship with the owners of a diploma. He took the allusion in the utmost good humor, as it was intended; and confessed himself honored and elevated by such a comparison.

He rarely raised his voice above a conversational tone when in the pulpit or public stand, and generally proceeded in that strain with his discourse; appealing to some acquaintance in the congregation for corroboration of facts.

Sometimes a sensitive preacher could hardly maintain the connected links in his chain of ideas, when Brother Thomas sat behind or near him; the latter was so much in the habit of responding, like all his Island brethren. When an emphatic sentence fell, he would startle all by saying, "That's good! give us more! Lord bless the brother!"

He could not brook those petty annoyances, however, that were of a different complexion. A timely hint to those laughing and whispering young men, or "girls," as he termed our modern ladies, and all became quiet in that quarter.

He stopped a minister one day in the midst of a fine oratorical flight, to appeal to a mother in the congregation, whose little child kept up an intolerably annoying squall: "Sister," said he, in tender tones, "do give that child a '*tater!*'"

His own texts when he preached, embraced an entire paragraph, or portion of a chapter; preferring, as he would remark, plenty of sea-room. His sermon on the history of Joseph was simply a paraphrase, but so inimitably rendered, that persons would go home after hearing it, and read, and re-read their Bibles with a new love and delight for the sacred record. Most of the prominent events that mark the course of inspired history, were grouped in their connections, and formed the subjects of his Sabbath discourses.

His figures were homely but very expressive. On the subject of "faith and works," and their intimate relations, he had the old illustration of rowing a boat against the current. One oar without the other, he showed, was worse than useless, but both in harmony, and simultaneous exercise, availed to "shoot ahead!"

On perseverance, as an essential element of success in prayer, he would refer to some of his own actual experiences in secular life; saying, "I once had occasion to borrow an article of a neighbor. I knew he did not like to lend; but I could not get along without the accommodation. I applied, and was put off. I tried again, and was denied. I went once more, and the man said, 'There take it, you stick like wax, when you want anything; and never let a fellow rest until you obtain it!' That's the way to pray, my brethren; pray and never faint, and the blessing will come; for, understand, our heavenly Father is willing; but he wants us to feel our need more than we do; and by seeming to withhold, he only tries our sincerity and earnestness."

When, after the lifelong exposure he had endured from cold and wet, at all seasons, and in all changes of weather, his robust frame became debilitated by an acute attack of rheumatism, confining him to narrow limits in his labors, and finally to his large arm chair; he found this lesson a difficult one to learn: that patience was a Divine requirement, and as necessary towards the purity of the soul, and the glory of God, in some instances, as the most active public life.

"They also serve that wait," he in due time ascertained; and after rejoicing in the abundance of grace through so many years of duty, he claimed, and obtained the promise so dear to a sufferer. "All things shall work together for good to them that love God."

He continued to preach, even when unable to stand or walk; and was as interesting—if not more so—to his neighbors in Sabbath ministrations, as when he made it his business and daily delight to "go about doing good."

His mode of conveyance to the Island Church, when in this enfeebled condition, was, to be carried by his family to the water's edge, and seated in his canoe; then glide up the thoroughfare to Captain Price's landing, where this good friend of his, met him with an ox cart, and conveyed him to the place of prayer.

One Sabbath morning the oxen became refractory, and upset the cart. The poor old man was severely hurt by his fall; but, after recovering a little, he insisted on going to the church. All their persuasions failed to deter him from his duty. He preached that morning with more than ordinary unction; and before dismissing the congregation, requested them to come out again in the afternoon, as he had another sermon, and a "still better text" to preach to them.

The afternoon service was crowned with the blessing of God, in a very especial manner. The people were made happy, and had "a time of rejoicing" together, in which he heartily joined.

Father Thomas, in closing the meeting, said, "The devil tried to prevent me from preaching to-day. He entered those oxen, and impelled them to run over a stump, that he might spoil my prospect for doing some good; but, you understand, I would not stop for that; and my Lord has wonderfully sustained and strengthened me this time. I thought it well, to make sure of a good victory over the enemy—to preach twice, instead of once; and the adversary is disappointed. Glory be to my Jesus."

It was a sad sight to hundreds of his old friends who assembled at the Deal's Island meeting in August, 1847, to see him helpless as a child, and in the midst of great bodily suffering. He tried to be cheerful, however; and had an appropriate word for all who dropped in to greet him in his tent.

The exercises of that meeting encouraged his soul greatly. Such preaching, he remarked, he had rarely, if ever, listened to before. The charm that lingered round his early recollections of camp meeting preaching, remained with him as long as memory held its seat. He could recall the day when a Solomon Sharp thundered forth the claims of God, or told his kindly care, in preaching from the passage: "My people shall dwell safely in the wilderness, and sleep in the woods;" and when Chandler moved the masses by his Sunday morning sermons. He also cherished the names of a Lawrenson, White, and others among the fathers; "but," said he, "our preachers now-a-days, and those at this very meeting, are, I feel, commissioned by the same great Shepherd, preach the same saving truths, and preach them as forcibly and powerfully as man, with his highest faculties in culture can do it.

Of the preachers at that meeting, we remember Rev. John A. Roche, and his eloquent discourse on the "great salvation;" Rev. James Allen urging home to the conscience, the startling question, "What shall it profit a man if he gain the whole world and lose his own soul?" Rev. A. Cookman, then a boy, but mighty as the intrepid David, before the enemy of his people, and their God; Rev. V. Smith, timid under the responsibilities of his ministry, but when nerved, and baptized by the Holy Ghost, irresistible in appeal; Rev. William Campbell, soon to lay his armor by; and others, a noble band of soldiers in the all-conquering army of Immanuel.

Well might the dim eye of the old patriarch kindle up, and his heart swell unutterably full, with hope for the church, and good to the world, from such preachers and such preaching.

While Brother Roche was contrasting the two great issues of human probation, on that occasion, men bounded to their feet, and stood out the sermon, without being conscious of the act.

His appeal to the colored people was hailed by shouts for Jesus and salvation; and, as the application ended, there was a pervading concern in that immense audience, which, if it found utterance, would have been in the question, "What must I do to be saved?"

A passage in the sermon of Brother Cookman was often afterwards dwelt upon by the Parson, to his solace, in loneliness, and his comfort in pain. The text was, "And they cast their crowns before the throne." "Every act of adoration," said the eloquent speaker, "will add a new and brighter jewel to that crown of joy! The tribulations of earth will, if remembered, sweeten the pleasure to God's redeemed, that they shall find at his right hand for evermore!" If this be so, thought Father Thomas, I'll do as the poet says:—

> " Suffer on my three-score years,
>   Till my Deliverer come,
> And wipe away his servant's tears,
>   And take his exile home."

CHAPTER XXVI.

Removal of the Camp Meeting—Park's Grove—New Church—Rev. J. D. Onins—Dedication—Rev. J. Sewell—Dr. Bunting—Elliott—Great Sermon—A cow subscribed to pay for church—Contrast—Last Sermon of Father Thomas—His prayer—A good Text—Preaching—Probation work —God speaking to men—Folly of procrastination—A forty days' shower —Exalted privileges—Danger of abuse—Weeping for sinners—The word let slip—Inattentive hearers—A leaky bucket—The seed in stony places —Earnestness—Neglect—No escape—The great salvation—Now is the accepted time—A hiding place from the storm—Last appeal—A pledge to try for heaven—Happy conclusion.

The last encampment held on Evans' Hill, Deal's Island, was in the year 1849. At its close there was an expression of opinion adverse to a continuance of the meeting at that particular spot. The constant washing away of the bank that formed a barrier against the dashing tides, had left but a limited space for tents. In other respects, also, the ground was rapidly losing those necessary advantages, in the way of shade, and accessibility to the main and populous parts of the Island, which seemed to be desirable. An intimation was given, that a new site was in contemplation, and was already selected for meeting the following year.

Accordingly, in August 1850, Park's Grove, a charming spot, thickly studded with vigorous oaks, and lying in one of the most beautiful and eligible neighborhoods on the Island, was prepared for the purposes of worship in the woods.

That same year, a neat new church had been completed, and stood in close proximity to the camp, awaiting dedication, in connection with the services of the meeting.

The engraving opposite is an exact representation of this building, and its picturesque surroundings. It presents moreover a view of the tomb where Father Thomas "rests in hope," and alongside, the stone which marks the grave of his youngest son, the beloved and lamented Aaron.

Near the church, and a little below it, there stands a tasteful structure, devoted to the important purposes of education.

Above the church, and by it, hidden from view, is a neat little hall with belfry and other appurtenances; which is owned and occupied by the Sons of Temperance; who have, through weal and wo, maintained an existence there for many years. One of the leading men in the Division, is Noah Webster, a merchant, residing on the adjoining premises. He also fills the office of Postmaster.

Clustered here, then, we find those elements that constitute the centre of population—The Church, Academy, Temperance Hall, Post Office, and Camp ground.

The work of removal from the "old hill," of the Islanders' tents, was arduous, but performed with a will, and almost in a twinkling. The new ground presented

DEAL'S ISLAND M. E. CHURCH.—GRAVE OF REV. JOSHUA THOMAS.

a magnificent appearance on the first assembling of the congregation there.

Rev. Mr. Kemp, and the writer, were on the circuit at that time, and necess rily in attendance at this very pleasant scene of religi us devotion.

We were favored with the aid of several excellent brethren from Baltimore, besides the Presiding Elder of the District, Rev. John Onins, and a number of preachers from adjacent circuits.

Rev. J. Sewell preached several very interesting discourses. A brother named Bunting, Dr. James Bunting also of the Baltimore Conference, preached, and labored with great acceptability and overwhelming effect. Rev. Mr. Elliott, well known of late years, as a regular attendant and an eloquent and successful camp meeting preacher, was there for the first time; and announced himself, in one of the most beautiful and effective sermons that, we have been assured, ever had been listened to in that locality, as a local minister from the business circles of Baltimore city.

The stand was occupied, also, by Rev. Solomon Prettyman, Rev. Robt. H. Pattison, and others.

The new church was dedicated by the Presiding Elder with an appropriate sermon from the words: "How amiable are thy tabernacles O Lord, God of Hosts! My soul longeth, yea, even fainteth for the courts of the Lord." Psalm lxxxiv. 1, 2.

When the sermon was concluded, it was found necessary to make a money effort, to free the house from debt. One of the first who evinced a desire to aid in this matter was Father Thomas, then a helpless cripple. He had, at his request, been carried in on a chair, and greatly enjoyed the discourse which had been delivered, setting forth the beauty and glory of God's earthly sanctuary, and the privilege and duty of all who love Him, to say of Zion, "Peace be within thy walls and prosperity within thy palaces."

" Come brethren, friends, speak out; how much will you give towards paying for this commodious Temple, in which you will henceforth worship God ?"

This question was the prelude to subscription, and the first response it found, was from the devoted Parson. The language of the text, he adopted as his own sentiment. He loved the courts of his God, and prayed fervently there, that "multitudes might be born from above, and *for* the upper sanctuary within those walls. But the money had to be raised, and in his simplicity he remarked, ' Silver and gold have I none ;' but my wife has an excellent cow, worth at least twenty dollars, and we will give the cow to help pay for the church. Please put down the cow !"

One or two visitors from a distance, were in the congregation, and were so much pleased with the old gentleman's offering, that they walked up and paid the money for him, and then returned the cow.

" That's the way my Lord always does," said he ; " he knows I have a willing mind, and that we would have had a hard time without our supply of milk ; and, understand, he has put it into your hearts, my friends, to do this noble act.   God bless you !"

The money was then speedily raised, the church opened for stated worship, and the exercises of the camp, sus-

pended for the time, were renewed, and moved on with
regularity and very marked interest.

The grove has been tented, with perhaps but one
or two exceptions, every year since then, but we have
looked in vain, so far, for such meetings there, as char-
acterized the old place. True, sinners are awakened
and converted at every meeting. Believers are quickened and encouraged, and an occasional shower of refreshing grace, like "manna in the wilderness," falls all
around; but when our older people ask, "Where are the
days of the Henry Whites—the John S. Taylors, and
others of *their* time? Where is the Lord God of Elijah?
The holy fire? The multitudes filled with joy?" Echo
answers, "*Where?*"

It was at this camp meeting, (1850,) Father Thomas
preached what proved to be his last regular public discourse.

The Baltimore brethren had taken their departure,
and quite a number of the preachers from adjacent fields
of labor had arrived on the ground. The Dedicatory
services in the new church had been satisfactorily performed, and undivided attention again secured to the
order of exercises at the stand. A general good feeling
pervaded the congregation, and was manifested in the
prayer meetings.

It was Wednesday. The meeting, it was expected,
would be concluded next day. Rev. Mr. Onins, the Presiding Elder, preached the morning sermon,—a warm,
winning appeal, from the words of Moses to Hobab, the
son of Raguel, the Midianite—" We are journeying unto
the place of which the Lord said, I will give it you:

come thou with us, and we will do thee good; for the Lord hath spoken good concerning Israel." Numbers x. 29.

This discourse had a fine effect. Its conclusion was reached amid loud exclamations of religious confidence and joy, from both the front and rear of the stand. White and colored participated in hearty responses, when the heritage of God's spiritual Israel was portrayed, and the church's hope of a "better country, that is, an heavenly," set forth. The preachers themselves were very much animated; and old Father Thomas, deploring his inability to shout, kept up a running response, and commentary, on the cheering truths of the sermon.

As the preacher sat down, Brother Thomas continued his remarks in exhortation and encouragement to his old friends who were there present, and announced his desire to preach once more before he died.

"I may not live," said he, "until another meeting here, or, if I do, the Lord may send for some of you, so that we shall never meet again till we cross the river, and stand on the other shore, where the hymn says, ' We'll be safe for evermore.' I will therefore preach my farewell to you this afternoon, if our good ministers have no objection."

"None at all," said the ministers, unanimously; and there was a decided sensation evinced, at the prospect of a sermon from one whom they all, both young and old, delighted to honor.

The congregation then joined in singing the old hymn, "Our bondage it will end," &c., during which, those awakened and seeking peace, bowed around the altar.

The time for afternoon service was announced by the pealing horn, and few on that particular occasion were laggard in securing a seat as eligible as possible, where they might hear the voice once more of him whose gentle monitions and striking anecdotes they had listened to, many of them from early childhood. Some were there who had not seen or heard him for many a year; and others, including the writer, who never had the pleasure to hear him preach before.

Many eyes were turned, as the moments passed, in the direction of his tent, and a number of persons remained standing near it, to escort him out. They waited respectfully until he had prayed for help and grace, in this his time of need. He then appeared seated in his wheelbarrow! and was trundled out to the public stand. They placed him directly in front, and handed him the books. His hymns had been previously conned, and carefully " turned down." His text, likewise, had been selected, and studied over with prayer, before leaving his tent.

Persons toward the outer edge of the congregation here crowded closer in, and took a standing position where they might catch his every word.

The hymn he announced was sung with spirit. His opening prayer was simple, touching, and very comprehensive. He seemed as one talking up into the open sky, as though his Father was within the range of his eye and voice; and the throne of mercy, where the great Intercessor presides, very near. He continued long his pleadings for the Island people, and all the strangers who might be in the camp. Various classes were alluded to; saint and sinner, both comprised in the outgushing love of his devoted heart.

"Never," said he, "shall all this people hear thy poor old servant speak in honor of Thy name again. Give him words to utter that may do them some good. Bless his feeble effort one time more, to hold up Jesus, the sinners' friend, and their only hope. May I see thy power, O God, unto salvation, this day, that thy name may be glorified, and my neighbors and their children converted and made happy by believing in thee."

The Divine Spirit softly came over the hearts of all around him, while the prayer was being offered, and tears were observed in many eyes, as the congregation arose and resumed their seats.

The stirring hymn, "Blow ye the trumpet, blow," &c., was next announced and sung; after which the venerable preacher slowly read his text twice over, as follows:

"*Therefore we ought to give the more earnest heed to the things which we have heard, lest at any time we should let them slip. For if the word spoken by angels was steadfast, and every transgression and disobedience received a just recompense of reward, how shall we escape if we neglect so great salvation?*" HEBREWS ii. 1, 2, 3.

"This," said he, "is a good text. I have heard it preached many a time; and so, perhaps, have you. Pray, friends; pray, that I may be able to say something on it that may do you good, as it doeth the upright in heart—something that may be remembered to your comfort, when I am sleeping in the grave.

"We are commanded to work while it is called day; for the night of death cometh, when no man can work.

Therefore, as the good Book says, 'Whatsoever thy hand findeth to do, do it with thy might,' or, as my text says, 'Give the more earnest heed to the things which ye have heard, lest at any time we should let them slip.'

"Now you need not look for much of a sermon. You see my situation, I cannot preach like these good brothers in the stand—never could. But as many of them have told me, 'Brother Thomas, you preach in your own way, and say whatever the Holy Spirit gives you, and the Lord will use your instrumentality for his own good pleasure.'

" The servant that in the days of Christ had but one talent, and used it well, had the pleasure to hear his Master say, 'Well done!' There is a good hymn which says,

> " Oh, that each in the day, of his coming may say,
>   'I have fought my way through :
> I have finished the work thou didst give me to do.'
> Oh, that each from his Lord, may receive the glad word,
>   ' Well and faithfully done,
> Enter into my joy, and sit down on my throne.' "

"We read in the chapter above this one, about the goodness of God to us in the gift of his Son Jesus Christ; and how that he has spoken to us himself in these last days. Yes, he has often spoken to me, and like one of old, I have always been ready to say, 'Speak, Lord, for thy servant heareth.' Who do you suppose that was, my little friends? Have you ever heard of Samuel, little Samuel? Well, it was he who said that, and God was pleased with the little boy, and loved him. Now do

you want God to love you? I hope you do; but if you
are heedless and sinful, he cannot tolerate sin, or accept
you until you give up your evil ways, by giving him your
heart.

"Remember, my text talks about giving heed to
something. But, as I was saying, the Son of God
speaks to us. When he said to me, long ago, 'Son, thy
sins are forgiven thee;' wasn't I glad? It was the
happiest feeling I ever knew. The hymn describes it
exactly:

> " Oh, how happy are they,
>   Who the Saviour obey,
> And have laid up their treasure above ;
>   Tongue can never express,
>   The sweet comfort and peace,
> Of a soul in its earliest love.
>
>   That sweet comfort was mine,
>   When the favor divine,
> I received through the blood of the Lamb ;
>   When my heart first believed,
>   What a joy I received,—
> What a heaven in Jesus's name !
>
>   'Twas a heaven below,
>   My Redeemer to know,
> And the angels could do nothing more,
>   Than to fall at his feet,
>   And the story repeat,
> And the Lover of sinners adore.
>
>   Jesus, all the day long,
>   Was my joy and my song ;
> Oh, that all his salvation might see ;
>   He hath loved me, I cried,
>   He hath suffer'd and died,
> To redeem even rebels like me.

Oh, the rapturous height,
Of that holy delight,
Which I felt in the life-giving blood;
Of my Saviour possess'd,
I was perfectly blest,
As if fill'd with the fullness of God."

"Jesus has often spoken to me since that first glad
hour I heard his pardoning voice. And he has spoken
to you, sinner. Whenever you hear his ministers, he is
speaking through them to you.

"He bids them warn the people from his mouth; just
as if your neighbor would send you word about some
matter, and tell his boy to say to you, 'I said so.' You
would rely upon it, wouldn't you? Well, Almighty God
says to all his preachers, 'I have set thee, O son of man,
as a watchman unto the house of Israel, therefore thou
shalt hear the words at my mouth, and warn them from
me.' You can read all about this in the thirty-third
chapter of Ezekiel.

"Now when the minister says, 'Come unto me, all ye
that are weary, and heavy laden, and I will give you
rest,' he speaks for Jesus, and Jesus speaks through him
to you.

"God used to speak unto the fathers, the old Patriarchs,
by prophets; and often by angels. I have read about
angels coming to Abraham, and visiting Lot, and appearing to Joshua, and guarding Elijah. But in these
last days, yes, these eighteen hundred years, since Christ
was born in Bethlehem, He has been speaking. He
went about preaching and doing good. Then he sent
his disciples into all the world, to preach the gospel to

every creature. He gave them his Spirit to attend them, and though 'He ever lives above for me to intercede,' yet he lives here in the hearts of the contrite ones, and says, 'Lo I am with you always, even unto the end of the world.'

"He is greater than all angels, superior to all the prophets, head over all things, and 'God blessed forever.' Therefore we ought to give the more earnest heed to the things we have heard.

"People who hear the gospel in these days, without improving their privileges, will be worse off than if they never heard at all. They are in more danger, and will meet a far more dreadful condemnation, than rejectors of truth in the times past. You .remember about the sinners who were drowned at the time of the deluge? they had plenty of warning, and time for repentance; but they were hardened against God, did not believe old Noah, laughed at his big ark, and called him hard names for his efforts to save them. But ruin came as he foretold. The rain poured down, the floods rushed along the valleys, and rose higher and higher, until those who climbed trees and rocks, were swept off into the whelming waters, and sunk in the ocean. Who laughed then? A man once told me that he read about one of the people who argued with Noah, and would not go into the ark; when the flood began to rise pretty high, he got in a canoe, and pulled on after the big ship, and wanted to get on board. 'No, sir,' said the captain, 'can't take you in now. The hatches are all down, and the gangway closed, you are too late.' 'Well,' said this man in the boat, 'go on, old fellow, I guess it won't be much of a shower after all.' He soon found out what kind of a shower it was, for it never held up, for forty days and forty nights, and where was he by that time? Now I believe that is only a kind of a story; but look at people now-a-days acting in the same way—reveling, mocking, and saying there is no danger near. Ah! my friends, you who go by water, there is always danger, only a plank between you and eternity. How many are drowned every year, and perhaps go to the bar of God unsaved!

"I heard of a brother who, in telling his experience, said he never pondered seriously his awful condition as a sinner until one dark night, bound up the Bay, he felt a solemn dread take hold of him, for he did not know but some passing vessel or steamboat might run foul of his boat and sink him; and in that case, said he to himself, 'Where would I go?' This thought brought him to repentance. He went to a camp meeting soon after, and determined never to leave that place, until God, for Christ's sake, should pardon his sins.

"He did not seek in vain, but was happily converted and joined the Church, to live and die among the people of God.

"But if there is no danger of a watery grave, how about the fire? Worse and worse. A deluge of flame will burst over this world at the last day, for it is reserved unto fire, the apostle says, and all this earth will be dissolved. If this be so, what manner of persons ought we to be, in all holy conversation and godliness?

"I must now come back to my text. It appears to me I have heard Brother Lawrenson and Brother James

Allen say, that it will be far worse on sinners who are lost by unbelief and disobedience, under the gospel dispensation, than it is on the antediluvians, and the wicked who perished in the city called Sodom.

"We read in the Testament, where Jesus said it will be more tolerable—that is, they will bear it better, they will not be so utterly wretched—it will be more tolerable in that day for Sodom and Gomorrah than for you. Why? If they had your light, your gospel privileges, they would have repented, like Nineveh, in sackcloth and ashes.

"This is the reason, the text says, 'we ought to give the more earnest heed to the things which we have heard, lest at any time we should let them slip.'

"The Lord of glory has come down from heaven to teach us the way, yet there are many who will not walk in it. He invites, but how few accept his great salvation, or care about their souls, that must live forever! How ungrateful we are to him who gave this life, that we might live a life concealed in him! I have often cried over my ingratitude of heart, when thinking about the goodness of the Saviour to poor sinners, of whom, like the apostle, I am chief. Why don't you cry over your hard-heartedness? Your eyes are dry, and you are ashamed to be seen, or even thought, serious about your everlasting welfare.

"Well, if you are, I am not. I feel like crying for you now."

Here he covered his face with his hands, and with bowed head, and low, plaintive wailings, deplored the unconcern of men, deprecated the wrath divine, and gave

evidence of being in deep distress for a few minutes.
This he really felt; and this was the great secret of his
power and wonderful success at all times, in enlisting the
attention, and controlling at will the emotions of his
hearers. He felt what he said, and said what he felt;
realizing truth, whether of a jubilant or fearful character,
and conveying to the mind and heart of his auditor, his
own emotions. He wept there before the people, until
they saw his tears trickle down, and melted into a tender
mood themselves. "Oh, Jesus, Jesus," he murmured,
"Thou didst weep over Jerusalem sinners, but these are
worse than they; melt their hardness down by the view
of thy cross, and bloody sweat, and agony for them.
Save them, Lord, they know not what they do! Help
me to-day to get hold of their hearts."

He then took a survey, with eyes full of tender com-
passion, of the scene around him, took up his handkerchief and wiped the tears from his face; while we were
all melted down; and strong, hard men appeared ready
to drop on the ground, sobbing convulsively, by the force
of sympathy, or under the power of the Spirit.

He here branched out in anecdotes and instances of
the times when he and his old neighbors were converted,
and how they labored to bring others to Christ, appealing to some one occasionally in the congregation, who
knew the facts, and could bear testimony to the truth of
what he was saying.

Returning to his text again, he began a brief exposition of the passage, emphasizing the terms, and illustrating in his quaint manner every point as he passed on.

"What things," he inquired, "are we to heed, so as

not to let them slip? The things this book teaches. The good word of life. The things our ministers tell us. What you heard from Brother Onins this morning, and from old Brother Sewell on Sunday, and from the brother Elliott, who preached such a glorious sermon to us. Don't let these things slip; that is, don't forget them. A schoolmaster had a boy who could remember nothing of his lessons, and he said what passed in at one ear just popped out at the other. He told him to get some cotton and stop one up, and then he might retain what he had learned. I wish some people who hear the gospel would do that, or anything else that would help them to remember the truth.

"Suppose a man took his bucket, and went outside there to the well, and filled it with water, and there was a hole in it, so that when he reached his tent, the water would all be gone; it would be labor for nothing. A good many persons go to preaching, and come to camp meeting, and everything they hear they 'let slip,' and return as empty as when they came, like that leaky bucket!

"I always make my children bring me something home from preaching, and while they are gone on Sundays, and I am alone at home, I can recollect many blessed sermons I have heard, and I feel happy in the midst of my pains and loneliness. They tell me the text that has been preached, and in trying to remember it, they generally catch some of the sermon too, and in this way I believe people could keep the devil from troubling them in meeting. When I hear what good text has been preached, I try to think what might be said upon it, and

they often tell me, 'That's just what the preacher said.'
This, friends, is all my comfort while I have to suffer
my Lord's will in affliction. I meditate on his law both
day and night, and like one of old, 'my meditation of
him is sweet.'

"I gave earnest heed when I could go about, and
treasured up many precious things to help me along in
my old age and infirmity.

"Don't let these good things slip, they are too precious to lose. A man went and bought some corn, and
started home with his bag on his back, but there was a
little torn place in it, and every step he took, out rolled
the corn. After a while his bag began to feel loose and
light; and when he examined the matter, he found he
had let his corn slip. But if you let the good seed of
the kingdom slip, it will be worse than a bushel of corn,
therefore give the more earnest heed.

"Some of you remember when old brother Henry
White preached that sermon on the 'hill,' about the
sower who went forth to sow, and the different places the
seed fell. Well, I thought that day I could see the
devil going about among the people, and busy at his
work of destroying the souls of men. In some he
choked the good seed at once by a few worldly thoughts,
in others he picked it up like the crows, as fast as it fell,
and there was none took root; and in a third class, he
trampled it down on the barren, beaten pathway of their
thoughtlessness. That was one great sermon, but you
let even that slip.

"Why, my friends, we must 'take fast hold of instruction,' as the wise Solomon says in the book of

Proverbs: we must hold on to the truth, as Paul says; and we must watch and pray, lest having a promise of entering into rest, any of us should seem to come short, and miss it at last.

" 'Give *earnest* heed.' That is about the same as 'Strive to enter in at the strait gate;' and means that we should wake up to strong effort, and hear in the spirit of prayer, 'the word being mixed with faith.' Let nothing you hear about the way of salvation, be neglected. Contend earnestly for the prize at the end of the race, and be as much engaged about getting grace, as about getting money.

"If you have a dollar or two, you will take mighty good care of it, and put it in your best pocket, or lock it up in your chest.

"A good brother once said, when he was here a begging money, to send the gospel off to the heathen, there were some people so stingy, that they held on to a quarter dollar so tight, as almost to make the eagle squall! This makes you laugh; but is it not strange that we don't hold on to our hope in Christ, with just as hard a hold as that? If you let go, you sink, you are gone.

"We ought to give the *more* earnest heed, seeing our privileges are so high, our time so short, and the judgment bar before our eyes. *We*, my dear friends, who profess religion: Paul said, *we*, meaning himself with others. We ought to feel for poor sinners, but we must 'take heed to ourselves.'

" 'Watch and pray that ye enter not into temptation.'

" 'For if the word spoken by angels was steadfast, and every transgression and disobedience received a just

recompense of reward;'—if those who sinned under the
old dispensation were punished for every sin,—if God
never falsified his own word, to let a guilty soul escape ;
—if this was the case before the world received the
blessed gospel of the Son of God with its light and motives to obedience,—then 'how shall we escape if we
neglect so great salvation ?'

"This is the last thing I will talk about, and this is
greatest of all, my unconverted friends. I want you
now to ask yourselves the question, to try and ascertain
it. As for me, *I don't know!* Perhaps you think you
can escape. I think not. For, understand, there is no
way but Christ. There is no time but now that you
can call your own. There is no place but this life, as
the hymn says :—

> " ' Life is the time to serve the Lord,
>   The time to ensure the great reward ;'

"And I bless God,

> " ' While the lamp holds out to burn,
>   The vilest sinner may return.'

"The lamp is your present life ; but it may go out
suddenly ; then where are you ? in darkness and blackness for ever. Some old people may be aroused to seek
religion, but it is hard work for them. I have seen a
good many old sinners made happy in the Lord, when
they repented, and began to cry like Peter, 'Save, Lord,
or I perish.' (Here he gave the names of several.) But
you who are young ought to seek this first of all. What
makes me so sorry is that I did not hear the pure gospel

plan explained, and feel the mighty power of the Spirit
when I was young.

"The text says it is a 'great salvation.' If you read
your Bibles, you will find out why it is so great.   Here
is one reason, ' God so loved the world, that he gave his
only begotten Son, that whosoever believeth in him
should not perish, but have everlasting life.'   This
teaches you what God—the Great God—had to do
with it.

"Then it is great on account of what it cost.   Did
you ever calculate what it cost to redeem a soul?   How
much money? No, something very different.   'Ye are
redeemed, not with corruptible things, such as silver
and gold, but with the precious blood of Christ.'   That's
it.   'The precious blood of Christ.'   Lord, seal this on
their hearts, make them think of it!   Now will you
trample on that price paid down for your sinful soul,
that it might be saved?   Oh! do not, do not.   Think
of the 'everlasting fire' from which this will save you if
you seek it, and then say, is it not a 'great salvation?'
Think of the glory world,—the saints of all ages,—the
paradise of God, where you may live, if you are holy
and faithful, and this shows how great the salvation is.

"You may be saved, hallelujah!—saved from sin and
hell, saved to endless life, for this is a *great* salvation;
great as your sins, though they were mountains high, or
more

" ' Than sands upon the ocean shore,

you may be fully, freely, and for ever saved.

"This makes me happy.   Oh! that I could shout!

Any sinner who comes to Jesus Christ the Saviour in the right spirit, will not be cast away, for ' He is able, he is willing, doubt no more.'

" Well, but will you *accept* this great salvation, you see the consequences if you neglect it. You have a part to act. *Will* you accept Christ? He said to a certain people, ' Ye will not come unto me, that ye might have life.' Is this the case of any here? Will they miss of it by neglect?

" Mind, it does not say ' reject,' but ' *neglect.*' Now a soul can be lost on either tack. I do not know which is worst of the two; but it appears to me I have heard preachers say, the one who neglects, that is, passes on with indifference, as if it were of no account, this precious blessing of God, is worse off at last than he who openly and boldly rejects it and takes the consequences.

" I hope you, my friends, will do neither. It would be to your shame if you did. Do you really think you can get along without it? If you do, you will find out your mistake in a dying hour, as some I have known, and many I have heard tell of, who professed to be infidels, or some foolish thing of that sort; but when they came down to the cold, swelling waves of death, ah! what did they do? they cried for mercy, but found their day closing in night, and all their hopes lost in the flood-tide that swept them away in one eternal storm.

" Is there anything you can prefer to this salvation? Anything to live with and die by equal to it? No:—

> " ' Nothing is worth a thought beneath,
> But how I may escape that death
> That never, never dies.

How make mine own election sure,
And when I fail on earth, secure
A mansion in the skies.'

" It is a great wonder to me how any of us will escape.
We would be undone forever, but—

" ' The voice of free grace cries, Escape to the mountain,
For Adam's lost race Christ has opened a fountain,
For sin and uncleanness and every transgression,
His blood flows most freely in streams of salvation.'

" That's good news for us. That will be our shelter
from the stormy blast, and our eternal home,—

" ' When the rocks and the mountains shall all flee away,
Then you shall have a sure hiding place that day.'

" But, sinner, you will not escape, you cannot, you
ought not, if you refuse Him that speaketh from heaven,
and now calls the wanderer back :—

" ' Turn to the Lord and seek salvation.'

" Now is the accepted time. When we learned that
good old invitation hymn, long ago, on the Tangiers, we
thought it was glorious; and many flocked home to
Christ the Shepherd and Bishop of their souls, while we
used to sing it. Those old pilgrims have gained the city.
Many are now in bright glory, and I shall soon meet
them there. They died as I expect to die, shouting
this great salvation free for all, for Jew and Gentile
too.

" Oh ! when I get up yonder, what do you suppose I
shall hear ? I expect to hear them sing with a loud

voice, 'Salvation unto our God, that sitteth on the throne, and unto the Lamb forever and ever.'

"My friends, will you meet me there? I am now going to do as old Brother White did one happy Sunday on the 'Hill.' He asked you to meet him above, and all who were there promised. Will you meet me hard by the throne? All who feel like trying for heaven and glory, now rise up!"

With a bound, nearly every person in the circle, not already standing, sprang to their feet, and at least a hundred clear off their feet, so intense had become the excitement of the moment.

The unconverted wept and trembled, crowding up to the altar, and believers shouted aloud, in their uncontrollable emotion, while they pressed forward to take the old man's offered hand in pledge to meet where pain and parting tears are shed no more.

Many were speedily converted that afternoon, and joined in the general joy. Brother Thomas was taken back to his tent, under great excitement, and there continued to exhort a crowd, that stood, around the entrance, to prepare for heaven, and live faithful.

Thus ended the public ministrations of this remarkable man;—remarkable for his simplicity, directness, and zeal for nearly forty years of effort in showing to others the gospel way of salvation.

He lived a few years after this, and continued his ministry of earnest, loving entreaty and prayer with all who visited him in his little Island home; allowing none to cross his threshold without a timely word of exhortation adapted to each case.

A very singular circumstance is told, as having occurred some time prior to this; and as a well authenti-
cated fact, proving that good man's power in prayer, we
introduce it here.

He owned a small island adjacent to that on which he
lived. It is called "Piney Island," and the original
patent, under which it is held, remains in the possession
of the family.

In the waters surrounding this island, large quantities
of fish were discovered, a seine was employed by some
of the family and neighbors of Brother Thomas, and an
abundant supply caught. The news spread, and others
came to share this blessing of Providence; but selfishness and avarice were allowed to gain such an ascend-
ancy that a quarrel arose, and blows were exchanged by
those laying out their seines. Father Thomas heard the
affray, and hastened to his closet—there spent some
time prostrate before God in prayer. He then came
forth, and said to the parties returning from the new fish-
ing-ground, " *There will be no more fish in that place!*
God sent us this blessing, and as it was likely to prove
a source of discord, I have prayed him to remove it."

The prayer was successful; his faith was sustained;
from that hour no fish have been found in those waters.

CHAPTER XXVII.

The Parson obtains a carriage—Going to church—Household words—Letter
from Rev. B. F. Price—Imposition of hands—Sordid selfishness rebuked
—A Chieftain in the host—Accidental fall—Dream—Dr. Jones—Visits of
the preachers—Adventure of the Princess Anne lawyers—Hon. Mr. C.—
" We must pray if you are all lawyers."—Character of the prayer—its effects—He prays for " their servants."

SUCH was the desire of Father Thomas to attend the
services of the sanctuary, and occasionally visit his
Island neighbors and friends, that a small carriage was
constructed for his use, in which he could recline as in
a large easy chair; and so arranged that he could be
lifted off, and carried into the house of God, without
having to change his seat.

The writer is happy to remember, that he had a hand
in the getting up of this contrivance; and personally
witnessed the grateful surprise it gave the good old man,
when conveyed to his residence; and he was informed
that it was a token of the affectionate esteem of his
friends, who sought, by this means, to alleviate a little
his deprivation, and aid him in moving about, to bless
the people with his presence, and continue his useful
labors in the church.

The engraving represents a Sabbath morning scene.

The Parson is on his way to the new church farther up the island; and is seen passing the old, or former place of worship; where, from the time of its erection, until supplanted by a larger and more elegant structure, he regularly ministered in holy things.

Turning the corner of the road at this point, we have a glimpse of the large building, which for many years was the residence of Brother Mister; now owned and occupied by Captain Thomas Bradshaw.

The persons represented as an escort to the little carriage and its occupant, are of his own family. There are Seymour and Aaron, his sons; Joshua, his little grandson; Mrs. Thomas, the companion and sympathizing participant in all his afflictions. There is also the wife of Aaron—now a widow—and her little daughter Catherine.

In the bright sunshine, they cheerily move along; and though living farthest from the church, are likely to be among the first to reach it, and the most happy in its services.

They will presently fall in with numerous companions on the way; and with kind, friendly interchanges of regard, and a frequent observation, containing weighty wisdom, from Father Thomas, the journey is a pleasure; to be near him, a privilege.

To the casual question, as to who may be going to preach, or whether he will preach a good sermon?—*He* replies, in words of gentle rebuke: "Never say a preacher or a sermon is *bad*, or *poor;* if it has Christ in it, and anything about the way to heaven, it will be a good, a rich sermon. Don't, my friends, underrate your ministers,

THE PARSON AN INVALID, ON HIS WAY TO CHURCH.

love them and hear their words, with hungering and thirsting; then you shall be filled, and blest."

So of "bad" weather, or what persons would call a miserable day, if rainy, cold, or even excessively warm, he would reprove their presumption, in thus passing judgment on God's weather, and unthinkingly reflecting on his wisdom and providence.

His sayings of this kind are still "household words," among the people of the Islands. "As old Brother Thomas used to say," comes with authority, to all who love his memory.

Rev. Benj. F. Price was the pastor of the Island churches, at the period of which we now write. He pays a truthful and beautiful tribute to that memory still precious among the people, in the following communication:

"DEAR BROTHER WALLACE:—In compliance with your request, to furnish you some reminiscences of Brother Thomas, I send you one or two particulars, which memory has preserved, of my casual and transient intercourse with that man of God.

"My first interview with him was at his own house, and although decrepid with age and disease, I felt myself in the presence of one, who, like Enoch, 'walked with God,' and who retained a freshness which neither age nor disease could destroy. His conversation was in the fullest sense religious. His bearing was that of a veteran, and a victor; and the smile that gladdened his countenance, and glistened with the tears that bedewed his eye lids, arched his time-and-toil-wrinkled brow like the rainbow of hope.

"I had not been with him long, before he requested me to find the hymn beginning with the words, 'The thing my God doth hate,' &c. (Page 305.) After singing, he desired me to pray, which I did. He then called me to him, and placing his hands on my head, gave me his blessing. I felt it was no mean imposition, and my vows were renewed by a fresh consecration.

"On another occasion, when at his house, conversation turned on his temporal necessities. After a life of active labor in the service of the church, Brother Thomas, in old age, found himself poor in this world's goods, and unable to accomplish any thing towards the support of his family. He had enterprising children, who were getting on well in the world, and willing to assist him; but he preferred to provide for himself. It was suggested that the church owed him much, and would gladly remember his wants, if he would allow his case to be mentioned at the various appointments. To this he consented, on the principle that the 'laborer is worthy of his hire.'

"He was so universally known and beloved, that many felt it to be a privilege to contribute to his comfort, as I mentioned the subject to them. Some time after this I again paid him a visit, which may have been my last. He told me, he understood that, at a certain place where I had mentioned his circumstances, objections were made by an individual; this I did not recollect, and told him I thought it was a misapprehension; but he had his suspicions, and remarked, that the person referred to had met with a serious loss of property, and that Providence had in that manner vindicated his cause.

"He related to me several instances of the kind, and said he had actually been afraid to make a request, lest the person refusing should be visited with some stroke of retribution. Great was his faith in the God whom he served.

"During the period of my ministry on the circuit, Brother Thomas was but rarely able to attend public worship, except at the camp meeting on Deal's Island, to which he was conveyed from his little Island home, and at which, by means of an easy chair, he was enabled to occupy a place on the preachers' stand, and listen to the word of life, to which he gave responses in earnest 'Amens,' and shouting 'Hallelujahs!' His presence at the camp meeting seemed to revive in his own mind blessed recollections, and to kindle in the hearts of his brethren, the spirit of holy zeal and perseverance."

He was like a chieftain among the Lord's hosts, waiting for his release from battle service, and when the chariot came, he mounted it and

"Passed through death triumphant home."

At one of the camp meetings, while in this enfeebled state, Father Thomas had a very severe fall, from the effects of which he suffered intensely. He called on a couple of persons to carry him back to his tent, from the stand, and while they were hurrying along, he slipped from his chair and fell to the ground.

He was in such a condition, that this fall jarred his body and limbs very much, and hastened on the period, when, to his regret, and that of his friends, he could leave his room no more.

An inflammation broke out, about this time, in one of his limbs, that could not by any ordinary means be subdued. He had a dream one night about this matter, and on awaking told Mrs. Thomas to procure some potatoes, scrape them in the raw state, and apply a poultice to the inflamed part. This was done at his request, without much hope of relief, by his attendants; but he was cured almost immediately.

Dr. Jones often visited him in his last days, and showed him all the attention possible. During his calls, Father Thomas inquired particularly if any were sick on the Island, the nature of their complaints, and their prospects for recovery. After his kind inquiries were all answered, he would ask the doctor to read a few chapters in the Bible, and then kneel down by him, while he offered prayer. In his petitions, he referred to every patient by name, of whom he had been informed, praying most earnestly for their recovery, and that God might bless the doctor with great skill and success in his practice, and give him grace, to turn him away from the vanities of earth, to seek an acquaintance for himself, with the great Physician of souls. These simple acts of his Christian sympathy, his concern for the suffering, and his desire for the salvation of all who crossed his threshold, gave the doctor unmistakable evidence of his sincere piety.

A friend of his, a lawyer in Princess Anne, presented him with a large arm chair, in which, with the family Bible on his knee, and his hymn book at hand, he spent the weary days of his declining years. In this chair, and just as the writer last saw him, is he intended to be represented in the portrait which has been prepared for this volume. That it is an exact likeness we cannot pretend, as memory was our only guide in the design; and a likeness of either of his sons, who resemble him very closely, would not have been his. If the result of our labor will but suffice to recall the sainted form of Brother Thomas, as his friends remember him in life, the object in view will have been attained.

The influence he exerted, and the prayers he offered for visiting friends, while an invalid at home, made deep and durable impressions on the minds and hearts of all with whom he came in contact. If one of the preachers could spend a day or night under his roof, he was cheered greatly; and seemed to feel his sufferings less, while conversation ran on the affairs of the church, or the prospects for a revival of religion among his acquaintances on the Islands.

Strangers sometimes made considerable journeys, to see for themselves, and spend a short time in the company of a man so much talked of in the community. These visits resulted in good to their souls, invariably. A more solemn feeling, perhaps, never rested on the mind of an individual, than that experienced, when, in obedience to his request, he knelt before him, and with his hands on the head, devoutly gave his blessing, or invoked the benediction of God on a visitor.

A number of gentlemen, most of them lawyers, from Princess Anne, had been making an excursion for purposes of recreation to the Islands; and happening in the

vicinity of Father Thomas' residence, agreed to pay him
their respects; and immediately started for the house.
Among the company was Hon. Mr. C., long a highly
valued friend, and, in many instances, a benefactor of the
Parson.   They entered, and found him with the holy
Book open before him, which he was perusing for his
edification and comfort.   After each had walked up to
where he sat, and shook hands with him, they were invited to sit down, and Brother Thomas inquired the
names of all he did not recognize, ascertained their business, and whether they had families, &c.   Conversation
had been continued for some time, and all were highly
gratified—the Parson in the unexpected honor and
pleasure of the visit, and his friends in the cheerfulness
he evinced under debility and pain, and the entertaining
anecdotes he repeated of his acquaintance with their
fathers in past days.

A movement was made by some of the party to end
the interview, and retire.   The others took the hint, and
all were about to leave, when he said, "Stop, friends!
you see my situation here.   I cannot leave this chair;
but, down with you, every man on your knees. *If you
are all lawyers*, we must have a word of prayer together
before you go!"   The company dropped into the desired
posture, in various parts of the room, and to some of
them the position was entirely novel; they were not
used to this holy exercise; while all felt the situation
into which they were brought in such an unexpected
manner, to be unusual, and its sensations peculiar.

But the memorable prayer began.   Simple and solemn,
touching every heart in a moment; and as it proceeded,

in appropriate scriptural terms, the interest and admiration of the kneeling circle was thoroughly enlisted.
When he came to personate them, and pray for the wives
of those who enjoyed that blessing, and their little children at home, and the servants of their households, tears
began to flow, handkerchiefs were hastily brought into
requisition; and when the prayer ended, and they arose
from their recumbent posture, silence prevailed to an em-
barrassing degree. No word was uttered, as one by one
the lawyers gave the good man their hand in farewell,
and took their departure from a place, of which they
could exclaim, as one of old, "Surely the Lord is here,
and I knew it not; this is God's own house, and the gate
of heaven." After walking some distance, an effort was
made by some one to rally his solemn visaged fellows,
and break the spell which hung around them. He addressed the pilot, or driver of the party, Mr. T. Smith,
—"Tom," said he, "the old gentleman did not pray for
you." "Oh yes, he did," rejoined Tom, "did you not
hear him pray for *your servants?*" This occasioned a
laugh, and brought the company back to their ordinary
spirits, and to the use of their tongues; but not a man
of them has lost the recollection, or will ever forget the
feelings of that hour.

CHAPTER XXVIII.

Nearing port—Cheerfulness and religious hope—Sorrows of old age—Dying young—Ministry of a devoted wife—"Son, I am not afraid to die"—Tranquil passage—In the harbor—Safe at home—"He is gone !"—Funeral sermon by Rev. Z. Webster—Doctrine of the resurrection—Certainty and glory—Consolation to the sorrowing—Security of the righteous—"He sleeps in Jesus"—Rev. A. W. Milby—Burial—Inscription on tomb—Death of Aaron Thomas—A widow's stay in trouble—The Thomas family—Reflections—Conclusion.

DURING the summer of 1853, it became evident to Father Thomas and his friends, that his end was nigh at hand. This gave him no concern, but was to his mind rather a subject of cheerful contemplation. "Don't look so gloomy and distressed," he would say to those who visited him, and could ill restrain their tears, at witnessing his feebleness, and increasing bodily infirmities. Some of the wisest and weightiest words, that ever fell from his lips, were uttered with a view to reconcile his family, and all others who shared his sympathy and affection, to the event that must soon remove him from the associations of earth.

He said to the writer, "Brother, never pray, or wish, to live until you are helpless and old. To die young, may seem, to hopeful youth, a hard thing; but it looks to me, to be a great privilege, if it be God's will, to call one away to the joys of heaven, before the weary burden of old age presses him gradually down into the grave. The sooner you reach heaven the better."

The seventy-seventh anniversary of his birth greeted him, and left him unable to be moved from his couch. There, he was attended by the ceaseless ministrations of that loving wife, who, as he firmly believed, had been selected for him by his Lord, nearly forty years before; and who, by reason of natural strength and endurance, never wearied in her kind and considerate attention to his every want. "What would I do without her?" was his frequent remark, as she nursed him with tenderness, and watched by his bed of pain. The goodness of God, in providing him with such a devoted companion, and such affectionate children, filled his heart with praise. His sons, Seymour and Aaron, were daily near him, to afford all the support and comfort possible, as his sun serenely declined, and his eventful life was closing, without a cloud on the horizon of his religious hope.

A short time before he breathed his last, he said to Seymour, who appeared to be filled with distress—"*Son, I am not afraid to die!*" From this moment he rapidly declined; and, satisfied that his work was done, bade all his family farewell, before his power of utterance failed him; then appeared to fix his thoughts on that world, the confines of which his spirit had reached: and in which his dim eye discerned "a building of God; a house not made with hands, eternal in the heavens."

His longed for release came at 2 o'clock, on the morning of the 8th day of October, 1853; and the transition was quiet, as a gentle slumber. With his last expiring energy he gave the signal, as he entered "death's cold stream," that all was well! Toiling hard, he at length found anchorage in the peaceful haven; fighting long, his victory came, and with "an abundant entrance" he gained the "crown of life."

"*He is gone*," was the subdued announcement of one to another, as the tidings traveled to every home on the Island that morning; "gone to heaven," was the thought of every heart.

"Lay me," he had requested, "in a plain coffin, when I die. Let Brother Webster preach my funeral sermon; and be sure you do not bear my poor decaying dust into the holy sanctuary during the services; leave it outside the door, while you enter and bow before the Lord in prayer, and hear his glorious word; then make my grave, where the sound of a preached gospel, Sabbath after Sabbath, and the shouts of happy Christians (from the adjacent camp ground) will linger over the spot where I shall rest in hope."

These arrangements were obeyed in every particular. The funeral cortege included nearly every person in the entire community. The church was thronged, and sadness fell on all, as the memory of that voice which was wont to instruct and comfort, but now hushed forever, came vividly before the people. Rev. Z. Webster, accompanied by Rev. A. W. Milby, ascended the pulpit: the former to preach the funeral sermon, and the latter, who, out of respect to the deceased, had come a long distance, to assist in the services.

(A full report of this discourse was prepared for insertion here; but owing to the limited space that remains to us, a bare synopsis is all that can be given.)

After the customary introductory services, Brother Webster rose and announced his text from 1 Thess. iv. 13, 14–18.

"*But I would not have you to be ignorant, brethren, concerning them which are asleep, that ye sorrow not even as others which have no hope.*

"*For, if we believe that Jesus died and rose again, even so, them also which sleep in Jesus will God bring with him.* * * * * * *

"*Wherefore comfort one another with these words.*"

The doubts and difficulties of many in the early Christian church, and through all subsequent time, on the doctrine of the resurrection; and the apostle's arguments, and explanations, to settle the faith, and cheer the hopes of sorrowing humanity, in its *certainty* and glorious consequences; formed the subject of preliminary remark.

The preacher then adverted to the solemn and afflictive dispensation of death—the death of the good, the venerated and beloved of earth. He intimated that sorrow from a sense of bereavement, was natural and irrepressible; but *hopeless* sorrow, for a Christian departed, was unnecessary, and unworthy those who accept and believe the revelation of God, which clearly shows that, under certain conditions, "to die is gain;" and that a reunion, beyond this vale of tears, is the happy heritage of all the sanctified.

The resurrection of the human body, he stated, is made dependent on the fact that "Jesus died, and rose again." This fact he then proceeded to notice at length; showing the numerous authorities which incontestably establish it, as the great basis of hope to man, that there will be a general resurrection at the last day. Christ, having risen from the dead, and become the "first fruits" of them that slept, has sufficient ability to accomplish the mighty work. Of this power, illustrations were given, and striking examples—in the case of Lazarus, and the saints, whose graves were opened at the time of the crucifixion—were adduced. Objections to the doctrine were noted and answered, and the faith of Christians encouraged by the view of God's omnipotence and faithfulness.

He then presented the effects—to all who "sleep in Jesus"—of a part in the *first* resurrection; urging repentance, faith, holy living, humility, watchfulness, and fruit-bearing, as the necessary means and evidences of this saving intimacy with Christ Jesus.

To such as "look for his appearing," and, bearing his cross, are found at his coming to be faithful servants, God will secure a triumph o'er the grave, a full and final victory over death. In this prospect the believer can sing, with a delightful poet :—

> "I would not live alway ; no, welcome the tomb!
> Since Jesus hath lain there, I dread not its gloom;
> There sweet be my rest till he bid me arise,
> To hail him in triumph descending the skies."

To the unconverted there is nothing pleasing in the prospect of that morning, when "many that sleep in the dust shall awake." The glorious provision of "everlasting life" may be forfeited and lost; and, consequent on impiety, only "shame and everlasting contempt" be realized as the result of the trumpet's call; and, while Christ's followers shall have the unspeakable privilege of being "ever with the Lord," those who despise or reject him "shall be banished from his presence" forever.

"God is gathering home his people," said the preacher, " one by one they have gone from among us, and while *we* lament their loss, are swelling the multitude which no man can number, and praising him above. Another is gone from his beloved and stricken family, from the Church, and society, where he occupied a place of prominence, for his deep piety and great usefulness. Father Thomas is no more.

"I need not add here, where his life, character, and labors are so well known, any extended remarks. He was a good man, full of faith and the Holy Ghost, did great good in his day and generation, and we have not the shadow of a doubt is now where 'the weary are at rest.'

"May God comfort the hearts of this bereaved family, and large circle of mourning friends, and may we all follow him as he followed Christ. Amen."

Rev. Mr. Milby addressed the people in some remarks following the sermon, and read the impressive burial service at the grave; after which, the mortal part of this beloved Father in Israel was committed to dust and ashes, in hope of a future and glorious reunion, when the saying shall be brought to pass, " Death is swallowed up in victory."

His tomb may be seen by the side of the Deal's Island church, and bears the following inscription :

IN MEMORY OF THE REV.

JOSHUA THOMAS;

WHO DEPARTED THIS LIFE,

OCT. 8th. 1853 ;

AGED 77 YEARS, 1 MONTH AND 18 DAYS.

> " Come all my friends, as you pass by,
> Behold the place where I do lie ;
> As you are now, so once was I ;
> Remember you are born to die."

This stanza, it is said, he selected and arranged himself, before his death ; as a silent and solemn call to the living to secure in life, the great end of probation.

Another grave had soon to be opened, near that of the father, for his youngest surviving son, the beloved Aaron. In *his* death, the church lost a jewel. He was converted when a boy, was rebaptized with the Holy Spirit at Tangier, and afterwards became a zealous and useful exhorter. Had he been spared, his destination was evidently the " walls of Zion," where he would have been a " bright and shining light."

In his death, also, the now doubly bereaved and widowed mother found her cup of sorrow full ; but the hand Divine, blended in its bitterness the sweet ingredient of resignation, and joyous anticipations of a meeting soon, where

> " Sickness and sorrow, pain and death,
> Are felt and feared no more."

Before concluding these memoirs, the writer may be allowed to notice the death of John Parks, one of the early contemporaries of Brother Thomas, of whom an extended sketch is herein presented.

He died on Thursday, the 24th day of January, 1861, and now rests from his labors. Of him it may be said, in the words of Charles Wesley:

"Weep not for a brother deceased;
   Our loss is his infinite gain;
A soul out of prison released,
   And freed from its bodily chain.

With songs let us follow his flight,
   And mount with his spirit above;
Escaped to the mansions of light,
   And lodged in the Eden of love.

Our brother the haven hath gained,
   Outflying the tempest and wind;
His rest he hath sooner obtained,
   And left his companions behind.

Still toss'd on a sea of distress,
   Hard toiling to make the blest shore,
Where all is assurance and peace,
   And sorrow and sin are no more.

There all the ship's company meet,
   Who sailed with the Saviour beneath;
With shouting each other they greet,
   And triumph o'er sorrow and death:

The voyage of life 's at an end;
   The mortal affliction is past;
The age that in heaven they spend,
   For ever and ever shall last.

The grave yards of Deal's Island have gathered in many, whose memory is precious to the church and community ; and whose Christian example for liberality to the cause of God, is a sweet memorial that shall never die.

The pious Aaron Bradshaw evinced his sympathy with that work which contemplates the conquest of the world by righteousness, and the establishment of His reign, whose right it is, "from sea to sea, and from the river, unto the end of the earth ;" by a legacy, the proceeds of which are realized from year to year, to send the gospel into " all the world."

His son Caleb, also departed, followed the example of his father in this respect, as he did in the service of his father's God.

Another name has been recently added to the list of those, whose influence and liberality continues to bless the church, they " being dead." We refer to that of Hamilton White : a brother beloved in life, and who passed away leaving a clear and emphatic testimony behind, to the power and preciousness of the religion of Christ, to enable the soul to triumph in its last hour of earthly conflict.

> " 'Tis religion that can give
> Sweetest pleasure while we live ;
> Religion only can supply
> Solid comfort when we die ;
> After death its joys will be
> Lasting as eternity."

The members of Father Thomas' family who remain, are John, to whom frequent allusion has been made ;

Elisha, one of the class leaders on Deal's Island; Seymour, who lives adjoining old Mrs. Thomas on the little island; Mrs. Webster, also referred to; and Lybrand, named after a favorite preacher—the late Rev. Jos. Lybrand. Most of these have large families of children, on whom, may *his* mantle, of whom we here make affectionate memorial, descend and ever abide.

And to this devout wish, the writer will only add, in closing up this labor of love, the prayer, that the Island people, whose generous liberality to the cause of missions, the Christian church, and whatsoever things are lovely and of good report, is unbounded; and whose hospitality to the ministers of Christ is proverbial—may abound more and more, in all the graces of godliness; be steadfast in the faith of their fathers, and find admittance at last to the society of the blessed at the right hand of God.

There may he who now sustains to them the endearing relation of pastor—himself through mercy saved—renew the hallowed intercourse of time with those who have crossed the flood, and among them, the glorified spirit of one we long to greet again—" The Parson of the Islands."

THE CHRISTIAN MARINER.

TO THE MEMORY OF THE REV. JOSHUA THOMAS

BY R. E. KEMP.

Full many a day has passed away—
    And days with danger rife;
Since first thy bark was launched upon
    The stormy sea of life.

And many a wave has spent its force,
    And oft the driving storm
Has swept across thy onward course,
    And broke upon thy form.

With quadrant, compass, and the chart,
    Which God's own hand has given,
To guide the sailor safe to port—
    Thy voyage led to heaven.

And now the clouds have passed away,
    The sky is bright and clear;
A star, the harbinger of day,
    Disperses doubt and fear.

The coast of bliss so long in view—
    Beyond the breakers' roar—
Is gained at last, and anchor cast
    Upon that shining shore.

Thy sails are furl'd, and safely there
    Thy weary soul may rest:
For thee, thy Captain did prepare
    A home among the blest.

And while we miss our brother here,
    And for thy presence sigh,
With humble hope, we wait the day,
    To greet thee in the sky.

FOR MARYLAND'S HONOR

A Story of the War for Southern Independence

By Lloyd T. Everett

Dedicated To
**"To my Father
Rev. Wm. B. Everett, M.D.,
A Confederate Veteran of the "Old Line State,"
and to Dixie's defenders everywhere"**

229 Pages -Reprint of rare and very desirable 1922 edition
by Christopher Publishing Co., Boston
Hardback, Black linen w/Gold Embossing
Just $25.00 plus $5.00 priority Shipping & Handling (USA)

New to this reprint: Photograph of 1ˢᵗ Maryland Infantry Regimental Colors
("Bucktail Flag") presented by the Ladies of Baltimore
(Maryland State Archives Special Collection)

Although *For Maryland's Honor* is a novel, the scholarly research and attention to detail is evident throughout the book. The author, Mr. Everett, informs readers, *"In the purely historical parts .... careful recourse has been had to the authorities."* Starting with the political fervor surrounding Maryland in October 1860, the author uses enticing and realistic dialogue, together with carefully researched historical facts, to very effectively set the stage for a progressive and informative narrative.

Included are details about Lt. Col. Bradley T. Johnson and his wife, known affectionately by the soldiers as Mrs. Capt. Bradley, who together were successful in recruiting and equipping Marylanders into Confederate service under the Maryland banner. In *For Maryland's Honor*, the woman's perspective of the "War for Southern Independence" on the home front is eloquently portrayed by Miss Marion Palmer who provides both the love interest and conflict...as her loyalty is to the North.

For Maryland's Honor is a must read for men and women alike who seek to "feel" what it meant to be a citizen of Maryland in those patriotic, yet sorrowful and heartfelt times.

About the Author – Historian Lloyd T. Everett practiced law, researched, wrote and lectured on Confederate history before historical associations in Washington, D.C., Maryland, Virginia and Florida. His many credits include publication in the South Atlantic Quarterly, Southern Historical Association Papers and Tyler's Quarterly Historical and Genealogical Magazine. He also co-edited the re-publication of R. G. Horton's *A Youth's History of the Civil War*, first published in 1866.

ISBN: 0-9703802-1-6
Library of Congress Control Number: 2001088654

FREE TO STAY

The TRUE STORY of Eliza Benson and the family she stood by for three generations

By Nan Hayden Agle

160 Pages – Paperback - Reprint of 1985 titled: "A Promise Is To Keep" by Zondervan Publishing House – Grand Rapids, Michigan

Just $18.00 plus $5.00 Priority Shipping & Handling (USA) – (5% MD Tax)

"I had to write Eliza's story. If I hadn't, it might have been lost, and that would never do. 'No-sir-ree Bob, horsefly in the buggy," as Eliza would say."

Slaveholder Marse Bradford Harrison, a citizen of the state of Maryland, gave four-year-old Eliza Ann Benson to his daughter Braddie in 1841. Eliza was to be a friend and a slave to her infant owner , but a friendship began and a promise was made.

Eliza stayed with Braddie through Braddie's married life, which included the Civil War and its aftermath. And when Braddie and her husband died leaving a family full of children and no one to rear them, there was one more promise that Eliza wanted to keep.

Author Nan Hayden Agle, Braddie's granddaughter, says, "Eliza was all good things rolled into one package – and she was smart, too. She could size up a situation and straighten it out 'before you could say boo to a goose.' She was warm when warmth was needed, strong when strength was needed, and brave when only bravery could lift sorrow about heartbreak. Eliza was the hub of our family for three generations."

This fascinating and true saga is illustrated with a photograph section comprised of pictures of Eliza, members of the Harrison and Spencer families, and documents from the Civil War period. It also includes priceless photographs released by the Baltimore Museum of Art and the Maryland Historical Society.

ISBN: 0-9703802-0-8
Library of Congress Control Number: 00-135279

The Second Maryland Infantry

AN ORATION

(1909)

by

Rev. Randolph McKim
Formerly 1st Lieut. And A.D.C., Third Brigade,
Army of Northern Virginia

40 Pages – Paperback – Illustrations
Just $8.00 plus $3.00 Shipping & Handling (USA) – (5% MD Tax)

This historical booklet is a compilation of research from Enoch Pratt Library, Baltimore and data in private collections. **An Oration** was given at the State House in Annapolis on the occasion of a captured Maryland Confederate Regimental Battle Flag being returned to it's homeland by the State of Ohio. In the audience were veterans from both the Union and Army of Northern Virginia.

As evidenced by the following quote, **An Oration** celebrates both unity and loyalty in a state and union that was once so bitterly torn.:

"There is in our hearts a double loyalty today; a loyalty to the living present, and a loyalty to the dear, dead, past. And that loyalty to the Lost Cause, as men call it, is the best pledge and proof we can give of our steadfast devotion to our Reunited Country. Fellow citizens, the people that is ashamed of its heroic dead – is already dying at the heart and we believe it will make for a greater strength and glory of the United States if the sentiments that animate us today shall be perpetuated generation after generation."

Included are copies of General Orders of Gen. Jos. E. Johnston and Maj. Gen. Ewell; Rosters and casualties of Co. H., 1st Maryland Infantry, CSA and Co. A, 2nd Maryland Infantry, C.S.A.; names and ranks of known Marylanders who served in units other of other states' regiments plus patriotic poetry.

A portion of proceeds from sale of this booklet will help benefit a scholarship fund to send a deserving high school student to The Civil War Institute held annually at Gettysburg College, Gettysburg, PA.

FUTURE OFFERINGS

Book based on the diaries and letters of a Maryland Civil War soldier who first served in the Union and then in the Confederacy

Children's Books based on Maryland History

Reprints of more rare and desirable titles

PUBLISHING INQUIRIES WELCOME

Family Memoirs
Church & Town Histories
Military Histories
Manuscripts
Poetry

BOOK SALES BY CONSIGNMENT

Local Authors
Books on Local History

OUT-OF-PRINT BOOK SEARCHES

Arcadia Enterprises, Inc.
1703 Carver Square
Salisbury, Maryland 21801

Website: www.buyarcadiabooks.com